Women Practicing Resili
and Wellbeing in Academ

Through a lens of self-care and wellbeing, this book shares stories of struggle and success from a diverse range of women in academia.

Each story highlights how these women mitigated and overcame various barriers as part of their academic trajectory and provides practical strategies for maintaining self-care and wellbeing. Taken from lived experience, the autoethnographic narrative approach provides a deeper, personal understanding of the obstacles faced by women throughout an academic career and guidance on how these might be navigated in a way that avoids self-sacrificing.

This collection goes further to illustrate the ways that higher education institutions can be more accommodating of the needs of women.

Ida Fatimawati Adi Badiozaman is the Executive Dean of Research in Swinburne Sarawak. An award-winning multidisciplinary researcher driven by equity and access issues, she has been involved in transformative and impactful research. In 2020 she won the United Nations' WEP Award for the Community and Industry Engagement Category. In 2021, she received the Special Recognition Award for her contribution to education at the state-level celebration of International Women's Day 2021 by the Chief Minister of Sarawak. In 2022 Dr Ida was highlighted in the book *Sarawak Women in Scholarly Writing*.

Voon Mung Ling is a Senior Lecturer and Research Cluster Leader for Human Resource Innovation in the School of Business, Faculty of Business, Design and Arts in Swinburne University of Technology Sarawak. She holds a PhD from UNIMAS in the area of leadership practices. Mung Ling's research interests cover organizational behaviour, leadership in organizations, strategic planning, and human resource management practices. She is an active researcher and has published several research articles in journals and a book chapter.

Kiran deep Sandhu is a John Maxwell Certified Leadership Coach. Her areas of research are gender, access, equity, and leadership. She is also the founder of the Give Back to Community Trust, a non-profit organization working on bridging the technological gap in rural education by supporting unprivileged children gain access to better education. In 2021, she was awarded among the "Most Admired Global Indians" by *Passion Vista Magazine*.

Wellbeing and Self-care in Higher Education

Editor: Narelle Lemon

For more information about this series, please visit: www.routledge.com/
Wellbeing-and-Self-care-in-Higher-Education/book-series/WSCHE

Women Practicing Resilience, Self-care and Wellbeing in Academia

International Stories from Lived Experience

Edited by Ida Fatimawati Adi Badiozaman, Voon Mung Ling and Kiran deep Sandhu

Routledge
Taylor & Francis Group

LONDON AND NEW YORK

Designed cover image: © Getty Images

First published 2023
by Routledge
4 Park Square, Milton Park, Abingdon, Oxon OX14 4RN

and by Routledge
605 Third Avenue, New York, NY 10158

Routledge is an imprint of the Taylor & Francis Group, an informa business

© 2023 selection and editorial matter, Ida Fatimawati Adi Badiozaman, Voon Mung Ling and Kiran deep Sandhu; individual chapters, the contributors

The right of Ida Fatimawati Adi Badiozaman, Voon Mung Ling and Kiran deep Sandhu to be identified as the authors of the editorial material, and of the authors for their individual chapters, has been asserted in accordance with sections 77 and 78 of the Copyright, Designs and Patents Act 1988.

All rights reserved. No part of this book may be reprinted or reproduced or utilised in any form or by any electronic, mechanical, or other means, now known or hereafter invented, including photocopying and recording, or in any information storage or retrieval system, without permission in writing from the publishers.

Trademark notice: Product or corporate names may be trademarks or registered trademarks, and are used only for identification and explanation without intent to infringe.

British Library Cataloguing-in-Publication Data
A catalogue record for this book is available from the British Library

ISBN: 978-1-032-37706-3 (hbk)
ISBN: 978-1-032-37703-2 (pbk)
ISBN: 978-1-003-34148-2 (ebk)

DOI: 10.4324/9781003341482

Typeset in Bembo
by SPi Technologies India Pvt Ltd (Straive)

Contents

Contributors

Akiko Nanami, Hiroshima Shudo University, Japan.

Anisha Kaur Sandhu, Monash University, Malaysia.

Betty Exintaris, Monash University, Australia.

Deena Kara Shaffer, Ryerson University, Canada.

Fareeha Javed, Lahore College for Women University, Pakistan.

Ida Fatimawati Adi Badiozaman, Swinburne University of Technology, Malaysia.

Khairunnisa Haji Ibrahim, Universiti Brunei Darussalam, Brunei.

Kiran Deep Sandhu, Swinburne University of Technology, Malaysia.

Louise Oldridge, Nottingham Trent University, United Kingdom.

Maranda Ridgway, Nottingham Trent University, United Kingdom.

Michaela Edwards, Nottingham Trent University, United Kingdom.

Moreoagae Bertha Randa, Sefako Makgatho Health Sciences University, South Africa.

Mumtaz Begum Aboo Backer, Universiti Sains Malaysia, Malaysia.

Nicola Sum, Monash University, Australia.

Nilushi Karunaratne, Monash University, Australia.

Roslina Abdul Latif, Taylors University, Malaysia.

Sampurna Das, University of Delhi, India.

Sana Rahim, Sheffield Hallam University, United Kingdom.

Soubakeavathi A/P Rethinasamy, Universiti Malaysia Sarawak, Malaysia.

Voon Mung Ling, Swinburne University of Technology, Malaysia.

A note from the series editor

Immediately after I sat down and began reading this volume, I was thrown into a deep empathetic response. With a rawness and vulnerability that was confronting, the words on the page from each of the authors in this volume resonate, are familiar. And with this vulnerability comes an invitation to "open yourself, contextualise that self in societal constructs and systems, co-learn, admit you do not know and be human" (Brantmeier, 2013, p. 2). As we negotiate ourselves as women within and across various contexts, we begin to interrupt what is and can be. We interrupt the "*un*caring neoliberal, competitive and individualising" (Gravett et al., 2021, p. 1) notions of the higher education system, and embrace a "responsibility to one another [based on] mutual and spontaneous regard" (Noddings, 2012, p. 232). Noddings reminds us that when we engage with deep listening, care, self-care, kindness, compassion, and appreciation we emphasise a care ethics that illuminates the "difference between assumed needs and expressed needs" and "from this perspective, it is important not to confuse what the cared-for wants with that which we think [they] should want. We must listen, not just 'tell', assuming that we know what the other need" (Noddings, 2012, p. 773).

As women we write so powerfully about our lived experiences. We live, tell, retell, and relive our life stories, we continue to learn and understand as we construct narrative accounts (Caine et al., 2019; Clandinin & Connelly, 2004). My vision for this book series is that we as authors and readers come together as a community learning with and from one another. By placing academic wellbeing and self-care at the heart of discussions around working in higher education, we are providing a narrative connection point for readers from a variety of backgrounds in academia. In this case the editors of this collection have curated 15 chapters from 21 authors located in nine different countries including Japan, Brunei, Pakistan, Malaysia, Australia, Canada, UK, and South Africa. Highlighted are the lived experiences. Honoured are the voices of our colleagues working in higher education. We are provided with an opportunity to connect deeply with and reflect upon a diverse range of strategies for how to put in place wellbeing and self-care approaches as an academic. By engaging this way, we begin to shift the rhetoric that self-care and wellbeing are selfish. Rather, we refocus, reconsider and position self-care as worthy of our attention. We are invited to consider new ways of working and being.

Professor Narelle Lemon
Series Editor
Wellbeing and Self-care in Higher Education: Embracing Positive Solutions

References

Brantmeier, E. J. (2013). Pedagogy of vulnerability: Definitions, assumptions, and applications. In J. Lin, R. Oxford, & E. J. Brantmeier (Eds.), *Re-envisioning higher education: Embodied pathways to Wisdom and transformation* (pp. 1–19). Information Age Publishing. https://blogit.jamk.fi/tecsummerschool/files/2013/05/Ed-Brantmeier-Pedagogy-of-Vulnerability-Definitions-Assumptions-Applications.pdf

Caine, V., Estefan, A., & Jean Clandinin, D. (2019). A return to methodological commitment: Reflections on narrative inquiry. *Journeys in Narrative Inquiry: The Selected Works of D. Jean Clandinin*, 265–277. https://doi.org/10.4324/9780429273896-16/RETURN-METHODOLOGICAL-COMMITMENT-VERA-CAINE-ANDREW-ESTEFAN-JEAN-CLANDININ

Gravett, K., Taylor, C. A., & Fairchild, N. (2021). Pedagogies of mattering: Re-conceptualising relational pedagogies in higher education. https://doi.org/10.1080/13562517.2021.1989580

Jean Clandinin, D., & Connelly, M. (2004). Knowledge, narrative and self-study. In J. L. Loughran, M. L. Hamilton, V. Kubler, & T. R. LaBoskey (Eds.), *International handbook of self-study of teaching and teacher education practices* (pp. 575–600). Springer, Dordrecht. https://doi.org/10.1007/978-1-4020-6545-3_15

Noddings, N. (2012). The caring relation in teaching. *Oxford Review of Education, 38*(6), 771–781. https://doi.org/10.1080/03054985.2012.745047

Acknowledgements

Gender inequalities in academia still persist, despite attempts to mitigate them. The genesis of the book came from wanting to capture the many voices of women in academia and the gendered challenges faced on daily basis. We wanted these voices to be heard and we wanted these voices to be understood.

We owe an enormous debt of gratitude to the detailed and constructive comments from Narelle Lemon, for helping more authors turn their ideas into stories, and for the opportunity to realise our academic dreams. We could not have done this without the support of our family and loved ones. We want to thank these inspirational ladies for sharing their stories. May it inspire others to create a space for self-care and wellbeing.

Part I

Women and the changing academia

1 Of glass ceilings and glass cliffs

Navigating the gendered academy

Ida Fatimawati Adi Badiozaman, Voon Mung Ling, and Kiran Deep Sandhu

Of glass ceilings and glass cliffs: navigating the gendered academy

> ### Prelude
>
> *Congratulations. You got the job. You were not the obvious choice, but we believe that you will be able to change the research culture in this institution. We will review your performance in six months. All the best.*

Back in my office, shell-shocked and slightly confused, I replayed the interview outcome in my head. I replayed the conversation and thought of the responses I should have said and questions I should have voiced. I felt utterly robbed of what should have been a joyous occasion and a meaningful career moment in a challenging year. I was unable to celebrate the promotion. Instead of elation, I was focused on the fact that I was given a near-impossible task. I was to curate a research culture in a traditional teaching institution and to enhance research performance with minimal resources. To add to the challenge, the position came with an expiry date. As I struggled to make sense of this information, I realised how sadly familiar this situation was, especially for women in academia. I broke the glass ceiling,[1] only to be met with a glass cliff.[2]

Introduction

The massification of higher education (HE), internationalisation, and globalisation have changed the governance and roles of universities (Badiozaman, 2019, 2021; Ghasemy et al., 2018) in Malaysia. The neoliberal practices in higher education have also intensified academic labour along gender lines. Although women's representation among undergraduates equals and often eclipses men's, the same cannot be said for doctorate completion, tenured faculty status, and senior administrative positions in higher education (Vaughn, Taasoobshirazi, & Johnson, 2020). Prior literature has attributed structural issues, family responsibilities,

DOI: 10.4324/9781003341482-2

gender bias and discrimination, academic culture, motivation, self-esteem, and impostor syndrome to the dwindling number of women ascending the academic ranks (see Brabazon & Schulz, 2020; Macfarlane & Burg, 2019; Spanò, 2020; Subbaye & Vithal, 2016).

Inside the marketised university, traditionally gendered divisions of labour see women concentrated in education, humanities, arts, social sciences, health, and social work – areas afforded increasingly less academic 'prestige' (Aiston & Jung, 2015, p. 206) or 'capital' (both literally and figuratively) than the traditionally male-dominated domains of science, technology, engineering, and maths, which are more amenable to quantification and industry partnerships (Brabazon & Schulz, 2020). Women occupy most junior or casual academic roles inside these divisions while assuming the greatest responsibility for teaching. Though there are success stories of career progression and women in leadership roles in academia, these stories, much like mine, are imbued with complexities. Brabazon and Schulz (2020) aptly sum this: "When women are granted positions of power, this typically means being placed in difficult institutions in difficult situations, with heavily circumscribed capacities to generate change" (p. 878). Consequently, women promoted to leadership and decision-making roles within this context often have to navigate considerable organisational pressure.

In academia, there has been a long history of struggle with gender equity (O'Connell & McKinnon, 2021). Over the last 50 years, most governments have attempted to implement appropriate policies in an effort to encourage gender equity (Harris Rimmer & Sawer, 2016). Academia has followed up with policies that would increase the participation of women in faculties and leadership roles (Vettese, 2019). In most countries, women comprise about 50 percent of under-graduate students (Strauß & Boncori, 2020), but they are under-represented in the senior academic ranks. Surprisingly, higher education has failed to achieve gender equity in key areas in most countries. For example, women make up only 27 per cent of full professors in the European Union (European Commission, 2018), and 32 percent of full professors in the United States of America (Hussar et al., 2020). Representative leadership requires gender equity, which underpins the need for changes in the higher education landscape (Cheung, 2021). As the numbers of female graduates and junior faculty members grow, proportional representation should be reflected in leadership roles in higher educational institutions. This issue is not unique to specific regions or countries, as fewer women hold key positions in virtually every part of the world (see Table 1.1). However, Bothwell (2020) noted signs of progress: in 2020, women led 39 of the top 200 higher education institutions in the world (19.5 per cent), an increase from 17 per cent in 2019 (Bothwell, 2020).

In 2020, there were only two (10 per cent) female Vice-Chancellors in the 20 Malaysian public universities, five of which were renowned public research institutions (Azman, 2021). It is common knowledge, but pertinent to note, that politics has had substantial influence on the management of the tertiary educational institutions in Malaysia. The incumbent government would typically appoint their preferred people to the posts of Vice-Chancellor, Deputy Vice-Chancellor, Governance Board members, and Chairs of Public Universities. Based on the data

Table 1.1 Women in higher education leadership

Region/Country	Year	Percentage of female leader		
		Institutional leaders (%)	*Executive leaders (%)*	*Academic leaders (%)*
Arab League	2018	6.8		
Australia	2016	25.0	34.0	34.0
China: 'First–class universities'	2019	4.8		
Latin America	2020	18.0		
Pacific Rim	2018		21.0	25.0
United Kingdom	2018	29.0	37.0	31.0
United States	2016	30.1		

Source: Assembled by Cheung (2019) based on American Council on Education (2017) [United States], APRU (2019) [Pacific Rim], Releraqi & Salahuddin (2018) [Arab League], UNESCO-IESALC (2020) [Latin America], WomenCount (2017) [Australia], WomenCount (2018) [United Kingdom], and Zhang (2019) [China].

Table 1.2 Number of academics by gender at Malaysian public universities, 2019

Academic rank	Male	Female	Total
Professor	1,128 (63.96%)	636 (36.1%)	1,764 (100%)
Associate Professor	2,285 (51.4%)	2,162 (48.6%)	4,447 (100%)
Lecturer	8,509 (39.2%)	13,223 (60.85%)	21,732 (100%)
Language Teacher	317 (28.4%)	801 (71.6%)	1,118 (100%)
Total	12,239 (42.1%)	16,822 (57.9%)	29,061 (100%)

Source: Azman, 2021: Ministry of Higher Education, Malaysia (2019).

gathered, only one (5 per cent) woman was appointed to lead the Board of Governors/Directors of a public university; moreover, women constitute only 21.1 per cent (42) of board members nominated by the government (Azman, 2021). Women are also inadequately represented in leadership positions in other public universities. In most cases, men hold the position of Chief Finance Officer (60 per cent), and women make up only 8 out of 20. The majority of Chief Administration Officers are men (75 per cent), while only 5 out of 20 are women (Azman, 2021).

In the 2019 statistics of the Malaysian public universities, women held more than half of the full-time teaching posts and more than 60 per cent of all lecturers and lower positions. However, a very small number of them filled the higher positions, such as Associate Professor and above (see Table 1.2). There is inequality in gender representation in the senior academic leadership positions; it is evident that more men than women are promoted to a professorship. On top of that, few women are recognised with the highest national awards in academia. Judging from the past National Academic Awards listings published by the Ministry of Higher Education (2020), more men than women received awards in the last 13 years.

Barriers to and enablers of career trajectory for women in academia

The challenges faced by women in academia is well documented. The ubiquity of these challenges remains in 2022. Women's experiences in academia are imbued with a fundamental set of issues pertaining to gender inequalities. Despite having come a long way in educational attainment, women in academia continue to lag in senior academic positions (Barnard, Arnold, Bosley, & Munir, 2021; Brabazon & Schulz, 2020; Vohlídalová, 2021). While women comprised approximately half of all students and over half of all staff at our institution, they were negligibly represented in senior positions within the university structure, a pattern reflected in HE institutions globally. Gendered organisational practices at higher education institutions have long been held responsible for the glass ceilings faced by female academics (Macfarlane & Burg, 2019).

To this end, this section discusses the barriers to and enablers of career trajectories for women in academic fields. Enablers are factors that facilitate advancements in career pathways, whereas barriers hinder women from progressing and lifting their careers to greater heights (Fazal, Naz, Khan, & Pedder, 2019). There are many career progression enablers: social capital, the support of family members and relatives, social norms and traditional gender choices for certain professional development, personal drive, and self-initiative (Fazal et al., 2019). Regardless of culture and nationality, women, more often than not, face career barriers or challenges (Hill, Miller, Benson, &Handley, 2016; Njiru, 2013), which may encompass gender discrimination, striking a balance between family life and work schedules, minimal opportunities in the workplace, lack of family understanding and assistance, broader social practices and general attitudes, as well as limited facilities, in the work environment (Ali & Rasheed, 2021; Fazal et al., 2019), and the existence of multi-level barriers encountered by academics when trying to succeed in their careers (Allen et al., 2021; Rickett & Morris, 2021). Similarly, Santos (2016) maintains that the organisational, professional career barriers pertain to three general themes: poor collegiality and workplace relationships, the lack of organisational support and employment precariousness, and career progression standards and expectations.

Organisational norms and cultural barriers

Even though the workplace culture constantly changes over time, it is the main obstacle to women's advancement in academia (Vongalis–Macrow, 2014). Many academic institutions remain "gender-blind" in their policies, resulting in a bias towards males (Cheung, 2021). It is no secret that the organisational culture is tainted with perceptions of preferred masculine leadership behaviours (Gallagher & Morison, 2019), which are related to male-dominant practices that covertly discriminate against women in various manners. For example, in Vietnam, there is a gender stereotype that women's leadership capabilities are inferior to those of their male counterparts (Truong, 2014). Management science researchers also suggest that women are less likely to take up a job if they think they are not fully equipped or qualified for the post. On the other hand, men are more likely to apply for a job (Vongalis-Macrow, 2014) and think they have the necessary skills or the confidence to overcome the challenges of the work.

Cultural norms and traditional behaviours may partly explain why women, by and large, are not ambitious enough to climb to the top of the corporate ladder and are content with secondary or less important positions (Azman, 2021). In Asian society, male dominance is woven into the fabric of everyday life; hurdles and obstacles premised on cultural practices and religious beliefs are set in place to confine women to so-called gender-appropriate work and acceptable lifestyles (Azman, 2021). Prejudices against female leadership and misconceptions about women's intellectual capabilities, their development potential, and work performance flourish in the corporate environment due to gender bias, and there is a minimal degree of transparency in the selection process and promotion criteria (Azman, 2021).

A balance between family and work

Despite the available support and more positive societal attitudes in the running of the family, women remain primarily responsible for carrying out household chores. They continue to assume the primary role of raising children and caring for the elderly (Gallagher & Morison, 2019). This adversarial work-life culture (e.g., the culture of long working hours) may make it more challenging to balance work and non-work. Consequently, women are often faced with an ultimatum in life decisions – have children or embark on a successful career. As shown in the statistics globally, women are more likely than men to dedicate themselves to and spend time caring for their families, such as teaching children and undertaking household duties (Cheung, 2021).

With their plate full of family obligations, women often have to reduce the amount of time devoted to professional career progression, although this may not necessarily affect their productivity and performance (Cheung, 2021). Many women struggle to strike a balance between their multiple roles as career woman, mother, wife, daughter, and daughter-in-law. In a highly competitive educational environment, the survival of a university is a major issue and concern; to achieve that end, the university management would demand more time and effort from the academic staff members, which inevitably increases the workload of the women academics (Cheung, 2021). For these reasons, women encounter more barriers to achieving objective and subjective career success.

In certain circumstances, some women teaching staff opt for part-time work when their children are in the growing stage, while others stay put in their full-time job by sacrificing other aspects of personal or family life such as fewer sleep hours or spending less quality time with the family members. Some women may defer their career advancements by forgoing opportunities for promotion or taking up managerial leadership roles in academia. Ultimately, without thoughtful planning, family commitments could slow down an academic woman's career development (Gallagher & Morison, 2019). On the whole, it is a daunting task for working women to sustain a balance between the multi-roles they play at home and the workplace, the burden of which may take a toll on their mental health and physical wellbeing.

Mentorship as an enabler

By forming a mentoring relationship between the older academic women and younger female academicians, the probability of the latter's career progression could be enhanced (Woolnough and Davidson, 2007). Research indicates that mentoring is a highly effective and beneficial method of training, which aids the mentee in his or her career development, and in turn, helps the person move up in the organisational structure (Locke & Williams, 2000; Martin-Chua, 2009; McKeen & Bujaki, 2007; Ragins and Cotton, 1999). There are two main categories of mentoring programmes – the formal and informal (Arokiasamy & Ismail, 2008). Usually, a formal mentoring programme is developed by the organisational management (Murray, 1991). On the other hand, an informal mentoring relationship is often formed by mutual agreement between a mentor and a mentee because of circumstantial or developmental needs (Arokiasamy & Ismail, 2008).

According to the observations of Altbach (1995), the nature and routines of work within universities have changed significantly in recent years. Some examples of major changes in institutions of higher learning are different weightages of resource allocation for different purposes, diminishing sources of funding, and an increasing emphasis on operational efficiency, all of which may exert pressure on the faculty members to raise their level of productivity. A mentoring arrangement can help women adapt to the ever-changing working environment, leading them to greater career advancement (Arokiasamy & Ismail, 2008). Through a mentoring programme, a more mature and experienced mentor can provide the necessary support and share her experiences with her mentee.

Based on Bilimoria, Joy, and Liang's (2008) study, leadership development is integral to fostering women's advancement to take up leadership positions. An effective mechanism must be established for inculcating in women leadership skills through formal development programmes, which should be undertaken outside of national and institutional structures. These training courses would enable female academicians to attain career advancement. Several universities have implemented initiatives to help females who have had career interruptions, such as leadership development programmes that empower women to take control of their career progression and provide any support needed to realise their dreams of their career goals.

Challenging the impossible: putting our self-care at the forefront

As academics, we are evaluated on our metrics. As women, we face structural and systemic disadvantages in our professional and personal lives. The following strategies have significantly helped the authors navigate academia and their career trajectory.

Strategy 1: Self-care in the form of a network of support

As reflected in literature, a network of support is needed for academic women across all career stages and not merely for graduate students or early-career researchers (Boynton, 2020; Vázquez-Cupeiro, 2021). These networks of support play multiple roles in academia (Heffernan, 2020; Lillis & Curry, 2018). In academia, the network of support provides social capital and is associated with positive outcomes such as promotions, salary increases, career advancement, or career satisfaction (Barrow & Grant, 2019; Barthauer, Spurk, & Kauffeld, 2016). Our networks of support come in the form of female academics and working women outside academia. The network of support in academia provides access and opportunities that may not necessarily be made available to women in lower levels (Level B, Level C), those not holding a management role, or those who are not tenured. This includes sharing information on opportunities for grants, research projects, academic positions, and teaching-learning resources (see Figure 1.1).

Looking back at when I applied for my academic promotion to Level C in 2017 and then to Level D in 2020, my network of support has played a crucial role right throughout all the stages; from the planning of the write-up, writing our applications together, providing affirmations to each other whenever imposter syndrome reared its head, to celebrating successes and consoling each other for failed

Figure 1.1 In the image above, the authors are meeting up in a café to share our plans for the year and support each other in their respective endeavours. We increase our productivity in academia by optimising the available research opportunities and consolidating our skills and resources. We check in regularly for work and personal matters. Our regular meetups are a form of self-care, a career-supportive relationship providing both emotional and social capital in academia.

applications. My support network also includes male allies (Madsen, Townsend, & Scribner, 2020; Moser & Branscombe, 2021) who read my numerous drafts, told me to be 'bolder' in my writing, and reminded me of the many achievements that I deemed insignificant. This informal network of support has also become an essential resource for sharing information, opportunities, and access to research activities throughout my career. This informal, collaborative network has mani-fested in many transformational projects, and the team won many international awards. This career-supportive relationship has helped me navigate academia and break through glass ceilings.

In my new role as the Executive Dean of Research, I often face many challenges stemming from unconscious biases. I was responsible for leading research strategy, innovation, and change across Swinburne Sarawak to build organisational research capacity, develop a research ecosystem, and ensure a high-performing team envi-ronment exists to deliver high-quality research outputs. My role also required that I build an overall culture of research excellence, both internal and external. The position description also stated that the Executive Dean (Research) contributes to the achievement of the University's Strategic Plan through leadership of Swinburne Sarawak's research activities, research training, industry liaison, intellectual prop-erty, and commercialisation of research outcomes.

Needless to say, it was a steep learning curve, and I was determined to prove myself. Hailing from the field of social sciences and securing one of the most coveted positions in the university meant that I had to be strategic, and quickly learn the ropes. No one day was the same, and as challenging and gruelling as the schedule was, I quickly learned how to position myself in external engagements, observe the conversations, identify power dynamics in meeting settings, and suc-cessfully secure research outcomes. In identifying research opportunities and col-laborations, I rely on multiple strategies. One strategy that has been very successful was the male allies I had formed over the years in academia through various inter-disciplinary research projects. My male allies (Dubow & Ashcraft, 2016) not only advocated gender equality, but their allyship provided a sense of belonging in a male-dominated work environment (Moser & Branscombe, 2021). Though impostor syndrome will rear its occasional head, I am thankful for my male allies who have supported and opened many doors for research collaborations for the university. As men have larger and broader networks, this gives them access to a broader audience and more opportunities. Male allies in senior positions thus can increase the visibility of talented women (Valerio & Sawyer, 2016). The same person that told me "I wasn't the obvious choice for the position" is now my mentor and a staunch supporter.

Outside academia, our support network builds support systems and provides resources to nurture existing close relationships and increase feelings of relatedness, competence, and autonomy in my role as a working mother. The complex and dynamic role that these social support networks play in the everyday life of work-ing mothers involves processes of creation, maintenance, and mobilisation of social ties. In general, social support refers to the physical and emotional comfort given to an individual by family, friends, co-workers, and others. For the authors, the other working mothers are our 'tribe' who understands the challenges and pressures of managing family and work. This support network consists of mothers who would help babysit or organise afterschool activities and school holiday excursions for our children. These career-driven mothers are the ones who would share health information, current activities, and social events, at which we could gather and further expand our network with like-minded women. With this informal support, we could navigate the demands of academia and motherhood and mitigate career interruptions.

Strategy 2: Membership in virtual personal development community

Research shows the positive impact of virtual communities on social capital, giving users a sense of strong network ties, collaboration, cooperation, innovation, access to sources of information and professional advantages, shared values, diversity of thought, and feelings of trust and safety (Santos, Oliveira, & Chaves, 2019). When the pandemic started in March 2020, I found the shift to online teaching-learning challenging initially because of limited experience in teaching online. However, soon I decided to improve myself as a virtual presenter. In my pursuit to get better, I explored virtual communities for personal development. Eventually, I joined a closed Facebook Public Speaking Forum, which had over 15,000, members and formally started learning the art of Public Speaking.

On a daily basis, a topic of discussion was given by the mentor, which required community members to make a video on their perspective and share it on the Facebook page. I started making videos, and over a period of time, it built my confidence in speaking virtually. Soon, I started mentoring other members on the Facebook forum to improve their public speaking. My students encouraged me to start a YouTube channel to share tips on how to communicate effectively. This had a rolling effect on other opportunities that had seemed impossible earlier because of geographical boundaries. Soon, opportunities to present as a keynote speaker and trainer at several virtual events came my way, giving me access to a global audience. I decided to build my credibility as a public speaker and so took the opportunity to present at a TEDx event conducted virtually by University Malaysia Sabah, which once again opened new pathways to my career progression. In 2021, I started a vodcast called Leadership Talk, where I invited leaders from different industries to share their experiences. This gave me the impetus to become a certified leadership, communication coach and start a Leadership Development Company. So, virtual communities can create new and broader networks and opportunities in career progression.

Strategy 3: Engagement in professional network

Due to a dynamic academia environment, including globalisation, a diverse workforce in higher education institutions, increased academic mobility, and pressure to produce high-impact research output, it is crucial for women academics to be actively involved in professional networks (Ehido et al., 2019). This platform can be an effective way to advance in their profession. One of the significant ways that networking may improve career success is through enhancing the academic's social capital (Gonzales & Rincones 2008; O'Meara & Campbell, 2011). Social capital is the outcome of people's relationships with others (Ehido et al., 2019). Academics can build up numerous networks across various settings by investing their time and energy tactically to achieve the desired returns on their investment (Niehaus & O'Meara, 2014). Regarding my personal experience, my involvement in several professional networks (associations and non-profit organisations) has provided me with many great opportunities to meet people from all walks of life. This has also allowed me to tap into valuable resources that can benefit my career advancement, such as consultancy projects and research grants.

In 2021, I was given the opportunity to lead a Global Facilities Management leadership project. However, I felt that I did not have the subject knowledge to take on the new responsibility. I approached my male ally who had worked in Corporate Real Estate and shared my hesitation to take on the project. He emphasised that I was definitely the right person to take on the job and offered his support in areas where I needed to upskill my knowledge. He introduced me to his network and encouraged me to join and actively participate in his team meetings. This indirectly increased my visibility in front of the other stakeholders and brought clarity to my own role. Later, I realised that my hesitation to take up the new role was for two reasons. Firstly, I was suffering from the initial "impostor syndrome," where I wondered whether I would be accepted in a male-dominated sphere, and secondly, I was suffering from "time poverty." From this experience, I realised that men prioritise, delegate, and create boundaries, whereas women constantly blur the work-home boundaries and, as a result, struggle with time-management issues.

Conclusion

At present, higher education institutions need to adapt to technological change, globalisation, and the Covid-19 pandemic; educational leaders and managers have to draw on diverse perspectives and innovative solutions to solve problems. This requires a bold move away from the culture of male-dominated leadership; a more balanced approach would be necessary by adopting gender-equal leadership that would represent the student and academician populations in a comprehensive manner (Cheung, 2019). Overall, there is much room to correct the gender imbalance in leadership in the global higher education system. Implementation of more empowerment programmes for females will help overcome the obstacles in their career pathways and gain access to higher leadership posts. A more holistic understanding of how women choose and navigate the complex path that leads them to and through academia is necessary. We offer the process that we have engaged in, to support academic women to navigate academia, through critical reflection and action.

Notes

1 Glass ceiling is a metaphor used to represent an invisible barrier that prevents a given demographic (typically applied to women) from rising beyond a certain level in a hierarchy.

2 Glass cliff is the phenomenon of women in leadership roles, being likelier than men to achieve leadership roles during periods of crisis or downturn, when the risk of failure is highest.

References

Aiston, S.J., & Jung, J. (2015). Women academics and research productivity: An international comparison. *Gender and Education*, *27*(3), 205–220.

Ali, R., & Rasheed, A. (2021). Women leaders in Pakistani academia: Challenges and opportunities. *Asian Journal of Women's Studies*, *27*(2), 208–231.

Allen, K.-A., Butler-Henderson, K., Reupert, A., Longmuir, F., Finefter-Rosenbluh, I., Berger, E., … Kewalramani, S. (2021). Work like a girl: Redressing gender inequity in academia through systemic solutions. *Journal of University Teaching & Learning Practice*, *18*(3), 1–19.

Altbach, P.G. (1995). Problems and possibilities: The US academic profession. *Studies in Higher Education*, *20*(1), 27–44.

American Council on Education. (2017). American college president study 2017. https://www.acenet.edu/Research-Insights/Pages/American-College-President-Study.aspx

Arokiasamy, L., & Ismail, M. (2008). Exploring mentoring as a tool for career advancement of academics in private higher education institutions in Malaysia. *European Journal of Social Sciences*, *5*(4), 21–29.

Azman, N. (2021). Malaysian women in higher education leadership: Promise without progress, in International Briefs for Higher Education Leaders, No. 9. Center for international higher education, Lynch School of Education and Human development, Boston College.

Badiozaman, I. (2019). Rethinking English language education in Malaysia *The Journal of Asia TEFL*, *16*(1), 349–359. doi:10.18823/asiatefl.2019.16.1.24.349

Badiozaman, I. (2021). Early career academics' identity development in a changing HE landscape: Insights from a Malaysian private university. *Asia Pacific Journal of Education*, *41*(3), 424–439.

Barnard, S., Arnold, J., Bosley, S., & Munir, F. (2021). The personal and institutional impacts of a mass participation leadership programme for women working in Higher Education: A longitudinal analysis. *Studies in Higher Education*, *47*(7), 1372–1385. doi:10.1080/03075079.2021.1894117

Barrow, M., & Grant, B. (2019). The uneasy place of equity in higher education: Tracing its (in) significance in academic promotions. *Higher Education*, *78*(1), 133–147.

Barthauer, L., Spurk, D., & Kauffeld, S. (2016). Women's social capital in academia: A personal network analysis. *International Review of Social Research*, *6*(4), 195–205.

Bilimoria, D., Joy, S., & Liang, X. (2008). Breaking barriers and creating inclusiveness: Lessons of organizational transformation to advance women faculty in academic science and engineering. *Human Resource Management*, *47*(3), 423–441.

Bothwell, E. (2020, March 6). Female leadership in top universities advances for the first time since 2017. *Times Higher Ed*. Retrieved from: https://www.timeshighereducation.com/news/female-leadership-top-universitiesadvances-first-time-2017

Boynton, P. (2020). *Being well in academia: Ways to feel stronger, safer and more connected*. London: Routledge.

Brabazon, T., & Schulz, S. (2020). Braving the bull: Women, mentoring and leadership in higher education. *Gender and Education*, *32*(7), 873–890.

Cheung, F.M. (2021). The "state" of women's leadership in higher education. *International Briefs for Higher Education Leaders*, *9*, 5–8.

DuBow, W.M., & Ashcraft, C. (2016). Male allies: Motivations and barriers for participating in diversity initiatives in the technology workplace. *International Journal of Gender, Science and Technology, 8*(2), 160–180.

Ehido, A., Ibeabuchi, C., & Halim, B.A. (2019). Networking and women academics' career success in the Malaysian Research Universities. *International Journal of Academic Research in Accounting, Finance and Management Sciences, 9*(12), 940–960.

European Commission. She Figures. (2018). In gender in research and innovation; Directorate-general for research and innovation: Luxembourg, 2019.

Fazal, S., Naz, S., Khan, M.I., & Pedder, D. (2019). Barriers and enablers of women's academic careers in Pakistan. *Asian Journal of Women's Studies, 25*(2), 217–238. doi:10.1080/12259276.2019.1607467

Gallagher, J.E. & Morison, S. (2019). Women in academic leadership: A chance to shape the future. *Journal of Dentistry, 87*, 45–48.

Ghasemy, M., Hussin, S., Megat Daud, M.A.K., Md Nor, M., Ghavifekr, S., & Kenayathulla, H.B. (2018). Issues in Malaysian higher education: A quantitative representation of the top five priorities, values, challenges, and solutions from the viewpoints of academic leaders. *SAGE Open, 8*(1), 1–15. doi:10.1177/2158244018755839

Gonzales, L.D. & Rincones, R. (2008). The role of faculty in global society: Carving out the public purpose of our work. *Teacher Education and Practice, 21*(4), 382–406.

Harris Rimmer, S., & Sawer, M. (2016). Neoliberalism and gender equality policy in Australia. *Australian Journal of Political Science, 51*(4), 742–758.

Heffernan, T. (2020). Academic networks and career trajectory: "There's no career in academia without networks". *Higher Education Research & Development 40*(5), 981–994.

Hill, C., Miller, K., Benson, K., &Handley, G. (2016). *Barriers and bias: The status of women in leadership (Research Report No. 091-16 05M)*. National Coalition of Girls' Schools. Retrieved from: https://www.ncgs.org/wpcontent/uploads/2017/11/Barriers-andBias-The-Status-of-Women-in-Leadership.pdf

Hussar, B., Zhang, J., Hein, S., Wang, K., Roberts, A., Cui, J., … Dilig, R. (2020). *The condition of education 2020*. Washington, DC: National Center for Education Statistics. Retrieved from: https://nces.ed.gov/pubsearch/pubsinfo.asp?pubid=2020144

Lillis, T., & Curry, M.J. (2018). Trajectories of knowledge and desire: Multilingual women scholars researching and writing in academia. *Journal of English for Academic Purposes, 32*, 53–66.

Locke, V.N. & Williams, M.L. (2000). Supervisor mentoring: Does a female manager make a difference? *Communication Research Reports, 17*(1), 49–57.

Macfarlane, B., & Burg, D. (2019). Women professors and the academic housework trap. *Journal of Higher Education Policy and Management, 41*(3), 262–274.

Madsen, S.R., Townsend, A., & Scribner, R.T. (2020). Strategies that male allies use to advance women in the workplace. *The Journal of Men's Studies, 28*(3), 239–259.

Martin-Chua, E. (2009). *Maximizing human capital in Asia: From the inside out*. New York, NY: John Wiley and Sons.

McKeen, C. & Bujaki, M. (2007). Gender and mentoring. In Kram, K.E. & Ragins, B.R. (Eds.), *The Handbook of mentoring at work: Theory, research, and practice*. New York, NY: Sage Publications.

Ministry of Higher Education (2019). *Malaysian higher education statistics 2019*. Ministry of Higher Education (Malaysia). Retrieved from: https://www.mohe.gov.my/en

Ministry of Higher Education. (2020). *Anugerah Akademik Negara*. Ministry of Higher Education (Malaysia). Retrieved from: http://jpt.mohe.gov.my/aan/

Moser, C.E., & Branscombe, N.R. (2021). Male allies at work: Gender-equality supportive men reduce negative underrepresentation effects among women. *Social Psychological and Personality Science, 13*(2), 372–382. doi:10.1177/19485506211033748

Murray, M. (1991). *Beyond the myths and magic of mentoring: How to facilitate an effective mentoring program.* San Francisco, CA: Jossey-Bass.

Niehaus, E., & O'Meara, K. (2014). Invisible but essential: The role of professional networks in promoting faculty agency in career advancement. *Innovative Higher Education, 40*(2), 159–171.

Njiru, F. (2013). Factors affecting career progression of women in the corporate sector: A case study of Standard Chartered Bank in Nairobi (Unpublished thesis). University of Nairobi, Nairobi.

O'Connell, C., & McKinnon, M. (2021). Perceptions of barriers to career progression for academic women in STEM. *Societies, 11*(27), 1–20.

O'Meara, K., & Campbell, C.M. (2011). Faculty sense of agency in decisions about work and family. *Review of Higher Education, 34*(3), 447–476.

Ragins, B.R., & Cotton, J.L. (1999). Mentoring functions and outcomes: A comparison of men and women in formal and informal mentoring relationships. *Journal of Applied Psychology, 84* (4), 529–550.

Releraqi, A., & Salahuddin, I. (2018, December 4). Arab women are left out of university leadership. Al-Fanar Media. Retrieved from: https://www.al-fanarmedia.org/2018/12/arab-women-are-left-out-of-university-leadership/

Rickett, B., & Morris, A. (2021). "Mopping up tears in the academy"–working-class academics, belonging, and the necessity for emotional labour in UK academia. *Discourse: Studies in the Cultural Politics of Education, 42*(1), 87–101.

Santo, R.F., Oliveira, M., & Chaves, M.S. (2019). Are you getting full benefits from the use of Social Media? A review combining the concepts of social media, social capital and knowledge sharing. Revista de Administração da UFSM, *14*(2), 349–368.

Santos, G.G. (2016). Career barriers influencing career success: A focus on academics' perceptions and experiences. *Career Development International, 21*(1), 60–84.

Spanò, E. (2020). Femina academica: Women "confessing" leadership in higher education. *Gender and Education, 32*(3), 301–310.

Strauβ, A., & Boncori, I. (2020). Foreign women in academia: Double-strangers between productivity, marginalization and resistance. *Gender, Work & Organization, 27*(6), 1004–1019.

Subbaye, R., & Vithal, R. (2016). Gender, teaching and academic promotions in higher education. *Gender and Education,* 1–26. doi:10.1080/09540253.2016.1184237

Truong, T.M.D. (2014). Exploring challenges of middle leadership in higher education: A case study of a Vietnamese university. *Malaysian Online Journal of Educational Management, 2*(3), 70–96.

UNESCO International Institute for Higher Education in Latin America and the Caribbean (UNESCO-IESALC). (2020, March 7). Where are the women university rectors in Latin America? UNESCO-IESALC data reveals that only 18% of the region's universities have women as rectors. Retrieved from: https://www.iesalc.unesco.org/en/2020/03/07/where-are-the-womenuniversity-rectors-in-latin-america-unesco-iesalc-data-reveals-thatonly-18-of-the-regions-universities-have-women-as-rectors/

Valerio, A.M. & Sawyer, K.B. (2016). The men who mentor women. *Harvard Business Review.* Retrieved from: https://hbr.org/2016/12/the-men-who-mentor-women

Vaughn, A.R., Taasoobshirazi, G., & Johnson, M.L. (2020). Impostor phenomenon and motivation: Women in higher education. *Studies in Higher Education, 45*(4), 780–795.

Vázquez-Cupeiro, S. (2021). Women's networking in Spanish academia: A "catch-all" strategy or strategic sisterhood? *Critical Studies in Education, 63*(4), 485–500. doi:10.1080/17508487.2021.1911820

Vettese, T. (2019). Sexism in the academy. *Head Case, 34,* 1–26.

Vohlídalová, M. (2021). Early-career women academics: Between neoliberalism and gender conservatism. *Sociological Research Online, 26*(1), 27–43.

Vongalis-Macrow, A. (2014). *Career moves: Mentoring for women advancing their career and leadership in academia.* Rotterdam: Sense Publishers.

WomenCount. (2017). WomenCount: Australian universities 2016. Retrieved from: https://womencountblog.files.wordpress.com/2017/03/womencount-autralianreport_screen-res.pdf

WomenCount. (2018). WomenCount: Leaders in higher education 2018. Retrieved from: https://womencountblog.files.wordpress.com/2018/11/womencountreport-2018_web-version_new-final.pdf

Woolnough, H.M. & Davidson, M.J. (2007). Mentoring as a career development tool: Gender, race and ethnicity implications. In Bilimoria, D. & Piderit, S.K. (Eds.), *Handbook on women in business and management.* Northampton, MA: Edwin Elgar.

Zhang, W.J. (2019, July 26). Double first-class university presidents. China Education and Research Network. Retrieved from: https://www.edu.cn/ke_yan_yu_fa_zhan/gao_xiao_cheng_guo/gao_xiao_zi_xun/201907/t20190726_1675835.shtml

2 The Holy Trinity of teaching, research, and service

Roslina Abdul Latif

A broadcast journalist by profession, I found the transition to teaching was a tough decision and an even tougher act to perform. Having had a decade of experience in broadcast journalism after landing a nifty job at a broadcasting house, Sistem Television Malaysia Berhad (TV3), I took up a lecturing position at one of the few (at the time) private institutions in Kuala Lumpur. I managed a Master'sof Communication in Broadcasting while I was still working shift hours at TV3. If my hours were already crazy, it became more hectic with the commute to university for classes after work. I took everything in stride.

I started lecturing on media subjects and later graduated to more specialised fields of broadcasting, including production and writing. I also dabbled in journalism and broadcast journalism as that was what I started out with. In two decades of teaching, ten years were spent training, and the other ten spent gaining industry experience. What started out as a challenge has become a norm throughout the years with different projects, a slew of diverse subjects, and of course the many students that passed through my classes, some with flying colors or others suffering from my strict ruling of "you miss my deadline, you die."

But now it's not about just teaching. Academia has other demands, such as doing research, writing, and publication, which is a waiting game on its own. When the semester commences, you're supposed to manage your time to do the different parts of your job. The demands become greater with the more positions you hold or titles in front of your name, such as Dr., Associate Professor, or Professor. Add to this your services to the school/department, the university, and the community.

Ask any academic how they like to spend their free time and they'll probably give you a wry smile. There's no such thing as free time in academia, not really. Free time is for replying to the string of emails that need attention, for grading the continuous avalanche of assignments from the numerous subjects you teach, preparing for lectures for the new subjects that were conveniently given to you, for submitting overdue referee reports or review of research papers; the list goes on.

An academic's weekend is probably having just that Sunday afternoon off before the madness starts again. So, how do we deal with this situation? Some say a "to-do" list would help but honestly, they don't. They only cause more stress because of the pressure to perform and complete the long list. Self-care and mental health are important if you are planning to stay in academia for a long time.

DOI: 10.4324/9781003341482-3

Past research

Given the present situation, with the pandemic and online teaching, conditions have been stressful, to say the least, leading to burnout or chronic exhaustion within the academia. At its core, burnout is caused by work that demands continuous, long-term physical, cognitive, or emotional effort.

Academics have been working from home since the lockdowns started and have experienced problems and limitations during this time. Giving lectures, guiding research, organising discussions, and conducting online exams have gradually become habits for many university academics. Some think that working via the Internet can save time for academics and control their work and progress (Petersen, 2017), but there is a downside to it.

There have been complaints about work efficiency (Gaillard, 2018) and concentration (Ammons & Markham, 2004) in academics when working online. Additionally, lecturing and researching are professions that require commitment, integrity, and concentration. Therefore, academic parents have experienced many problems with balancing work and life during the pandemic.

Complaints include having to sacrifice private time, demanding employers, a lack of work-life balance, solving employer-employee conflicts at group meetings, and workers' reluctance to speak up from fear of losing their jobs (*New Straits Times*, 2021). Gajendra Balasingham, group Chief Executive Officer of GKK Consultants Sdn Bhd. revealed that an ugly side is unfolding with growing discontent and rumblings about WFH where the fine lines of virtual abuse and work-life balance are being compromised (*New Straits Times*, 2021).

He further stressed that employers' stress needs to be managed well, to ensure that their health and that of their employees is not compromised. Employers must respect each employee's space and draw the line between work and life and avoid encroaching on employees' personal lives. Employees also must respect work time and devote themselves 100 per cent towards accomplishing their tasks while not compromising their self-care.

Self-care is not new, so it's not surprising that there has been an increase in the amount of self-care research in recent years. A search on PubMed conducted in June 2019 revealed that the first self-care publication was in 1946, with publications peaking in 2015, when 2,457 articles were published on the topic. Godfrey et al. (2011) identified 139 different definitions of self-care in 2011, and little progress has been made since then to find an established uniform definition integrating related concepts (Matarese et al., 2018).

Patel (2020) defines self-care as part of the answer to how we can all better cope with daily stressors. A wellness expert, she explains work stress as the stress of trying to keep up with the pace of daily life, which technology has hastened more than ever. People have become lonelier and less able to unwind, which makes them feel more anxious and overwhelmed by even the simplest tasks.

Self-care interventions are among the most promising and exciting new approaches to improve health and wellbeing, both from a healthcare system's perspective and for people who use these interventions. The World Health Organization (WHO) uses the following working definition of self-care: Self-care is the ability of individuals, families, and communities to promote health, prevent disease, maintain health, and cope with illness and disability with or without the support of a healthcare provider.

> The scope of self-care as defined includes health promotion, disease prevention and control, self-medication, providing care to dependent persons, seeking hospital/specialist/primary care if necessary, and rehabilitation, including palliative care. It includes a range of self-care modes and approaches. While this is a broad definition that includes many activities, it is important for healthcare policies to recognise the importance of self-care, especially where it intersects with healthcare systems and healthcare professionals.
>
> (World Health Organization, 2019)

Riegel et al. (2021) identified six specific knowledge gaps that, if addressed, may help to combat these challenges. For example, issues with behavioral changes could be addressed to some degree with habit formation. The effect of stressful life events that interfere with self-care could be addressed somewhat by building resilience. Other issues such as the influence of culture on self-care behavioral choices, the difficulty of performing self-care with multiple chronic conditions, and self-care in persons with severe mental illness are issues about which we know relatively little. Finally, the influence of others (care partners, family, peer supporters, and healthcare professionals) was identified as a challenge because of our growing recognition that these others influence all the reasons that people struggle with self-care. Other research also supports this idea (Riegel & Jaarsma, 2019; Jaarsma et al., 2012).

Cluver et al. (2020) also agree with the above and stress that without support from colleagues and guidance from leaders, employees must manage mountains of work independently. In the long run, the pressure from work will create discomfort and lead to burnout. Garbe et al. (2020) also state that academic parents struggle to get their job tasks done while taking care of their children and completing other housework when working from home. In addition to cooking and taking care of children at home, parents, in place of teachers, must also ensure that their children study. These tasks reduce work efficiency and cause stress and fatigue for these parents.

However, Akash and Shreya (2020), who did an analysis of the sentiments regarding WFH on Twitter, found that 73.10 per cent of the tweets had positive sentiments as compared to 26.10 per cent negative sentiments. This signifies that in general, people had a positive outlook towards the concept of work from home. There were eight emotions evaluated in their research which included fear, joy, anticipation, anger, disgust, sadness, surprise, and trust. The analysis of the emotional quotient of the tweets found that the majority of the tweets across the globe involved three emotions: trust (24.03 per cent), anticipation (29.74 per cent), and joy (16.45 per cent). Emotions like fear, sadness, anger, and disgust were found in relatively smaller portions of tweets, with shares of 10.17 per cent, 8.60 per cent, 6.69 per cent, and 4.32 per cent, respectively. These results prove that people had a positive outlook and preferred the WFH experience (Akash & Shreya, 2020). These results become more important when a report from Gartner stated that

74 per cent of CFOs and finance leaders were willing to shift at least 5 per cent of on-site employees to remote work permanently (Lavelle, 2020). It should be noted that this research was done at the beginning of the pandemic, so feelings about WFH would have changed since.

In a study by Holgersen, Jia, and Svenkerud (2021) in Norway, they found that approximately 38 per cent of Norwegian jobs can be performed from home. This result also suggests that the pandemic and the government's attempts to mitigate this crisis may have an uneven impact on the working population. They also found that there is a clear difference across genders. Female workers are more likely to have WFH-friendly jobs than male workers. However, they argued that WFH might not be beneficial for female workers, as they often must take on additional housework in this situation (Collins et al. 2020).

Hence, WFH is suitable for fields that do not require direct interaction, but for fields that need information exchange and human interaction like academia, this format can cause depression and burnout symptoms, reduce working productivity and job performance, and cause conflicts in family life (Chung et al., 2020).

Methodology

Autobiographical research is a group-related qualitative research method for dissecting autobiographical text materials (interviews or written episodes and stories), that was developed in the early 1980s by Zech (1983, 1988; in Roth, 1989), but still relevant. The theoretical background of the autobiographical research was provided by the cultural-historical school of Soviet psychology and critical psychology. It has been noted that it is the individual process of becoming a particular subject or the formation of the subject's capacity to act in different social situations that form the general subject of research.

Past and present research has examined how individuals actively and independently develop the social conditions of their lives, their personalities, and their capacity to act during these processes of change. They also realise how existing ideologies offer adjustments that cause individuals to abandon possibilities for their own development. Hence, it is the relationship between the objective situational conditions of acting and the subjective explanation for acting that affects the individual development of personality that is analysed (Thomas, 2000). Abrahão (2012) understands life history as a methodology in autobiographical research. Autobiographical research uses various empirical sources (life narratives, oral stories, documents – both official and personal – diaries, memorials, epistles, videos, photos) and techniques (triangulation of information and in-depth analysis of the sources).

Life history is a (re)constructive view made by the researcher, where the researcher analyses empirical sources, as mentioned above, in a critical dialogue with research findings from elsewhere and with a global view of a socio-economic and cultural environment where the studied lives and the research takes place. She stresses that "life history is a product, not a process." The act of giving a new meaning to a narrated fact indicates that the researcher is consciously trying to capture that fact and is aware that it is being reconstructed by a selective memory, whether intentional or not (Abdul Latif, 2019).

Discussion and strategies of self-care

The literature has given us an overview of what self-care is in terms of research and intervention, but what is self-care, really? Iowa Family Counseling (2020) describes self-care as simply practicing behaviors and activities that help you to feel good and be mentally and physically healthy. That seems straightforward, right? Unfortunately, self-care has become a whole industry that overwhelms us with messages that tell us what we should do to take care of ourselves and imply that there is only one right way to do it. There is so much information on self-care that we don't even know where to begin. If you are finding the thought of adding self-care routines and practices into your life overwhelming and anxiety-inducing, you are not alone, and it is okay to feel this way (Iowa Family Counseling, 2020).

Life can be stressful, which complicates self-care further. Dan Mager (2013), a psychotherapist, clinical supervisor, and clinical director across a wide range of behavioral health and substance abuse treatment settings defines stress as "[a]n imbalance between your current coping abilities and the demands placed on you, including demands that you place on yourself – both real and perceived." So basically, we are doing a balancing act where we try to cope with the stress in our lives. We are out of balance when our stress is too much for us to handle. What we need to do is balance our stress with our coping abilities. Unfortunately, it is not that easy.

Here are a few strategies that can be used when we are trying to manage stress, work, family, life, and everything in between. For starters, I would recommend (*a*) taking long walks (see Figure 2.1). Depending on when you decide to exercise, wait for the sunrise or sunset. If you are game, you could also join virtual walks/runs and get rewarded for your workouts. According to Dr. Gill Lopez, Psychology Program Director, Department Chair at Fairfield University, "It could be anything that floats your boat – anything that puts a smile on your face or anything that makes you feel cared for, even if it's you caring for yourself" (Lawler, 2021). She expounds on the idea that physical self-care, such as prioritising sleep, adopting an

Figure 2.1 The researcher on her walks. There's this saying that "If you are good at building bridges, you will never fall into the abyss!" But then again you could always "burn the bridges" once you get across.

exercise routine you can stick with, and choosing healthy and nourishing foods over highly processed ones, is a good example.

Dr. Ellen Baker, a psychologist based in Washington, DC, also agrees with this idea. There's a lot of research, for example, showing that things like exercise, yoga, and mindfulness are supportive of mental and physical health (Lawler, 2021). An article published in the *Journal of the American Medical Association* (Pizzo, 2020) noted that longevity in the 21st century depends on abiding by healthy practices, such as exercising, not smoking, following a healthy diet, and embracing a positive lifestyle all around.

While you're on these walks, (*b*) enjoy the flowers. It's very calming to be one with nature. If you'd rather (*c*) cycle than walk, you could shake it up and do both alternatively. Equipment does not have to be expensive, just safe, so this is manageable. According to a 2019 study published in *Lancet Planetary Health* (Rojas-Rueda et al., 2019), spending time in green spaces is associated with a lower mortality rate, so it's good to be outside. Although the benefits of green spaces and mortality were found to be robust in the study, there were also negative effects of increasing green spaces in the urban environment (such as gentrification), but evidence of an inverse association between proximity to green spaces and all-cause mortality were positive.

A study by Saint-Maurice et al. published in the *Journal of the American Medical Association, Network Open* (2019) also concluded that people who exercised between two and eight hours per week throughout their lives reduced their risk of dying by 29 to 36 per cent. They also discovered that maintaining higher leisure-time physical activity levels in later adulthood were associated with relatively low risk of mortality, suggesting that midlife is not too late to start physical activity. Inactive adults may be encouraged to be more active, whereas young adults who are already active may strive to maintain their activity level as they get older. My self-care physical activity is walking, which you can see in Figure 2.1.

Next, (*d*) have a schedule and only work the hours you are paid for. Nguyen (2021) agree that both the university board of management and academics must accept that achieving work-family balance is difficult, especially with the social distancing requirement of Covid-19. The side effects of this imbalance can cause mental stress, health fatigue, conflicts in family relationships, and ultimately reduce job performance.

They further suggest that the university management board should implement more robust organisational support policies to remove the burden and stress of job-related activities. This includes sharing all necessary information and giving detailed guidelines, deadlines, and quality assessment methods for work duties, and maintaining constant and mutual effective communication between academics and management departments to strengthen direct and instant support from universities. Technology-related steps include teaching academics applications and digital tools and providing 24/7 support to ensure the ability to deliver good online lectures and discussions to the students regardless of where they are and how they access them. These technological interventions may enhance lecturer engagement with students and the university (Nguyen, 2021).

A study by Laura et al. (2018) titled "Communication in the Digital Work Environment: Implications for Wellbeing at Work" stresses a similar point. Their result is in line with the results of previous studies (Barley et al., 2011; Brown et al., 2014; Diaz et al., 2012), which showed that a large quantity of digital communication is exhausting and often spills over from work to non-work hours. This kind of spillover can be highly problematic, as it may induce unpaid overtime, impede recovery, and cause work-life conflict, which hinder employees' ability to detach from work and take time away from non-work activities.

Having a schedule will also give you relaxation time for (*e*) a movie night with the family or (*f*) quiet reading. It doesn't really matter what movie you watch – just enjoy the time together – but it does matter what you read, so be selective.

Ultimately, your self-care routine should make you a better version of yourself. Brighid Courtney (Lawler, 2020), a client leader of wellness technology, says that a rule of thumb is, "as long as the activities that you choose are adding to your well-being and are not detrimental to the other areas of your life, then there is a benefit." She emphasises that you are better suited to take care of others, foster strong relationships, be resilient, and balance personal and professional responsibilities.

(*g*) Leave meetings early to fetch kids from school, tuition, or work. Use this reason to start dinner or do workouts. Sometimes these meetings tend to drag, especially the ones without proper agendas, so let them know that you have a life after office hours. Bosses who call these meetings sometimes forget that we are mothers, sisters, and daughters who have other responsibilities after working hours.

(*h*) If you can go on short holidays, go ahead, but stay true to your auto-reply. Do Not Reply! I sometime get this: "I know you're on leave but could you …?" No, stop right there. Believe me, if you entertain one request, they will keep coming, and people around you will have this notion that you are still working even when on leave. In a way, we are, but it is "catch-up" time for all the other things that have been shelved because of work. This is the time for all those abandoned projects to be taken off the shelf and be completed – that book chapter, that paper for publication, or that novel you've been working on.

Nguyen (2021) also stress on this point, that academics individually should get familiar with saying "no" to the unimportant and taking care of themselves. Because of lack of time, learning how to prioritise things that matter most and saying no to things that matter least is an excellent way to manage limited time. Moreover, self-care is vital during this challenging period; thus, relaxing to get rid of mental stress and fatigue is important. Lopez (Lawler, 2021) also concurs with this point.

(*i*) Don't tweet or post about how busy you are with work as it sends mixed signals, that you are a workaholic and enjoy the burden.

(*j*) Take a longer drive and enjoy the sunset. If you stay in the city, you can take pleasure in the sunset wherever you are, but it would be nice to take a walk on the beach or cove to enjoy the sun disappearing beneath the horizon.

(*k*) Get a pet if you don't already have one, as they are very therapeutic. My family has a few kitties as members of our family, but this one is mine. She's a rescue from SPCA and I call her Rey (see Figure 2.2). She's in my study most of the time while I conduct online lectures and discussions but will plop on my desk when it's time to stop. She seems to know exactly when office hours are over so that's a good indication to end the day's work.

Figure 2.2 Rey signaling it's time to stop for the day.

Oh, did I mention (*l*) coffee? Coffee is a must because "coffee is blood," as I told my surgeon when he told me to reduce my coffee intake after a life-threatening surgery in 2019. I told him I needed coffee to write, and he frowned at me. I have since reduced to a mug a day and alternate it with Oolong tea with rosebuds in the evenings. If you're wondering, it used to be three mugs of black coffee before 11:00 a.m., if I needed to write research papers.

Now that Covid-19 is endemic and most people are fully vaccinated, restaurants allow dine-in, so go and have those catch-up (*m*) lunches with close friends. As we grow older and hopefully wiser as the years go by, our circle of friends becomes smaller and tighter. These are the comfortable companions that you could vent your frustrations to and pour your heart out to. They will listen and be empathetic and you will both end up laughing at the situation. It's always good to be able to laugh at yourself.

This is also known as emotional self-care as prescribed by Baker (Lawler, 2021). This includes self-talk, weekly bubble baths, saying "no" to things that cause unnecessary stress, giving yourself permission to take a pause, or setting up a weekly coffee date with a friend.

If you enjoy writing like I do, you could (*n*) write for a column in a newspaper or a magazine. Amid all the craziness of online classes, I sometime took time off to write for a few organisations that have invited me to write for their columns. As a columnist for AstroAwani, Bernama, and recently, TV Sarawak, I contribute in terms of ideas and discussions but only when I have something to say.

You could also just write for your own pleasure. The last two years of the pandemic gave me time to finish the sequel to my novel. *Sidelines* was my debut novel in 2018. Since then, *Sidelines* has won a place as one of the 50 Best Malaysian Titles for International Rights 2018/2019 at the Frankfurt International Book Fair 2018, become a finalist at the International Book Awards in the United States (2019), and won a grant from the National Library as a writer's award, to spur further writing. The grant money came in a day after my surgery, so I started writing the book during my chemotherapy. It was a very dull and sad time for me, so I turned to writing as my therapy. The idea was just to write; never did I imagine winning anything, let alone on an international level. The experience has been rewarding indeed.

If you have trouble getting started with a self-care routine, it might be worth examining where that roadblock comes from. Baker (Lawler, 2020) says that if there is a stuck-ness or a difficulty in getting started or sustaining a self-care program, something might be going on. She encourages journaling, as some people can unravel that mystery through independent journaling, but also suggests that you may need to visit a therapist to get to the root of the issue. A therapist will be particularly helpful if the question you keep running into is, "Am I worth it?"

Finally, (*o*) skip the grant rotation and publish less. Although I should caution you that this would be frowned upon by the bosses, you need to choose what to prioritise, and how, in your life. This concurs with recent research done by Nguyen (2021), who concluded that the administrative workload should be reduced for academics. The administrative task is considered truly a nightmare for all university academics. It not only takes a lot of time and effort but also causes stress to academics.

Conclusion

Life history is an interesting way to (re)construct a view using empirical sources as mentioned above, in a critical dialogue with either a local or global view of a socio-economic and cultural environment where the studied lives and the research takes place. Life history is a product, not a process. Therefore, it gives new meaning to a narrated fact that consciously tries to capture life as it is being reconstructed by a selective memory, whether intentional or not.

The above discussion is fluid and should remain intact even after the pandemic. Although some of these self-care practices started during the lockdown, these habits can continue if they benefit your mental health and, more importantly, become a part of your lifestyle. One popular method to build healthy habits is called the 21/90 rule (O'Brien, 2020). Commit to a personal/professional goal for 21 straight days. After three weeks, the pursuit of that goal should become a lifestyle. Courtney (Lawler, 2020) also approves this technique. After seven days, evaluate. Once you've completed a seven-day streak, reflect on how you're feeling and note any positive benefits. Use this as fuel to maintain the behavior throughout the period or even for a longer duration.

I close with some words that I live by, "When the mind is agitated, walk to come down. When the mind is distracted, write to focus. And when the mind is tired, read to get more material."

References

Abdul Latif, R. (2019). Mere observations, fair comment, and actual facts: The voice of Rehman Rashid. *Malaysian Journal of Communication*, 35(1), 252–267. E-ISSN: 2289-1528. https://doi.org/10.17576/JKMJC-2019-3501-17

Abrahão, M. H. M. B. (2012). Autobiographical research: Memory, time, and narratives in the first person. *European Journal for Research on the Education and Learning of Adults*, 3(1), 29–41.

Akash, D., & Shreya, T. (2020). Analysing the sentiments towards work-from-home experience during COVID-19 pandemic. *Journal of Innovation Management*, 8(1), 13–19. https://doi.org/10.24840/2183-0606_008.001_0003

Ammons, S. K., & Markham, W. T. (2004). Working at home: Experiences of skilled white collar workers. *Sociological Spectrum*, 24(2), 191–238. https://doi.org/10.1080/02732170490271744

Barley, S. R., Meyerson, D. E., & Grodal, S. (2011). Email as a source and symbol of stress, *Organization Science*, 22(4), 887–906. https://doi.org/10.1287/orsc.1100.0573

Brown, R., Duck, J., & Jimmieson, N. (2014). E-mail in the workplace: The role of stress appraisals and normative response pressure in the relationship between e-mail stressors and employee strain, *International Journal of Stress Management*, 21(4), 325–347. https://doi.org/10.1037/a0037464

Chung, C. O. Y., Ping, D. C., Zahari, P. S., Ravindran, T. S., & Kannathasan, K. (2020). The association between self-esteem and academic stress among undergraduate medical students. *International Journal of Biomedical and Clinical Sciences*, 5(2), 64–74.

Cluver, L., Lachman, J. M., Sherr, L., Wessels, I., Krug, E., Rakotomalala, S., & McDonald, K. (2020). Parenting in a time of COVID-19. *Lancet*, 395(10231). e64. https://doi.org/10.1016/S0140-6736(20)30736-4

Collins, C., Landivar, L., Ruppanner, L., & Scarborough, W. (2020). COVID-19 and the gender gap in work hours. *Gender, Work & Organisation*, 28 (S1), 101–112.

Diaz, I., Chiaburu, D. S., Zimmerman, R. D., & Boswell, W. R. (2012). Communication technology: Pros and cons of constant connection to work. *Journal of Vocational Behavior*, 80(2), 500–508. https://doi.org/10.1016/j.jvb.2011.08.007

Gaillard, A. W. (2018). *Concentration, stress, and performance. Performance under stress.* London: CRC Press.

Garbe, A., Ogurlu, U., Logan, N., & Cook, P. (2020). COVID-19 and remote learning: Experiences of parents with children during the pandemic. *American Journal of Qualitative Research*, 4(3), 45–65.

Godfrey, C. M., Harrison, M. B., Lysaght, R., Lamb, M., Graham, I. D., & Oakley, P. (2011). Care of self – care by other – care of other: The meaning of self-care from research, practice, policy, and industry perspectives. *International Journal of Evidence-Based Healthcare*, 9(1), 3–24.

Holgersen, H., Jia, Z., & Svenkerud, S. (2021). Who and how many can work from home? Evidence from task descriptions. *Journal for Labour Market Research*, 55(4), 1–13. https://doi.org/10.1186/s12651-021-00287-z

Iowa Family Counseling (2020). Self-care in times of stress. https://www.iowafamilycounseling.com/post/self-care-in-times-of-stress

Jaarsma, T., et al. (2012). Self-care research: How to grow the evidence base? *International Journal of Nursing Studies*, 105(2020) 103555. https://doi.org/10.1016/j.ijnurstu.2020.103555

Laura, B., Jussi, O., Jaana-Piia, M., & Kirsi, K. (2018). Communication in the digital work environment: Implications of wellbeing at work. *Nordic Journal of Working Life Studies*, 8(3), 29–48. https://trepo.tuni.fi/bitstream/handle/10024/103342/communication_in_the_digital_work_environment_2018.pdf?sequence=1

Lavelle, J. (2020) CFO survey reveals 74% intend to shift some employees to remote work permanently. *Gartner*. https://www.gartner.com/en/newsroom/press-releases/2020-04-03-gartner-cfo-surey-reveals-74-percent-of-organizations-to-shift-some-employees-to-remote-work-permanently2

Lawler, M. (2020). How to start a self-care routine you'll follow. https://www.everydayhealth.com/self-care/start-a-self-care-routine/#tips-for-coping-in-uncertain-times

Lawler, M. (2021). What is self-care and why it is so important for your health? https://www.everydayhealth.com/self-care/

Mager, D. (2013). *Some assembly required: A balanced approach to recovery from addiction and chronic pain.* Central Recovery Press. Las Vegas, USA.

Matarese, M., Lommi, M., De Marinis, M. G., & Riegel, B., (2018). A systematic review and integration of concept analyses of self-care and related concepts. *Journal of Nursing Scholarship*, 50(3), 296–305.

New Straits Times (2021, June 13). Ugly side unfolding about working from home. https://www.nst.com.my/news/nation/2021/06/698384/ugly-side-unfolding-about-working-home

Nguyen, H. N. (2021, December 14). Burnout, inter-role conflicts, and job performance among bankers who have children during social isolation. https://www.businessperspectives.org/images/pdf/applications/publishing/templates/article/assets/15907/BBS_2021_04_Ninh%20Nguyen.pdf

O'Brien, C. (2020, January 10). The 21/90 Rule: Make life better. https://www.activeiron.com/blog/the-21-90-rule-make-life-better/

Patel, K. J. (2020). *Burning bright: Rituals, reiki, and self-care to heal burnout, anxiety, and stress.* New York: Harmony Books.

Petersen, B. (2017). The relationships of role conflict with role ambiguity, role efficacy, and task cohesion: A study of interdependent university sport teams. (Unpublished thesis). Wilfrid Laurier University.

Pizzo, P. A. (2020). A prescription for longevity in the 21st century: Renewing purpose, building, and sustaining social engagement, and embracing a positive lifestyle. *Journal of the American Medical Association (JAMA)*, 323(5), 415–416. https://doi.org/10.1001/jama.2019.21087

Riegel, B., & Jaarsma, T. (2019). Self-care in long-term conditions: Old news or new thinking? *International Journal of Nursing Studies*, 90, A1–A1. https://doi.org/10.1016/j.ijnurstu.2019.01.008

Riegel, B., et al. (2021). Self-care research: Where are we now? Where are we going? *International Journal of Nursing Studies*, 116, 103402. https://doi.org/10.1016/j.ijnurstu.2019.103402

Rojas-Rueda, D., Nieuwenhuijsen, M. J., Gascon, M., Perez-Leon, D., & Mudu, P. (2019). Green spaces and mortality: A systematic review and meta-analysis of cohort studies. *The Lancet Planetary Health*, 3(11). https://doi.org/10.1016/S2542-5196(19)30215-3

Roth, W. (1989). Auto ethnography as a method for reflexive research and practice in vocational psychology. https://www.sensepublishers.com/catalogs/bookseries/boldvisions-in-educational-research/autobiography-and-autoethnography/

Saint-Maurice, P. F., Coughlan, D., Kelly, S. P., Keadle, S. K., Cook, M. B., Carlson, S. A., & Matthews, C. E. (2019). Association of leisure-time physical activity across the adult life course with all-cause and cause-specific mortality. *JAMA Network Open*, 2(3), https://doi.org/10.1001/jamanetworkopen.2019.0355

Thomas, A. (2000). Comparative – Leipzig contributions to universal history and comparative social research. 10(H 5/6), 182–193.

World Health Organization (2019). Self-care can be an effective part of national health systems. https://www.who.int/news/item/02-04-2019-self-care-can-be-an-effective-part-of-national-health-systems

3   The dancing lecturer

Crafting the strong woman in the academia

Mumtaz Begum Aboo Backer

To dance is to move the body in ways that the soul, mind, and heart coordinate, giving absolute power to the dancer to voice out through her dancing body. Dance in most of its forms and genres has prepared the space for women to express themselves, discover and be discovered, and acknowledge women as significant and powerful patrons. Women dancers-cum-educators have navigated their ways to teach, research, practice, and perform whilst portraying a strong commitment to their professionalism as both art practitioners and educators/academics, hence binding them in an intertwined relationship of "artist-educators", with the multi-faceted demands of both worlds.

The academic fields of arts and performance studies in Malaysia see more women artists discussing their thoughts intellectually as they position their artwork and illuminate critical discourses. Inspiring art luminaries Marion D'Cruz, Aida Redza, and Faridah Merican have paved the way for many more women artists to be trailblazers in art making, art advocacy, and art scholarship. Nonetheless, the higher educational institutions yet prefer to measure intellectual discourse through the lens of academic publications rather than the creative works of women artist-academics!

Pertinent questions – How does art position women in academia? How do women artist-educators negotiate between their personal and public space within their homes, offices, and minds to craft their works? How do art and women speak for each other in both the artistic and the academic scenes? How do art, women, and academia empower each other? And have the arts and academia considered the wellbeing of their women patrons and has the wellbeing of women even been discussed in the arts and academia? – need to be addressed. As the author tries to unravel each question and write the narratives in this chapter, she takes a step back to reflect on her journey as a performing artist (dancer/actor/choreographer) and on how the field of performance (dance and drama) has enabled her to posit her thoughts critically and with decorum through her artworks, constantly reminding and being reminded that arts (dance) is worthy of academia and not illusory, nor just a sign of longing for the gazes and applause of the audience.

The visual that follows is a photograph of Galeri Adiwarna (colourful gallery), a mini–art gallery, located at the School of the Arts' main building at Universiti Sains Malaysia (USM) (see Figure 3.1). This gallery illustrates the efforts taken by

DOI: 10.4324/9781003341482-4

Figure 3.1 Galeri Adiwarna (School of the Arts [SOTA-USM]).

the faculty to accord equal recognition to artistic practice and academic scholarship. This multi-functional purposeful space was set up to serve various events ranging from exhibitions, performances, art talks, and classes to conversations between staff, students, artists, and stakeholders from the community and industry. The gallery ensures a space for artist-academics to exhibit and display their work and thoughts where, importantly, no works by staff or students will go unnoticed Galeri Adiwarna envisions a deep sense of belonging to the school that cares for the wellbeing of her community.

Literature review

The dancer or the educator, first? Dancer or woman, first?

Women artist-educators, and the author herself, constantly battle between the roles they are immersed in: to be a dancer/actor or to be an educator? On the other hand, to the question of, "What do you do?" they are quick to reply, "I teach dance, drama, and performance studies at the university." So, are they dancers or educators? They are both, dancer-lecturer, artist-educator, practitioner-academic! Although this may appear opinionated and quite celebratory, contrary to the traditional scholarly practice of academic discourse, the notion is to explore the intertwined relationship between the artist/dancer, her artwork, and academia. As the author begins to write, once again, she is challenged and probed to think deeper, whether to look from the perspective of a woman or a dancer first. The above questions are the starting point for the deeper understanding of the complexities in the triangulated relationship between the woman, the dancer/practitioner, and the educator. The premise "I am a woman first" asserts the tone of the discussion in this chapter.

The discourse on women throughout history has mostly been fixated around her image (Ling, 2018), her body, and her feminine roles, while secluding the facets from mainstream discussion (Richardson & Robinson, 1993) and eliminating her capability to theorise for herself. Artistically too, women have mostly become the centre of attention as the objects of discussion and of gaze, rather than as subjects. Austin (1998) claims that women have been left out of codified knowledge, rendered as invisible, and denied autonomy. The generally accepted praxis to omit women out of knowledge, theorisation, and mainstream discussion can further be explored by the theory espoused in *The Second Sex* by the French feminist and theorist Simone de Beauvoir (1972), in which she contends with the works of Levi-Strauss and Dumezil (Leon, 1995) that the primary explanation for women being objectified is in the androcentric postulation from which is derived the concept of duality, distinguishing between the "self" and the "other." The "self" is understood as being independent and having the ability to be the "subject," in this case, meaning man, whereas the "other" is identified as being dependent on the "self," this being the woman. The framework further explains that the omission and exclusion of women is structural due to social conditioning and political and economic discrimination.

The continuous discussion on the power relations between man and woman in almost all fields of study, the arts included, have always been sexually centred by the roles defined by man himself, challenging women's studies, gender studies, sociology, and feminist thoughts. The fact that early great liberal thinkers, such as Jean-Jacques Rosseau, Edmund Burke, Thomas Pane, and Emmanuel Kant, were not only men, but their works, which focused on liberal thoughts, emancipation, justice, and equality, had politically excluded women from their discussion, proves that women were subjected to being second-class citizens. Rosseau's work, *The Social Contract* (Grimshaw, 1986), confirms the notion of a perfect citizen in which he offers his views on education for the boy, Emile, but systematically omitted the need for Sophie, the girl, to be educated. His argument further asserts Sophie's standing as only the companion for Emile and nothing more. Similarly, Paine's work, *The Rights of Man* (Watkins et al., 1999), illuminated the tyranny of the monarchy and the government over man, his life and property, but did not include the rights of women, further excluding women from rationality, politics, and economics. In addition, Mill & Mill's (1983/1869) argument on the position of women being socially recognised only through contractual marriage binds her in "bonded servitude to her husband," further keeping her in a demeaning position.

These past works and the systematic exclusion of women from knowledge, rationality, purpose, and economics gave impetus to the emergence of feminist thinking and works with the birth of Mary Wollstonecraft's *A Vindication of the Rights of Woman* (Grimshaw, 1986; Ollenburger & Moore, 1998), which counter-argued against and rejected Rosseau's idea of education that was different for boys and girls. Her argument asserted that human virtues or excellence should be dependent only on the fact that they are human beings, and not on their sex. The systematic exclusion of women from social and political life is explained by Aksiah Adam (1994), through her simple syllogism:

> domestic life is private and invisible,
>   women are at the heart of domestic life, therefore, women are invisible!

The battle continues, so how do women artist-academics make a difference?

Across the world, female artists have been stigmatised for either making artworks that are too feminine, safe. and of no great value or significance to the art community (Ling, 2018), let alone to academia! In response, women artists/dancers and feminist scholars negate these assumptions by questioning the impartiality of the art evaluation processes, which are dominated by men as curators, art directors, art producers, collectors, art critics, and art scholars (Haviland, 1998). In addition, Elwes (1985) states that even in the field of arts, men and women are unfairly compared, especially in the higher arts (literature and humanities) which is perceived as intellectually stimulating due to its nature of being theoretical as compared to the performing arts, which are visually emotional and naturally connected to the body of the performer. In response, Forte (1988/1998), however, states that women's performances are genuinely concerned with women because they are derived from the relationship between women and the dominant system of representation. Conversations with women artists/dancers, such as Aida Redza, Nur Hilyati Ramli, and Tetriana Fauzi (2021),[1] reveal that they truly believe that only women understand and can relate to the experiences, feelings, and perceptions expressed by fellow women. It is with this certainty that women artists/dancers pay attention to women when they appear as characters and when they do not.

Women artists have come a long way towards earning their rights and places both in the arts scene and academia, exhibiting their skills and discourse in the public domain as performance artists, visual artists, art directors, actors, dancers/choreographers, curators, and many more positions that allow them to make powerful statements (Copeland, 1998). These women artists-cum-academics, who are lecturers/guest lecturers and artists in residence at art colleges and higher institutions, deal with diverse issues. They range from issues of identity, placement, and displacement to national agendas – societal, political, economic, religious – and fanaticism, sexual politics, and violence against women and children. They include global agendas such as the rights of marginalised communities, environmental issues, sustainability of culture, and heritage. These are issues that not only raise awareness but also encourage women at the heart of the subjects who theorise, decide, and execute.[2]

Dance performance can further be noted as a "real-life presence" of the performer as she takes on no roles but her own through her consciousness, research, deep understanding, and provocation of the issues that concern and surround her. Real-life presence refers to the situation of dancers/theatre actors who experience unfair treatment when they are invited to a performance but are not paid fairly, have no proper waiting rooms before the show, and have no proper meals nor beverages prepared. This situation is also presently seen in universities and academic institutions whereby dancers, both lecturers and students, are either underpaid or expected to perform for free. Sadly, there are many situations where they must fork out their own expenses for make-up, costumes, and even transportation! What's even more disparaging is the unacceptable demeaning nature of the "gaze" on the bodies of the women dancers and their works, implying that their only purpose is for entertainment, even by other academics from different fields. More specifically, not only are the contributions of women dancers-educators considered to be undeserving for intellectual discourse and academe, but the well-being of the dancer-academics is also not given proper attention, both in the public art scene and academia.

On an encouraging note, however, contemporary dance in Malaysia has received much attention over the years from the art community, media, researchers, and academic institutions that offer dance as a field of study. Efforts to canonise contemporary dance are undertaken by artists, dance scholars, the dance community, and the media (mainstream and social media). Works paramount to the discussion of women's struggle, her freedom, and her voice emerged within the communities that she chooses to practice, communicate, and engage in. This is also evident in the increasing numbers of postgraduate students researching, publishing, and performing contemporary dance at dance and arts festivals and conferences, whether they be local, regional, or international. But the bigger question is, how much importance is given to the role of the artist, the artwork, the educator, and her wellbeing by higher educational institutions?

Methodology

> Dancing on tiptoes, positing the strong woman …

The author's personal journey and experiences as a dancer-lecturer is interpreted in this chapter, employing an autoethnography methodology to reflect her thoughts, works, and critical discourse in academia. Her academic journey in the field of Performing Arts began at the Arts Centre,[3] Universiti Sains Malaysia (USM), a pioneering art institution in the country offering three major disciplines: theatre, music, and fine arts. The experience of learning, discussing new ideas, discoursing critically, engaging in art theories, researching, performing, observing, and reviewing artistic works led to priceless discoveries both in the arts and art scholarship. It is here where she decided to follow her passion and vocation for both the arts and academia.

Trained formally in Bharatanatyam (Indian classical dance) from the age of five, danced countlessly on stages, temples, and cultural events, she performed the *Arangetram*[4] (solo debut) at 19 before enrolling in university. Understanding discipline, hard work, technical precision, movement execution, and absolute respect to the Guru (teacher) through her training in Bharatanatyam, Malay *Minang* dances (ethnic dances of the Minangkabau community), and Silat (Malay art of self-defence), she was mentally, physically, and emotionally prepared for the journey of a performance student at the university.

Her doctoral studies researching the presence of feminism in contemporary dance (2003–2007) further pushed the boundaries in examining the power relations that exist in the art scene and the scarcity of research and resources in publications on women choreographers and their works, struggles, and discourse. She began to question the "liberating effects" that many claim to exist in dance, whether it is paradoxically just a romantic assumption of "liberation/freedom" as Wolf (1998) puts forth. Wolf's argument on the extent to which dance is liberating is based on her observation on choreographic processes in dance, which are simultaneously controlled, systematic, and artistic and can be either subversive or progressive. On the other hand, this chapter also argues that the ideas, thoughts, and emotions in the works of these women are "free" and depict the "real-life presence" of women dancers who are academics as well. The paradoxes in the study between "free" and "controlled" portray the real-life situation of women who keep striving to free themselves from being shadowed by the constraints of their surroundings. This scenario is also applicable to women artists/dancers-cum-academics who use dance semiotically and symbolically to free themselves, but, at the same time, find themselves controlled, restricted, and bound by the curriculum, the demands of the institutions usually governed by men, limitations in terms of logistics, materials, performative elements, and the constant need to remind viewers that it is not their bodies that are on display, but the ideas/thoughts conveyed through their bodies!

Returning as a young lecturer to serve her alma mater was a surreal experience, charting a new chapter in her academic journey of teaching dance and acting. Overwhelmed by being the only female surrounded by all-male senior colleagues, she was inspired and aspired to be tough, knowledgeable, and creative. She observed closely her mentors and works of others, being open to suggestions and criticisms, and looked out for opportunities to collaborate, research, perform, and jointly publish. Likewise, the male artist-academics, too, respected her artwork and scholarship. She knew she had come a long way, just like her strong women dancers (Aida Redza, Marion D'Cruz, Mew Chang Tsing),[5] and she was here to stay and earn her rights to teach and practice. She was determined for her colleagues and students to see her as a lecturer and artist capable of organising, managing, teaching, and creating, to become a complete woman who is not afraid to make mistakes, learn from them, share her fears, and confirm her analyses. Quick to learn about the dos and don'ts once linked to a public institution, such as performances deemed as sensitive to Islam, politically seditious, socially demeaning, or unacceptable, she learned to negotiate and navigate between the grey areas, thus creatively cushioning her thoughts via her artworks. The ideas of "free" and "controlled" are once again contested, with the questions How little freedom and how much control? or vice-versa, and How can we surreptitiously use the arts to navigate between the gatekeeping systems?

The appointment to the Chair of the Drama department and Deputy Dean of Academic and Student Affairs further affirms her acceptance and rights in academia. Fitting into the system dominated by mostly men at both middle- and top-management of the faculty and the university brings different challenges, such as requesting and justifying additional resources to purchase books, costumes, make-up, equipment, facilities, properties, and technological software, programme reviewing, and curriculum development. The development of a new curriculum was met positively and was a great opportunity for the author and her colleagues to identify the weaknesses of current programmes and draw up new courses with a balance between practice and theory that engages the collaborative expertise from the industry and community towards a competitive and relevant programme. Thus, these artist-educators became curriculum reviewers, developers, and most importantly, the owners of the programme, asserting their thoughts and opinions via research, sharing knowledge, and exchanging ideas and communications with their national and international counterparts within the same disciplines.

Her current role as the Dean of the Faculty is the most interesting and challenging one that she has ever performed. Becoming the first woman dean from one of the smallest departments (Drama & Theatre) in the faculty and leading the only arts school in a science-based university, is an extraordinary feat. But the promotion also got her thinking: Why was she chosen and how was she going to live up to the expectations of the top management, her fellow colleagues, both men and women, her peers, the junior staff, the administrative staff, and the students? This appointment not only marks the recognition of women with administrative power but also signals to fellow women academics that the university is ready to take them seriously. The challenge then is to show the university that she represents both women and men, the artists-cum-academics, the psychedelic and the analytical, as an administratively and academically competent woman. The role requires her to demonstrate wise decision-making, manage human resources well, engage in two-way communication and, at the same time, portray strong leadership and mentorship academically and artistically as an educator, dancer, performer, director, scholar, and researcher.

In reconstructing the image and identity of the school (faculty), she begins with the mission of curating the arts school as a space to empower future talents to lead and serve the creative industry and communities artistically and intellectually. The school was propelled into a vibrant centre triangulated between students, staff, and the community to constantly engage and exchange dialogue and conversations. Artist-academics, designers, the industry, the community, and the students were key players in the creation of an oasis for dynamic ideas to take shape, thus creating tangible and intangible impacts through networking. Some of the strategies for advocating towards the betterment of the faculty are prioritising the wellness of her fellow colleagues and students, proposing a creative arts promotional pathway to the top management of the university (ensuring due recognition for artworks), ensuring a safe working space sexually, physically, and mentally for both women and men to work and study, creating a strong sense of belonging for all staff and students, and linking everyone through a web of sustainable support systems that encourages and allows for positive growth in the academia.

Discussion

Being the dancer-researcher

Simultaneously, the author must balance between being a lecturer, practitioner, and administrator while working with her students, colleagues, fellow researchers, community, and industry experts to build her scholarship in dance and theatre. Among some of her works and research that speak deeply about her thoughts and concern on social, environmental, cultural, and marginalised communities are theatrical works with children of special needs (cerebral palsy, trauma, and Down syndrome, 2008–2019), Rohingya refugee children (2018–2019), the voices of Malaysian children through heritage folktales (2017–2020), the extinction of the Malayan tapir (2017), and performances for healing (2015–2019).

These theatrical works and performances are derived from deep discussions, interactions, participation, and observations held with selected and affected communities. These research projects are funded by grants received from the university, Ministry of Higher Education (Fundamental Research Grants and Long-Term Research Grants), the Cultural Economy Development Agency (CENDANA) Performing Arts funds, and from certain non-governmental organisations (NGOs). The grants enabled workshops with affected and selected communities, creating opportunities for students and artists from various backgrounds to collaborate.

Among some of the works that were brought to the forefront of public and academic community discussion are grave issues concerning the wellness and well-being of marginalised children. "Tree of Dreams and Hope" (2015), a project with special-needs children with various disabilities such as cerebral palsy, autism, and trauma from physical, sexual, or emotional abuse, deals with issues of stigmatisation against these children and how theatre has enabled them to express their thoughts, fears, desires, and hopes artistically. Another challenging project was "Wayang the Boy and the Forest" (2015–2017), using Wayang Kulit (shadow play) as an innovative performance to stimulate the cognitive development of children with cerebral palsy. The project explored three important performative elements – storytelling, role-playing, and space – to enhance the cognitive abilities of children with cerebral palsy to learn, to sequence, and to reason. Linking the environment to the conservation of animals and children through the arts, the author produced "Everyone Is Special" (2017) and "Tapir Oh Tapir" (2017), two intertwined projects raising awareness about blindness and the extinction of the Malayan tapir with children from St. Nicholas School for the Blind. The projects too included several children with learning disabilities around Penang. Semiotically intertwining the tapir and the special children, the projects advocated strongly against animal endangerment, love, and care for the blind, and support for children struggling with learning disabilities. The methods employed, findings, and accomplishments of the projects were also discussed at academic platforms, conferences, and art symposiums. These projects and the struggles of the children were further documented as published materials in proceedings and peer-reviewed journals. More importantly, the projects are testaments to the fact that arts and the children empower one another.

Bridging the university and the community, the author, together with her colleagues from academia and the industry, went one step further to tackle the social issue of refugees that was affecting the country. "Jungle Book: The Musical" (2019) sheds light on the plight of the Rohingya refugee children and their fears and crushed dreams as displaced and marginalised communities. The project, an adaptation of Rudyard Kipling's book, juxtaposes the harsh realities of the Rohingya community with the light-hearted plot of the theatre. The theatrical illuminates the predicament of the Rohingya community fleeing persecution by the Myanmar military through the representation of Mowgli (man calf), running away from his enemy Sheer Khan, the tiger. The musical further positioned the faculty and university as being sympathetic and responsive towards the needs of the bottom billions and communities at risk. The impact of these projects can be seen and felt through the awareness raised and knowledge transferred to students, children, participants, and communities through observation, participation, understanding, concern, and commitment. These projects further reaffirm the author's roles as artist-educator and the use of artistic practice and academic scholarship as platforms for arts and communities towards empowerment.

Being the administrator-dancer

The administrative roles encouraged collective decision-making based on dialogues held with stakeholders, university officials, industry, community, staff, and students. Decisions were made on a "need basis" for teaching, learning, research and performing or exhibiting the artworks and were well communicated to all staff and students through appropriate channels and platforms. Resources, budget, and funding for the faculty, programmes, and projects were dispersed fairly among all departments, taking into consideration the number of students, the ratio between lecturers and students, graduate studies, studios, labs, nature of the artwork, and the impact of the project on students, community, the faculty, and the university. Priority is given to community projects with greater impact on knowledge transfer, conservation, and environmental and cultural sustainability.

Wellbeing of staffs at the heart of the leadership

The budget for the faculty must take into consideration a safe and comfortable working space for both women and men. The faculty established a breast-feeding room for nursing female staff and students, allowing them to nurse, express, and rest with comfort and privacy. The air-conditioned room is equipped with a sofa, a refrigerator, and a small changing space. Considering safety as one of vital elements in creating a healthy working environment, a separate women's prayer room was established within the office's main building, ensuring women's safety while performing prayers even after working hours. To nurture and support artist-academics' creativity, the leadership commits to creating a stimulating working environment, with coffee corners, a beautiful landscape with both indoor and outdoor relaxation corners, vibrantly coloured walls with paintings, sculptures, and shady green trees surrounding the faculty.

Taking a more humanistic approach, women staff are allowed to bring their children to the office if they are unattended or while transiting between school and tuition or extra-curricular activities. This is important to ensure the safety of the children and the peace of mind of working staff, further maintaining the wellbeing of staff and their children. The faculty encourages staff to conduct workshops, projects, and programmes for the staff's children during school holidays. These events not only enable children to learn new things and gain additional knowledge by being creative but also to be under the watchful eyes of their parent (mothers). Family days have become a tradition at the faculty, especially during Ramadan, Eid celebration, team building, or any major workshops at hotels. The staff are welcomed to bring their spouses and children for these events. This is highly important for staff to feel that the office is an extended family whereby everyone feels comfortable with each other's families. The author herself has included some of the staff's children in her theatre programmes and dance workshops. The faculty's welfare unit is also active and supportive. Through the small contributions made by staff yearly, the unit purchases and sends out gifts, cards, and cakes to celebrate birthdays, birth of babies, flowers, fruits for those unwell, wreaths for funerals, and donations for staff who lost a close family member as supportive and appreciative gestures.

The faculty supports flexible working hours and working from home (online), which was introduced during the pandemic, and plans to continue this system by moving into a hybrid mode for appropriate courses/subjects. Considering that the artist-academics work overtime, even into the night due to rehearsals/performances usually held at night, the flexible working hours are suitable. To prevent abuse of the system, staff are required to "clock in" online through the university's staff portal, record their work/activities for the day, record their classes and events for validation purposes, and respond promptly to work-related emails, text messages, and phone calls.

A steady mentoring system was encouraged between professors, senior lectures, and younger lecturers at the faculty to stimulate the production and sharing of knowledge, research experiences, supervision techniques, co-teaching, co-publishing, and peer-reviewing to help young lecturers improve and hone their skills. Realising that young lecturers lack teaching, researching, supervising, and publishing experience, the guidance and the "know-how" from their seniors is very helpful. Consider that some of the junior lecturers, having just returned from their studies, have also begun raising their young families and are juggling between their families and their careers, which both demand their attention, time, and energy. Among many of these young lecturers are women who have just launched their careers as practicing artists, academics, and young mothers. A mentoring system helps these young lecturers to feel encouraged and inspired, and not despair.

Strategies

Curating for a standing ovation …

For a dancer/actress, a curtain call with a standing ovation and continuous applause makes her day, for she knows that she has left a significant mark in the audience. Likewise for academics, their thoughts, works, and research are presented in conferences, seminars, and symposiums and further published in reputed journals or books. For a dancer-lecturer, artist-educator, it is the double run of getting the standing ovation and at the same time being able to speak about their artwork and research and be recognised and accepted both in the art scene and at academic events. Thus, it is important for the leadership of an art faculty to help the top management of the university or higher institutions recognise the efforts, research, and intellectual discourse of the artist-educators, artist-academics in the university. A special score/marking system must be discussed, identified, set up, and proposed to the higher management of the university on ways to appraise and promote the creative arts. Justification must be given to support the reasons for a different marking system for those in the creative arts as the nature of artist-academic works is different from the other faculties. The current appraisal system at most public universities in Malaysia does not recognise the different and unique works and demands of artist-academics and expects them to publish and apply for the same type of research grants as the academics from the pure arts, such as the humanities and social sciences and the sciences. This may not seem fair for the artist-academics as the outcomes of their projects are usually dances, performances, workshop-performances, and exhibitions and not paper publications in high-indexed journals as expected by the mainstream research grant funders.

The leadership must also strategise and formulate a well-thought-out succession plan to direct the faculty in terms of human resources at every level and determine vital positions that are significant for the operation of the faculty. The wellbeing of the staff must always be kept in mind and be of utmost importance to the leadership in educational institutions. A happy staff is a happy faculty, and this drives everyone to be passionate and committed to their artwork, teaching, research, and performances, and to do their all simply because they want to and not because they are made to. Communication channels must be kept open and viable to give and receive input to and from staff, students, and stakeholders for the betterment of the faculty.

Conclusion

> Dissecting the performance … The journey has just begun …

More work needs to be done in academia for the equal recognition of artistic practices and academic scholarship by artist-academics without being discriminating against because of their sex, gender, artwork, and the nature of their performances. The author continues to play many roles and uses her artworks for the benefit of the larger community, for therapeutic purposes, social interaction with inclusivity, and cultural and religious tolerance, through performances and research. The appointment of women artist-lecturers as administrators in the academy brings hope and recognition to women in the arts, and their discourse. Women's occupation as lecturers-cum-artists/performers has enabled us to raise awareness, coalesce our positions within the academy to promote the arts, and enable change within our institutions. The change includes the call for strong support systems looking at the overall wellbeing of the staff and nurturing platforms to prepare and mould young academics, who balance between advancing their careers and raising their young families. The job of a lecturer never ends and even enters the private sphere of her home. Contrastingly, even dance performances come to an end with a thundering applause from the audience. On the contrary, what keeps the academic going is seeing her students' proud performance on the graduation stage and scene. This chapter illustrates the journey of a woman academic, synonymous with the journey of a dancer, "standing on a perfect pointe," undergoing rigorous training, perseverance, and with positive attitudes, determination, and grit – all the characteristics needed to put up a strong performance by a strong woman. Finally, the achievements of women-artist in the academy have shifted the paradigm of traditional inquiry in academia and allowed the arts to be recognised as a legitimate field of study that is worthy of academic discourse.

Notes

1 Conversations with dancers/performers/artists – Aida Redza, Hur Hilyati Ramli, Tetriana Ahmad Fauzi, Siti Rohaya – about women's artwork recognition in the art scene and the academy. These conversations and personal communications were held separately on 24 September 2021, 4 October 2021, 16 October 2021 at Panggung Sasaran (USM), Pentas Studio, Bangunan Lip Sin, Taman Pekaka and at School of the Arts (USM).
2 Celebrating Malaysian women in the arts. https://penangartdistrict.com/celebrating-malaysian-women-in-arts/
3 Art Center, USM was transformed into School of the Arts in 1999.
4 *Arangetram* is the inaugural debut of a Baharatnatyam dancer after undergoing years of training, mastering the dance form and movement techniques. Arangetram consists of the standard seven-to-nine dances which are known as the *Margam* or the complete repertoire of Baharatanatyam. The Arangetram marks the accomplished dancer who has mastered the art of performing and teaching.
5 Aida Redza, Marion D'Cruz, and Mew Chang Tsing are the women choreographers that the author studied with and researched for her doctoral studies. Her thesis, titled "Performing the Strong Woman: A Study on the Relationship between the Female Role-Type and the Presence of Feminism in Contemporary Dance in Malaysia," is one of the first to discuss and theorize "Dancing the Strong Woman" in Malaysia. It was later published with the title *Dancing the Strong Woman in Contemporary Dance in Malaysia*, by Lambert Academic, Germany (2011).

References

Aksiah, A. (1994). Gender: A social factor in political consciousness and active participation. In Haas, R., & Hashim, R., (Eds.), *Malaysian women creating their political awareness* (pp. 1–15). Kuala Lumpur: Asian Institute for Development Communication.
Austin, G. (1998). Feminist theories: Paying attention to women. In L. Goodman & D. J. Gay (Eds.), *The Routledge reader in gender and performance* (pp. 136–142). London: Routledge.
Copeland, R. (1998). Sexual politics. In S. E. Friedler & S. B. Glazer (Eds.), *Dancing female: Lives and issues of women in contemporary dance* (pp. 123–138). Amsterdam: Harwood Academic Publishing.
De Beauvoir, S. (1972). *The second sex*. Harmondsworth: Penguin Books.
Elwes, C. (1985). Floating femininity: A look at performance art by women. In Jacqueline Morreau & Sarah Kent (Eds.), *Women's images of men*. London: Writers and Readers Publishing.
Forte, J. K. (1998). Women's performance art: Feminism and postmodernism. In L. Goodman & J. De Gay (Eds.), *The Routledge reader in gender and performance* (1st ed., pp. 236–240). Routledge. (Original work published 1988)
Grimshaw, J. (1986). *Philosophy and feminist thinking*. Minnesota: University of Minnesota Press.

Haviland, L. C. (1998). Women in dance in higher education. In S. E. Friedler & S. B. Glazer (Eds.), *Dancing female: Lives and issues of women in contemporary dance* (pp. 97–104). Amsterdam: Harwood Academic Publishing.

Léon, C. T. (1995). The second sex: Differently other or otherly different?. *Simone de Beauvoir Studies, 12*, 139–153.

Ling, B. I. C. (2018). Postmodern feminist identity through artworks by selected Malaysian female artists (2000–2015). (Master Dissertation, Universiti Sains Malaysia)

Mill, J. S., & Mill, H. T. (1983). *The enfranchisement of women and the subjection of women*. London: Virago Press. (Original work published 1869)

Ollenburger, J. C., & Moore, H. (1998). *A sociology of women*. New Jersey: Prentice Hall.

Richardson, D., & Robinson, V. (Eds.). (1993). *Introducing women's studies*. London: MacMillan Press Ltd.

School of the Arts, Universiti Sains Malaysia (2022). *Galeri Adiwarna* [Online Image]. Universiti Sains Malaysia. https://art.usm.my/facilities/

Watkins, S. A., Rueda, M., & Rodriguez, M. (1999). *Introducing feminism*. Cambridge: Icon Books.

Wolf, J. (1998). Dance criticism: Feminism, theory and choreography. In L. Goodman & D. J. Gay (Eds.), The *Routledge reader in gender and performance* (pp. 241–246). London: Routledge.

4 Carrying the world on your back

The burden of self-care for under-represented women

Sana Rahim

In this chapter, I place the lived experiences of under-represented women at the heart of the discussion around wellbeing and self-care in higher education. Through their visual narratives, lived experiences, and practical strategies, I provide a deep insight into the quest for wellbeing policies and self-care practices that are useful for minority diasporic communities as well as under-represented women in higher education in and from the Global South. In doing so, I draw upon critiques of power, practices, and the positions of the marginalised within the institution, academia, and the community to explore how various spaces in self-care and wellbeing both empower and restrict women at different stages and in different contexts. Here I also open the conceptual space in which we can see indications of the many social realities in operation within the wider context of neoliberal wellbeing ideas. Thus, in this chapter, I raise some key questions on the conceptual challenges that the practice of offloading self-care burdens onto the individual subject pose and what that means for the individuals already bearing the double burden of being on the receiving end of harassment and discrimination whilst also working towards dismantling it (Ahmed, 2012). Having to deal with a third burden of taking care of the self with wellbeing responsibilities is a luxury for those trying to simply survive (see Figure 4.1).

Literature

Recently, there is a growing body of research on self-care and wellbeing in academia (Fetherston et al., 2020). However, self-care still needs to be "more closely and extensively studied" to create a more supportive academic culture, particularly in relation to gender disparities (Gaudet et al., 2021, p. 2). Gaudet et al. (2021) argue that little attention is given to women's experiences with caring as they navigate the "careless doxa" of academic institutions. In the context of neoliberal institutions, women are paying a higher price than men to pursue their careers (Rosa & Clavero, 2020). On the same note, Bisaililon et al. (2020, p. 135) argue that with the pushing of neoliberal forms of logic, "what emerges is a working environment rife with expectations that may not be achievable unless a worker foregoes their health and equilibrium." They further point out that people of colour, people with an illness or disability, and all those individuals "with intersecting and intimate knowledges of being marginalised" report facing sickness most acutely

DOI: 10.4324/9781003341482-5

Figure 4.1 Context of who I am to the visual narrative/positionality. The image here shows indigenous herbs and oils that are used for self-care routines. This was provided by one of the study participants.

(Bisalilion et al., 2020, p. 135). Thus far, I have touched upon current studies that are critiquing the neoliberal workload expectations for women in academia. My study investigates the way in which neoliberal self-care and wellbeing notions contribute to these pressures for already marginalised and under-represented women in academia. From this perspective, a more nuanced analysis is needed when we talk about self-care, wellbeing, and foreign women in academia – particularly, the concept of the double-strangers between productivity, marginalisation, and resistance (Strauβ & Boncori. 2020). In this way, I would argue that marginalised women cannot contribute to the epistemic landscape in similar ways to those who do not experience discrimination (Dotson, 2012), and this can then be a harmful consequence and compromise self-recognition (Hänel, 2020).

One way of better understanding the relationship between the marginalised scholar in academia and their wellbeing is to draw upon Ahmed's (2012, p. 40) scholarship *Being included*. Ahmed's conversation about comfort is very useful here. For Ahmed, the word *comfort* suggests wellbeing and satisfaction, but it can also suggest an ease and easiness. Comfort is about an encounter between bodies and worlds, the promise of a "sinking" feeling. "If white bodies are comfortable, it is because they can sink into spaces that extend their shape." She points out that bodies stick out when they are out of place. "To inhabit whiteness as a non-white body can be uncomfortable: you might even fail the comfort test." Ahmed argues that it can be the seemingly simple acts such as, for example, walking into the room that cause discomfort (2012, p. 40).

> The body that causes their discomfort (by not fulfilling an expectation of whiteness) is the one who must work hard to make others comfortable. You have to pass by passing your way through whiteness, by being seamless or minimising the signs of difference.
>
> (2012, p. 40)

This analysis can allow us to understand and re-establish the links between the failure of the current institutional wellbeing policies and the needs of these groups of women in academia.

Methodology

The current study is a phenomenological examination of under-represented female academics in higher education and their understanding of self-care and wellbeing in the academy. Phenomenology is a qualitative research approach that is uniquely positioned to support this inquiry (Neubauer, Witkop, & Varpio, 2019, p. 92). For the purposes of this study, the term *under-represented* is used to denote people that are both diasporic minority communities and nationals as well as those in the Global South. Thus, in this study, I do not use the terms BAME (black, Asian, and minority ethnic) and BME (black and minority ethnic) specifically because they emphasise certain ethnic minority groups (and exclude other minority groups). However, the terms have been useful for me in recruiting participants for purposive sampling.

Facebook groups, both public and private, as well as LinkedIn, were useful and provided me with a diverse population for the recruitment of participants. I conducted ten interviews that were initially designed to be 30–40 minutes but were all around 60 minutes each. The sample included two women living and working in the Global South, two British-born ethnic minority women, and six women from the diaspora. Women in the study were from various ethnicities and did and did not neatly fit into the BAME category. This sample includes mixed-race, Pakistani, Indian, Bangladeshi, Mexican, Iranian, and African American women. All names have been randomly picked and all participants are fully anonymised.

Discussion

Self-care and its practices and advancements have been a challenge to everyone in higher education for a long time now. This has been heightened during a pandemic and particularly for women with extra care burdens. Over the past few years, in discussions of the need for self-care and wellbeing for academics, there have been increased acknowledgement and confessions in writing from positions of privilege. One such example is as follows. In their paper "Self-care for academics: A poetic invitation to reflect and resist," O'Dywer et al. (2018) reflect on their positions as being "white, able-bodied, and currently employed in established universities in Anglophone nations." "Each of us," they say, "holds a full-time continuing teaching and research position," and they acknowledge that the divide in experiences is stark. They then invite readers to dialogue through a collaborative construction of a poem that they used to explore their process of caring for the self. This poem comes as a representation of their self-care and reflective practice. A short excerpt from the poem is as follows:

Self-care: A manifesto

Eat apple pancakes smothered in Nutella.

Practice yoga
Watch *The English Patient*
Turn off email notifications
Walk.
Drink wine
Have a massage
Eat fish and chips
Swim.
Bake cookies
Eat cookies
Read to small children
Meditate.
Drink coffee
Buy flowers
Watch *RuPaul's Drag Race*
Gossip.
Eat hot cross buns
Read *Pride and Prejudice*
Plant seedlings in the dirt
Dance.
Drink champagne
Watch *Pitch Perfect*
Stand in damp grass and name the constellations
(O'Dywer et al., 2018)

Survival, self-care, and institutions

I do not write this chapter and present these experiences of under-represented women in academia in any way to suggest that the above poem of practices and other such work that looks at self-care from similar standpoints are not beautiful experiences and/or should not be done. And I appreciate that we under-represented women of academia do attempt to do some of these. Our strategies or tips may overlap in some cases. But what I do want to say and highlight in this chapter is that this sort of material needs to be presented with caution – particularly if we name it self-care instead of, for example, a reflection on luxuries. Self-care for some is still very much about survival.

The authors of this poem encourage dialogue and their article, they say, "serves as an invitation to other academics," so I take this opportunity here in this chapter to talk to the many advocates of self-care and wellbeing in higher education and present a glimpse of what self-care means to us as under-represented women from the Global South and diasporic minority communities or other marginalised communities, including those that do and do not neatly fit into the box of BAME (Aspinall, 2020). From my discussions with participants and my personal experiences, our poem, if there was one, would consist of words and phrases such as "survive harassment and racism," "find money to fund therapy," and "work more to prove yourself." Our wish lists consist of being able to say no and getting paid for the work we do. Thus, self-care and wellbeing are very different for those of us that are under-represented in academia. Simply acknowledging that racism exists or that some of us are privileged is nowhere near enough if the wellbeing of women in academia is to be taken seriously. We are not only fighting against ridiculous workloads, under-funded institutions, gendered structural and systemic disadvantages, and pressures of publishing as our colleagues are; we are also managing 'invisible work' (Social Sciences Feminist Network Research Interest Group, 2017) such as educating people on decolonising their curriculums, educating about recognising racist biases, inspiring students that they can make it regardless of who they are, and, more often than not, carrying with us historical trauma.

In this first section, I present some of the specific challenges under-represented women in academia may go through. In this way, I present context for, and set the scene for, the conversation on self-care being, for some, still very much about survival. The data reveals that in each case, the women were painfully aware of the challenges and struggles imposed on them in higher education. For example, one participant spoke about how: *"academia causes an environment that requires self-sacrificing" – Liliana.* Another participant spoke about the difficulties she faced with what academia presents as *"normal"*: *"the situation was very hard and it took me to a breakdown after two years. I went to the hospital and everything because I didn't have the emotional tools to manage the situations that in academia are very normal" – Sofia.* Participants reported that on a daily basis, they were dealing with uncomfortable situations and struggles. Many spoke about facing racism, tough visa processes, and unpaid labour. Comments include:

> When the bottom falls there's no net for me. You cannot self-care your way out of a bad structure. And care isn't about that. Self-care is about survival – when we're talking about survival we're talking about care. You can't thrive until you are able to survive.
>
> – Hannah

> I didn't know that it was not just the pressure or the stress of my PhD or my work, but it was the stress of being in a white institution that [has] no idea where I am coming from or what I am talking about.
>
> – Sally

There is cultural capitalism. It's just terrible that there is no support for artists or academics. The situation here is unacceptable, and all the venues are managed by white women.

– Mia

The visa is looming over my head – the home office is a fascist, notoriously racist organisation and so is border control. I feel like a woman really without a country. I don't want to go back now after living here for four years, I'm not sure I really want to live here either. I know I can never outrun racism, which is disgusting when you think about, it but yeh I don't know what I'm going to do.

– Sofia

Because I was working on race because I was talking about the narrative. The importance of actually recognising racism bias. That went very poorly. It was not very uncommon for me to walk into rooms where they were bragging about not letting any women into the club – despite it being illegal. I've been physically assaulted by people; I've been shaken; I've had people get in my face; I've been chased in parking lots, being yelled at – So that was my first year.

– Hannah

When I was working and when I was asking for money for this work, I was being told that there is no budget for this and a month later a student who was doing this same admin work was being paid to do it "a white British kid." It was – that really damaged my mental health. Now that I think back, I didn't have the tools at the time to navigate academia – I took it very personally. I was applying for post-docs and it didn't happen. Any offer I did get I was told to bring my own funding. I was totally disappointed. Young male British students were offered paid work that I had been doing for free.

– Sally

Though participants often spoke about the need to look after themselves or worried about their wellbeing, and were aware of the importance of doing so, they did not find any support in the institutions they were at. For these academics, self-care and wellbeing discussions were at best superficial and at worst added to their problems. The participants in the study noted that the self-care practices they were being pushed to do did not work for them or suit them. Not surprisingly, yoga came up in numerous interviews and the conversations and experiences were unique each time, revealing the dangers of the one-size-fits-all approaches in policies. One academic described her experience of being offered a chance to attend yoga by other academics as troubling for her:

If one more woman tells me oh do you want to try yoga? Yoga? I'm a big girl. My body is very comfortable here. This whole get-healthy narrative. Well, if you weren't healthy before you went into a pandemic, you're not going to get healthy during a pandemic, and this whole pressure of get healthy. If I say to someone I'm depressed, and they say go for a walk, because I didn't do that before the pandemic. So, what I'm saying is this whole self-care against me is colonialization. It is whitewashed; it has nothing to do with care.

– Sofia

Another participant explained how yoga had been taken over by white women and particularly venues and their management. A teacher of yoga herself, she spoke about how yoga had been altered to become something to make money from instead of its original peaceful purpose of promoting wellbeing. Sofia says, *"I find you can't talk about mindfulness without talking about where it comes from. There are many, many ways to mindfulness – many indigenous practices co-opted by unis/corporations without acknowledgement."* She goes on to say that *"This whole self-care thing has become so commercialised."*

Participants indicated that being mentored on or overly encouraged to pursue wellbeing "websites" and "wellbeing committees" at institutions was not valuable and in fact disregarded the real problems in higher education and academia:

To sit there and talk about mindfulness, to sit there and have wellbeing committees. Those committees really, really should be focused on how do we end precarity for graduate students, how do we make sure things like conferences are affordable. You want to talk about wellbeing – wellbeing starts with basic needs being met, and (not like Maslow, stolen from hierarchy, which was stolen from indigenous knowledge and inverted) we know that children who do not have access to food and good rest don't do well in school and they act out. Why do we think it any different for adults? – if you know most of your student body is paying to be here and you're demanding more labour of them – you know all of these inequalities exist to sit there and put out some nonsense about wellbeing practices that don't deal with structural issues. It's kind of a slap in the face.

– Hannah

This whole rhetoric – to describe this self-care movement is mind-numbing and again more damaging than it is good – and the burden of self-care is vitally important, particularly when we're facing a pandemic. Most of us are mothers, partners, wives, and we work. Not only do we have to get through all of this but we also have to identify it because it's not even defined what self-care is.

– Sofia

We have no support. The university has the resources and I think the white women didn't understand that I needed the community more than them.

– Sally

The biggest thing I've told students is don't go for mindfulness from the university. Get real help! If you don't know how to access it, I will help you access it. The mindfulness stuff that the faculty represents. I mean I don't need to be told how to notice the feel of freedom right now. That's not going to do anything when I'm an international unfunded student under duress to finish in a certain amount of time watching resources go to other people with nothing I can access.

– Hannah

I don't think I realised until I got this far – this far in my PhD journey – how little support you get as postgraduate students. Self-care for the university is a joke. The mental health waiting lists are months and months. There is absolutely no support at all.

– Sofia

Academics spoke about what they do need versus what they were being offered. Mia says, *"I already have two apps (Mind and Calm); how many more?"* One academic explained to me that

we do need to emphasise self-care, but you see, I do not need pampering. I need a good listener that I can tell my sorrows to, who can guide me, give me suggestions. If we get proper care, we will flourish.

– Liliana

The idea that one more plant or one more facial can solve all our problems is far from the truth. Another participant tells me that all she needs is some time off: *"Self-care advocates think why don't you meditate? I don't even have a day off."* – Sally. Others talked to me about their own specific challenges in their own institutions and academic communities. For example, one academic from the Global South tells me that *"there are unwritten codes here, for example, if you enter a park, you cannot run around very fast if you're a woman, so we need to focus on spiritual self-care more than, for example, physical self-care."* – Clara. Self-care and wellbeing advice for academics is often not culturally diverse or aware. She found that the overall narrative of self-care and wellbeing did not consider any cultural struggles or differences.

Therapy

Of the participants in my study, nine out of ten had been to therapy sessions for stress, depression, or anxiety-related issues. This is an overwhelming majority, with eight out of the nine participants that had been to therapy having to get this support and treatment outside of the academy at their own cost. Women from the diaspora struggled to find therapists that understood their issues, adding to the pain. Researchers and clinicians have pointed to the need for culturally sensitive interventions, where racial matching or concordance is described as an element of culturally responsive care that can reduce mental health disparities for ethnic minorities (Meyer, and Zane, 2013). However, this does not play out smoothly in practice. Participants found that they rarely received care from a therapist of colour even in cases where they specifically asked for this. Some experiences are described here:

If you are not from this country and you live in this country, you need therapy. Everyone needs therapy in general anyway, but if you are from the diaspora and English is not your first language, you need to have therapy with someone who understands racial injustice. During the long term, I had therapy that helped me a lot – a humanistic approach – but you don't get that everywhere.

– Sally

Women of colour, they have the extra burden of finding a clinician of colour, because how am I going to sit there and complain to this white person about my problems being black. Black patients have a 95 percent chance of never being seen by someone that looks like them. To be taken seriously, again that alone is traumatic because if you're ill, then you have to fight at the same time. And then you see black doctors being neglected by their own structures. I had childhood trauma that I had been dragging behind me like a dead body. So, I paid for my own therapy. I realised I have got a lot of trauma myself and how can I advocate for women and their trauma if I'm so f—— myself. And excuse my language. We are in constant survival mode and we don't have the luxury that white women do – where we can cry victim – they have no clue what being a victim is.

– Sofia

Women academics from the Global South are still very much battling stigma around mental health. For these women, using mental health services presented its own set of challenges:

Whenever our faculty member is on the committee – I will not be comfortable with sharing my own personal problems with them. We know that mental health treatment costs a lot of money, for a student. Here we will get stigma, not love. The idea that they are mental, that's why they will go to a mental psychiatrist. We would expect mental hospitals to be crowded, but here they are empty. But we do have to do this secretly. Our university has a high rate of suicide. There is a lot of pressure. Especially for girls, e.g., marriage.

– Lilana

I had therapy outside the academy. There are unwritten rules. If there are psychologists, I didn't use them. I prefer to use one from outside because … I don't know why, maybe I feel unsafe – the stigma. I want to be a professor and I think it would be a stigma.

– Clara

Resilience

Interview data and my own experiences reveal that resilience is something we are very much in a problematic relationship with. Women have to negotiate their actions in relation to rest and care within the environment that they find themselves (Nicol & Yee, 2017). Participants spoke about how they internalised the need to work harder, do better, and prove themselves, and how this was a difficult challenge to overcome. The line of thinking here is usually that resting is wasting valuable time that could be, or should be, used to be more productive. Similarly, saying no is rejecting an opportunity that others may not have been given, and thus is in some way ungrateful. It will come as no surprise that under-represented women feel the need to put more effort in, do more work, and prove their worth. Although used in a different context, Alison Howell's study on military psychological resilience training (2014) can be applied here to understand how academia pushes people to not only keep working in tough circumstances but "thrive" in them, where "resilience is a means for contributing to the production of these forms of precarity" (2015, p. 28). The following excerpts illustrate some of these dilemmas and how the participants have been dealing with them.

> I don't know what it is. It's always this inhibition of what the other person is thinking of me. That if I'm from a certain background and I'm here then I have to prove myself and I have to work extra hard and I have to put in more hours even though I have already done this by being shortlisted and through a proper process. I know that I deserve it, but still, there is this urge to be on my toes all the time. No matter how high a position you reach, you will always worry about what the white person in the room is thinking about you, and you will be always seeking validation in some sense from them. In hindsight I ask myself am I resilient? am I pushing my boundaries? or am I moving towards a more toxic work culture that I am setting for myself?
>
> I have been very lucky to get all the opportunities that I got, and I am aware of it all the time [that] I have to make every minute count and I can't take anything lightly. A lot of people that come from the same background have not had the same opportunities and in the past year I don't think I've done this – it's on my wish list to say no. this is something I have always struggled with. Social media has made it worse with toxic positivity all the time.

> If I want to watch a fun, useless, senseless show on Netflix, I'm like, no I will watch a documentary. Being a woman, I have to work extra hard to get somewhere. When I see someone do well, I'm like omg I have to step up. The culture differs – a major factor is the need to prove themselves.
>
> – Avery

> Everything was an opportunity. That idea of saying yes to everything – even with the postdoc, I have so much anxiety, and I'm going to do it anyway. But my idea of resilience has shifted from being able to handle everything to resilience has now become about feeding my soul. Saying yes to new experiences but which one is going to feed me – reserving the right to change my mind. Something about that loyalty and that I've given my word. It is impressed upon us that we are never misrepresenting ourselves. That idea/thought that

we are – "everyone that someone might perceive us to be we are suddenly emblematic for" and that is such a heavy thing to bear. And resilience really is about claiming in a certain way your own right to be an individual with individual needs.

– Hannah

The tropes about us manifest in different ways. There [is] still the problem [of] dressing up too much or looking a certain way – I have personally struggled with it. You don't want to be someone who is too out there. The burden is always on you to control the situation and maintain the situation.

– Avery

What doesn't kill you makes you stronger – I absolutely refute that because if that was the case, there wouldn't be suicide or trauma, I don't agree with that sentiment. The trope of the strong black woman has been more damaging to black women then empowering because what it does is rob us of our emotional responses to trauma.

– Sofia

Strategies unpacked as tips: "Connecting to the self"

The women interviewed for the study all did practice self-care in various ways and, as mentioned earlier, were aware of the need for and importance of doing so. Each participant was asked whether she was happy to share her own experiences and suggestions for others regarding their own self-care strategies. Participants talked at length about their own interests, hobbies, and, in some cases, coping mechanisms. Many women talked to me about making friends and creating communities outside of the academy or faculty. For example, one participant says: *"I had to go out and meet other people from the diaspora." – Avery*, and another says:

You have to be patient; it is a journey. It took me a while to find my own group even outside of academia; you have to build networks, you have to get out of your comfort zone. Mentally that has been the most satisfying thing.

– Hannah

Indigenous knowledge and self-care practices were valuable strategies given by participants:

My coping mechanism was the help of communities that were working on topics of race and displacement and my creativity has been my coping mechanism.

– Sally

I used herbs – I used steaming – infusions, oils, and body-based practices. Being with different substances, flowers and items.

– Faith

Ancestral knowledge indigenous groups helped a lot – I was doing this uncon-sciously during my PhD and consciously after. This opened a new world for me and was one of the best things I could do. I decided to be better by myself.

– Sally

Self-care for me is very much about accepting pain and coping with it through the three pillars: emotional, physical, and spiritual awareness. Letting go of what I can't control, forgiving people that hurt me and putting it away. An old proverb of ours: I can't always want people to love me, I have to forgive them. I have to be mindful – sometimes I can do this, other times I cannot. Trying not to compare myself to others (in different environments); that can be very harmful for myself. Looking back and thinking about why I am where I am. My current situation is the outcome of my past decisions, so I am responsible for my decisions. Consider myself a tree – and the outcome the fruit. And of course, music, walking, communication – these are all forms of emotional self-care for me.

– Clara

I think everyone has their own strategies and coping mechanisms. I would suggest switching off my phone when it's near to me at night. Learning to quit the circles that are not good for me. Balancing my diet well and getting proper sleep. *Bullet journaling and reading for pleasure have been great strategies.*

– Liliana

It's important to find places where you do see yourself as normal, and the academy doesn't afford those. Find spaces, take long walks, build friendships, poetry groups; exercise is paramount and we forget about that. The idea that mindfulness is a break from your life and that's so much at odds; it is a part of your life.

– Hannah

I have tried to connect to myself recently. I did a lot of introspection. I have tried hypnotherapy. Now I've understood what self-care is and asked myself what you can do outside of this PhD because you're not going to do Zumba and you're not athletic (my knees don't allow it anymore), so I have taken up cryptogram and colouring. I'm thinking back to what I used to like to do and I have started audiobooks too.

– Sofia

Some strategies that have been useful
* Bullet journaling
* Hypnotherapy
* Dance
* Walks and dinners with the family
* Saying no and being comfortable with doing nothing
* Creating or and being a part of communities with others in similar positions

- Working on topics that help to break the silence
- Therapy
- Spiritual awareness
- Infusing oils, herbs, and aromatherapy
- Cryptogram, colouring, and paint by numbers
- Reflecting back to your own childhood hobbies

Conclusion

This chapter and the study it presented sought to help us to better understand the relationship between self-care and wellbeing and under-represented women in academia. The findings suggest that self-care and wellbeing are very much at home with all women in academia, but there are some serious and real negative and harmful implications for women that are already carrying the burdens of (i) being on the receiving end of discrimination and trying to achieve self-recognition, (ii) educating and taking on extra care work, and now (iii) being put on the spot for either taking up or conducting neoliberal self-care and wellbeing policies and practices. In order to make academia a safer place for marginalised female academics, we need to open up spaces for them to speak and be heard. We need a clear and active focus on ensuring that self-care and wellbeing notions, policies, and practices progress from the stage of designing to implementation, taking into consideration the diversity in academia, and celebrating it rather than hindering it.

Consequently, the aim of this chapter was to highlight the need to disrupt the current climate of encouraging "resilience" and the "winner takes all" approach in academia, and to uncover ways in which the dialogue of self-care can be transformed from "managing the self" to a "connect to the self" approach. Ultimately the answers to how social practices of self-care within academia can be beneficial for under-represented women will come from (i) them having the space to voice their own individual experiences and needs in relation to self-care, with policies and practices developed from this rather than the "one size fits all" approach currently adopted in institutions, and (ii) institutions structured by representative standards and values that do not encourage self-sacrifice.

References

Ahmed, S. (2012). On *Being Included: Racism and Diversity in Institutional Life*. Duke University Press.

Aspinall, P. J. (2020). Ethnic/Racial Terminology as a Form of Representation: A Critical Review of the Lexicon of Collective and Specific Terms in Use in Britain. *Genealogy*, 4(3), 1–14. http://doi.org/10.3390/genealogy4030087

Bisaillon, Cattapan, Driessen, Van Duin, Spruit, Anton, & Jecker. (2020). Doing Academia Differently: "I Needed Self-Help Less Than I Needed a Fair Society". *Feminist Studies*, 46(1), 130–157.

Dotson. K. (2012). A Cautionary Tale: On Limiting Epistemic Oppression. *Frontiers: A Journal of Women Studies*, 33(1), 24–47. https://doi.org/10.5250/fronjwomestud.33.1.0024

Fetherston, C., Fetherston, A., Batt, S., Sully, M., & Wei, R. (2020). Wellbeing and Work-life Merge in Australian and UK Academics. *Studies in Higher Education*, *46*(12), 2774–2788. https://doi.org/10.1080/03075079.2020.1828326

Gaudet, M. I., Bujaki, M., & Bourgeault, I. L. (2021). Women and Gender Equity in Academia through the Conceptual Lens of Care. *Journal of Gender Studies*, 31(1), 1–13. https://doi.org/10.1080/09589236.2021.1944848

Hänel, H. C. (2020). Hermeneutical Injustice, (Self-) Recognition, and Academia. *Hypatia*, *35*(2), 336–354. https://doi.org/10.1017/hyp.2020.3

Howell, A. (2014). Resilience, War, and Austerity: The Ethics of Military Human Enhancement and the Politics of Data. *Security Dialogue*, *46*(1), 15–31. https://doi.org/10.1177/0967010614551040

Meyer, O. L., & Zane, N. (2013). The Influence of Race and Ethnicity In Clients' Experiences of Mental Health Treatment. *Journal of Community Psychology*, *41*(7), 884–901. https://doi.org/10.1002/jcop.21580

Neubauer, B. E., Witkop, C. T., & Varpio, L. (2019). How Phenomenology Can Help us Learn from the Experiences of Others. *Perspectives on Medical Education*, *8*(2), 90–97. https://doi.org/10.1007/s40037-019-0509-2

Nicol, D. J., & Yee, J. A. (2017). "Reclaiming Our Time": Women of Color Faculty and Radical Self-Care in the Academy. *Feminist Teacher*, *27*(2–3), 133–156. https://doi.org/10.5406/femteacher.27.2-3.0133

O'Dwyer, S., Pinto, S. & McDonough, S. (2018). Self-care for Academics: A Poetic Invitation to Reflect and Resist. *Reflective Practice*, *19*(2), 243–249. https://doi.org/10.1080/14623943.2018.1437407

Rosa, R., & Clavero, S. (2020). The challenge of neoliberalism and precarity for gender sensitivity in academia. In Eileen D. & Siobhán C. (Eds.), *The Gender-Sensitive University*, (pp. 16–28). Oxfordshire: Routledge.

Social Sciences Feminist Network Research Interest Group. (2017). The Burden of Invisible Work in Academia: Social Inequalities and Time Use in Five University Departments. *Humboldt Journal of Social Relations*, *39*, 228–245. http://www.jstor.org/stable/90007882

Strauβ, A., & Boncori, I. (2020). Foreign Women in Academia: Double-Strangers between Productivity, Marginalization and Resistance. *Gender, Work & Organization*, *27*(6), 1004–1019. https://doi.org/10.1111/gwao.12432

Part II

Identity formations and the career trajectory

5 Solitude, sanctuary, and pseudo-mentors

A pandemic lens on an early career transition into doing and being research/researcher

Nicola Sum

Buried deep in the pandemic lockdown of Covid-19, I am drawn to Deepak Chopra's blog for hope, which begins with the statement "When your mind and heart are truly open abundance will flow to you effortlessly and easily" (Chopra, 2020). It is a fitting reminder of the previous moments of transition in my lifetime where his books, or reflections, seemingly appear unsought during times of decision-making and change that I have been facing. Now as I seek to draw some lines, turn some pages, leave some luggage behind at the last station, or whatever your choice of metaphor may be, and move forward with my decision to be part of academia, it is past the shadow cast by those two words – *being* and *doing* – omnipresent in the mind of a fledgling academic. Given the dearth of literature accounting for the experiences of new scholars working in the intersectional spaces of colour and gender (Bhopal et al., 2018; Moss-Racusin et al., 2012), the purpose of this study is to explore the challenges of this transition. While the disruption of the pandemic brought with it further economic, social, and political tensions for work in the Australian higher education sector, it also provided potentially new and different opportunities to find other pathways to be and do (Barrow et al., 2020; Monk & McKay, 2017). As an early career researcher, I aim to provide a narrative that may resonate with other scholars of similar experiences, who may be working in different settings at this time. In doing so, I hope to engage in much-needed discourse and reflexivity on considered ways of working in higher education at this critical time. When public sentiment is driven by the need to reimagine education, what are we reimagining for ourselves? I am hopeful that finding and defining care and self-care on our own terms, through balanced moments of solitude, sanctuary, and interactions with pseudo-mentors, contributes to communities of practice that extend beyond campus gates and nation-states. Reimagining how we work provides us with opportunities to define and shape the relationships and aspects of work that we value, choose to belong to, and work alongside with. In light of this, I share my visual narrative, a cryptic crossword, followed by my positionality to my work as an early career researcher (ECR). I explain the context of this narrative and discuss the key themes of fight or flight, identity, and mentoring that scholarship provides in relation to ECR experiences in higher education. Most significantly, thinking about and writing this piece has led me to reconnect with the ways in which women write and work in solitude, and the sanctuary that

DOI: 10.4324/9781003341482-7

home provides for this creative expression. Through a lens of positioning theory (Van Langenhove & Harré, 1999), I analyse my lived experience as an early career researcher (ECR) and discuss these implications for being a researcher and doing research work.

Visual narrative

The *Cryptic crossword of Doing Words* (Figure 5.1) gathers my reflections of being (and doing work as) an academic when the lockdown of the pandemic began in 2020. It is accompanied by an attempt at *poetry* on the right-hand side and the *suggested solutions* at the bottom-right corner. It is an attempt at poetry because I am not a poet, just as I am not an academic, or at least I was not sure how to be one at this time. The solutions are harder to see, and possibly not obvious to all, at times even seeming completely unclear. The opaqueness speaks for itself, and speaks to my quest to understand how and why work in the academe is as it is. As importantly, it is a pondering on how I might work productively and not be swallowed up by the system – a whole and undigested mess. My visual narrative may be my attempt at triptych art but in disorganised panels, capturing some part of a pilgrimage for an academic holy grail of how to sustain life in academia. It could be a triangulated idea framed in a quadrilateral shape, which holds a mirror up to my sense of being a misfit, or what scholars often insist on labelling as impostor syndrome (McGee et al., 2021). However, it is more than likely the seemingly organised and structured screen to a tumultuous collection of ideas and emotions located backstage behind the black square curtain.

Positioning

My adult life has been shaped by not only career and work transitions, but also life relocations. Beginning with the end of a business degree, which led to an early foray into chartered accounting, I chose to retrain and follow my passion for teaching. That transition came without the fanfare and thunderbolts that one would imagine should accompany an epiphany. Nonetheless, education opened a door to happiness and satisfaction that made me giddy with glee. It also became a job and a role that opened the world to my wandering spirit. Over two decades, I had immersed myself in schools and education systems in various countries (Hayden, 2011). Across curricula, culture, and community, change and transition had become a way to knowing myself and understanding the world around me (Bunnell, 2016). Having grown up as a third-culture child in Australia, I find being somewhat of an outsider has never been a new sensation (Walter & Auton-Cuff, 2009). The shift into this working life positioned me more as a global citizen than I imagined (Bunnell, 2016). My attitude to education has always been driven by an underlying moral purpose. Leadership roles and responsibilities arose from my need to address problems and find solutions (Fullan, 2013). This need for problem-solving led to my doctoral study, which in turn led to an ongoing role in an esteemed university, and the transition from school principal to student to academic. Moving from a life's work in schools to a novice in research and seemingly

Cryptic crossword of doing words
For much I hope to be doing
But all the while knowing
There is too much I don't know how to do
Forces roiling in an atmosphere
Agents of priorities not centred on my own
Even as I stare at what I need to be doing
I see all the black space of not enough done
Not enough words
Not enough doing words
Doing, doing and doing and some more
To leave a dent in the black space
Why? For whom?
Can it sit on the coffee table till next Saturday?
Will the doing words have changed?

Across:
1. Reinvented many times
2. Air is raining messages
3. If your mind were only
4. Will be sharp enough

Down:
1. Words before words
2. Questions endlessly worth answering
3. As much below ground as above
4. Something you need to hear
5. Laugh at a single name they're forced to share
6. Life runs alongside them, unseen

Figure 5.1 The *Cryptic crossword of Doing Words*.

to an expert upon conferral was seamless on paper but silent in practice. The silence was isolating and exclusionary. Out of the black curtain of silence came frequent directions and expectations to be met. I was emailed things that I would be doing and taken aside for pep-talks on how I should be. This is disjointed from the work I see and hear around me and that I expected to be doing myself – thinking about research findings and writing about it to contribute to the field (Petersen, 2011; Lahiri-Roy et al., 2021).

I am privileged by the hard work of my parents, which enabled me to access an education and transition into work. Both my parents held high expectations for study, and university qualifications were always a priority in our family (Jones & Ludhra, 2019). My parents raised two daughters. We looked after ourselves, because it took both parents working full-time to build a life for us in Australia. We grew up with bullying and name-calling because of the empty assumptions people made about Asians in Australia at that time. As teenagers, we both worked part-time in retail. It was a rite of passage for high school life in Melbourne. We were often congratulated on our English by customers, who would accompany their comments with exaggerated hand gestures, as though they might have been right about us in the first place. I am brought back to this example not for the casual racism or for the many accompanying moments where we put on our *thick skin*. My positioning is grounded in these childhood examples. Knowing who we have been, what we have done, and why we are doing what we choose to do at this time has always been something we carry in us and unpack in safe spaces for meaning and value (Lahiri-Roy & Belford, 2021). Knowing what I know about schools and education, being inducted through the doctoral study, and making the transition into ECR is a journey of finding safe spaces to create meaning and to be of value. The black curtain of silence was the unexpected challenge. I am inclined to step back from the silence, but am not sure how, and then the pandemic began its journey around the world and across our workspaces. The silence became irrelevant; the practice was mine to find.

Context and methodology

Early in the lockdown stage for Melbourne, a team of senior scholars circulated an open invitation for an experimental gathering of autoethnographic researchers (Markham and Harris, 2021). The experiment used Facebook as a vehicle for communication, with the choice to share work as an option to all. This became a 21-day writing project for me (Ellis, 2004). I sought to use journal writing as a reflexive tool to understand my own journey from PhD into full-time academic (Ellis, 2004; Ellis et al., 2011). My visual narrative was taken from my work on this autoethnographic project. As my positionality implies, this journey began from a completed doctorate in 2019, into the black and empty space of Covid-19 lockdown in early 2020, and the struggles to understand academia that had preceded it. The narrative and discussion are shaped by positioning theory (Van Langenhove & Harré, 1999), situating the patterns of reasoning and behaviour in the way that academia is encountered and experienced. I provide an autoethnographic exploration of my transition from doctoral student to early career researcher, disrupted by the onset of the global pandemic. In doing so, I identify my positioning as a successful South Asian woman (Jones & Ludhra, 2019), stepping out of my career in school leadership and into a new career with little guarantee of success (Fisher et al., 2019; White, 2004). I identify the tensions of school as community and belonging manifested, with the cold opaqueness of the academy (Hemmings, 2012). Further contrast is evident in the pressure of being and doing as an early career researcher, as disconnected to my previous responsibility and accountability of being a school leader. The struggle to publish (Petersen, 2011), to network (Noy & Ray, 2012), for mentorship, and to access research opportunities contributes to a landscape with little guidance (Petersen, 2006). These experiences were then compounded by the onset of the global pandemic (Blackmore, 2020). I represent these experiences as the cryptic crossword shown above. These opaque experiences of navigating the work of being an academic are framed in extant literature as the socialisation, or the institutional logic, of working in higher education. I explore the literature which brings together these concepts of identity, institutional logic, and the discourses of solitude, specifically in relation to women, to consider how such dimensions informed my experiences through the pandemic, and the resultant implications for sustaining productive and meaningful work habits.

Early career transitions and mentoring

According to the Australian Research Council (ARC), early career researchers are generally identified as being within five years of having completed their doctoral study and in full-time employment as an academic or in a research role (Bazeley, 2003). While there are nuances in the journeys made by ECRs during and directly following the completion of their PhDs, this is the definition applied by the ARC. Further to this definition, Bazeley (2003) also concluded that the "promising early career researcher is well advanced from being a beginner in research" (p. 277), distinguished by the likelihood of having already completed a "major independent project" (p. 277). Operationalising this idea of an ECR, and of one that is promising enough to potentially secure the level of funding driving university metrics, already sets in motion the significance of being a researcher and doing research. Moreover, this being and doing must be set against such ideas of "promising" versus "beginner." Exact terms, beyond the reference to a major independent project, are not clear, but it would seem that ambiguous expectations are implied.

In light of this external expectation, the risk of frustrated researchers opting out and concerns about the potential inability to retain quality researchers, scholars have continued to study trends in the experiences of ECRs. Findings on identity development highlight the tendency for ECRs to adopt positions such as administrative roles, tutored students, and academic writers, related to the level of organising and the complexity of supervision during their doctoral studies (Monereo & Liesa, 2020). Positions can be adopted concurrently, and may vary in relation to the ECR, who consider their work as more or less research oriented. Experiences during doctoral study also influence their sense of wellbeing and preparedness, and perceptions of success. Unsurprisingly, scholars in STEM fields have identified that students who feel less prepared through their studies perceive themselves to be less successful in comparison to their peers, which in turn seems to lead to lower levels of publishing (Fisher et al., 2019). In their study of attrition amongst ECRs, Petersen (2011) found that "stress was rampant" (p. 35), time at work was spent on aspects away from what ECRs considered their core work, and many had strategies for exiting the profession. Furthermore, when unable to face leaving the job, many ECRs had adopted coping mechanisms. Petersen (2011) identified these coping strategies as working to the terms (contractual requirements), withdrawing care to reduce emotional investment, and reframing the role as a career rather than a passion or calling. The concerns here pertain to the purpose of research and how such work is done (Petersen, 2011). While implementing these coping strategies, the identity and authenticity of early career researchers is being re-shaped in ways that are ambiguous at best.

Barrow et al. (2020) considered the theoretical frameworks used in the field of research pertaining to academic identity. They propose that identity becomes a focus when we are uncertain about where we belong, pointing to the way that the autonomy of an academic to choose their own research agenda has been impacted. Accountability and performativity initiatives have centred institutional metrics as the measure of academic success, and the trend towards casual employment in the higher education sector has particular impacts on early career and female academics (Barrow et al., 2020). In response to such challenges, the professoriate proposes that they represent a potential intervention. Specifically, Boyd and Horstmanshof (2013) identify that the professoriate is not able to address the "institutional concerns," instead championing the "the age-tradition, that of the master-apprenticeship mentoring process" (p. 76). This mentoring approach is viewed as supporting new academics' survival in the modern university. Survival as a goal seems disheartening. Is there an option where ECRs might thrive rather than merely survive? Interestingly, a more recent survey found that 38 per cent of ECRs reported not having a mentor, and 41 per cent found the performance review process to be unhelpful (Christian et al., 2021). Other scholars have also shown that in fields such as the physical sciences, female students are not only judged to be less competent but are offered lower salaries and less career mentoring (Moss-Racusin et al., 2012). During the Covid-19 pandemic, the strain and challenges of transition into an academic role have been compounded by the volatility and uncertainty of the Australian higher education sector. Blackmore (2020) claims that "Covid-19 has exposed the carelessness of both government and university executives" (p. 1333). Pressures resultant from the marketisation of universities and fractured by the government response to Covid-19 resulted in vice-chancellors making decisions about job redundancies, with those staff remaining also having to cover extended duties (Blackmore, 2020). It is Blackmore's (2020) contention that academics continue to gift hidden labour, which reflects their passion and commitment for their work, and which remains significant for university life. This is particularly poignant for ECRs, who carry heavier and more unbalanced workloads (Petersen, 2011; Christian et al., 2021), requiring some sense of solitude or sanctuary.

Solitude and sanctuary

In philosophical terms, solitude is framed as the conscious choice to extract oneself from society as a means of "transfiguration of self" and a "way of life" (Groff, 2020). Such practice points to a tension between autonomy and the possibility of reconciling self to community (referred to as city – virtuous or not). In the instance of the *city* lacking virtue, the philosopher cultivates solitude as a means of "insulating himself from it spiritually and intellectually" (Groff, 2020). In exploring this journey of transition, conceptualising solitude as a choice to self-insulate positions the academe as the city, which threatens to overwhelm and pollute the philosopher. Solitude is also recognised as a state, complex and multifaceted, characterised as a continuum from punishment to respite (Coplan and Bowker, 2014). According to Coplan and Bowker (2014), on its negative face, solitude is imposed through experiences of peer exclusion and ostracism, while its productivity lies in its capacity for restorative work and creative expression or, as philosophers often view it, in relation to spiritual transformation. As a means of self-care, I ascribe to solitude as the "title for processes that are actively initiated and not suffered" (Macho and Rashof, 2021, p. 9). For example, in facing the challenge of the black curtain of silence, and seeking a way to be an academic during that initial transition, I used the onset of Covid-19 and the work-from-home mandate to initiate a writing space. I chose to sign on to the autoethnographic project, which enabled me to interrogate my sense of self as researcher and writer. This creative process, in the solitude of a newly created home office, provided respite from frustration and the early steps towards clarity in my own writing. It is the extraction of self from the city, the academe, in order to learn and practice the cultural technique of reading and writing, that meets the challenge of being and doing as an ECR. Macho and Rashof (2021) propose that solitude techniques enable one to step out of a logic of being possessed and, as such, enable a defence in response to external claims of ownership. As Groff (2020) points to the insulating properties of solitude, the notion of solitude as a cultural technique (Macho and Rashof, 2021) identifies the discipline of listening to one's own voice.

Long and Averill (2003) examined solitude as a social phenomenon because it is based on the capacity for human reflections of experiences, which are inherently a product of socialisation. Solitude is distinguished from loneliness, and freedom is the precondition to many of its benefits (Long and Averill, 2003). This freedom from constraint, named "positive freedom" by Long and Averill (2003), is about the capacity to use solitude constructively – for creativity that is an expression of ideas valued by us (self) and others. This theme of socialisation is also a consideration in a time of technological immersion. Deresiewicz (2009) reflected that we are losing our ability to choose to be alone. The argument here is that celebrity, and connectivity, induces such a high level of interconnectedness, that solitude is squeezed out from our lives. Furthermore, as much as the Internet has brought potentially isolated people together, there are questions about the authenticity of connections if self-esteem is determined by visibility on social platforms. Deresiewicz (2009) speaks to suburbanisation, and the exacerbation of boredom and loneliness, noting that the modern tendency is to the "networked or social mind" (p. 4). While solitude may not be easy in a time when "universities do everything they can to keep their students from being alone, lest they perpetrate self-destructive acts, and also perhaps unfashionable thoughts" (p. 5), understanding solitude is a path to restoring our integrity in self.

These ideas of solitude as generative, chosen, and cultural practice are related to the ways in which women's relationship to solitude has also been considered. Wear (1993) identifies themes of identity, culture, and work. Bindings of interdependence, and views of self as only in relation to others, fade into the solitude of "moments of impenetrable, profound silence, moments in which I am alone" (Wear, 1993, p. 4). Such time is critical for women to analyse experiences, else they find themselves driven by the demands of others predicated by the responsibility to care for others first. Wear (1993) advocates that women "stalk those moments of solitude often wedged in daily life" (p. 11), and recognise that we are more than what is shown to us in reflections of those around us. Over time, multiple literary figures have also held up a mirror for women to consider their relationship to private space, home, and solitude (Garner et al., 2014). In Garner et al. (2014) we find multiple illustrations of women choosing to step away from expectations about connectivity, and as Wear (1993) intimated, stalking moments of solitude so that they may engage in writing, alone, and as owners of the space. Solitude generates the connection to self, the insulation from disruptive influences of academe. It is a choice to find time to for creative output. It is a qualitative assessment of circumstance and a philosophical choice to position away. It is also a cultural technique and an alignment to identity which is authentic and of integrity.

Discussion and implications for self-care

My positioning to my new role in academia was largely characterised by a sense of confusion and the frustration of being met with silence. Informed by my previous experiences as a successful educator in schools (Jones & Ludhra 2019), I found moving into a new role as ECR brought with it an expectation of growth, challenge, and expansive opportunities for work (Petersen, 2006). For a South Asian woman, success continues to be "layered and weighted within a configuration of physical, psychosocial, cultural, religious, historical, economic and socio-political factors" (Jones and Ludhra, 2019, p. 240). The risk associated with the invisible labour of negotiating these dimensions is the overemphasis on women's agency and choice, especially in the context of inequalities and complex power operations experienced by women of colour (Jones and Ludhra, 2019). While terms such as change and transition are used to indicate difficulty following the completion of the doctoral study, there are deeper questions to be asked about the nature of said difficulties imposed on ECRs by the academe (Petersen, 2011; Christian et al., 2021). Furthermore, there is a need to recognise that ECRs, like women, are not a homogenous consideration (Bhopal et al., 2018). It is possible that in preparing to become an academic, I perceived myself to have more freedom and choice than the reality, and the silence I reference is that stark moment of realisation that "women's choices (particularly girls and women of colour) are therefore mediated through dimensions and intersecting differences" (Jones and Ludhra, 2019, p. 241).

We need a more holistic response to such difficulties than the vague suggestions of ambiguous mentoring (Moss-Racusin et al., 2012). My choice to invest in solitude and focus on creative writing enabled a sanctuary for thinking, being, and doing research. Until I made this choice, my positioning to notions of success and job satisfaction had hit a silence unbending.

The pandemic disrupted my experience of this transition, but I would argue that it was well timed. The challenge, represented in my cryptic crossword, was mitigated by the opportunity to invest time in the creativity of solitude. It provided me with a sense of respite – the opportunity to stalk privacy of space. In that house, and with my family, came the space for private grief. I grieved for what I had hoped the role would be, like other ECRs before me, who carried visions and ideas about contributing (Petersen, 2011; Barrow et al., 2020). They seemed like childish dreams, swallowed up by the carelessness of the neoliberal structures (Blackmore, 2020). Yet my home, and yes in the lockdown, brought me new privilege. It allowed me to set up an office – a room – the privacy of space (Garner, et al., 2014). In this office I located beauty in the view of the green lawn across the backyard, and I gave myself time to think. This solitude of my making proved generative, in contrast to the silence imposed on me which had felt as punitive. Perhaps it is akin to philosophers separating themselves from the ugly city (Groff, 2020). In this privilege of solitude, valued and practiced by women before me, and elusive to my senses until the pandemic extracted me, my work has found sanctuary. That safe place to unpack ideas, to learn, to think, and to know, has revealed itself to be in my domain. New project ideas begin to formulate themselves in terms that align to the values and ideals which had mattered to me before I started my doctoral study (Long & Averill, 2003). Sitting down to write is a relief. It enables an unburdening of questions and possibilities that I hope to imagine and understand like the literary role models in Garner et al. (2014) and the cultural technique of Macho and Rashof (2021). Here I will say that the practice is not therapeutic. It is an adventure. I am inspired by great pieces I read and excited to fall down that rabbit hole of literature we are warned about. There is also a need to acknowledge, as Coplan and Bowker (2014) did, that solitude may carry negative associations. This may be a point of fear for some, and a sense of apprehension that solitude is about loneliness. It is also a fear identified in Deresiewicz' (2009) notion of technology and implications on our sense of self. To this, we must consider which mirrors we choose to look into, for they reflect back to us possibilities as solitude may provide, or they reflect back to us the black squares of the cryptic crossword.

When the world is full of possibilities, then all the possibilities are doors you must open. I do. I find the pandemic has moved so many opportunities to virtual spaces, and in my solitude, I am able to enter many rooms full of different people and not be met with silence. I am met with enthusiastic sharing and the polyvocality of other women (Lahiri-Roy et al., 2021). I find new networks of writers, of thinkers, and of researchers sharing different epistemologies in virtual spaces. It may appear as a contradiction to Deresiewicz' (2009) concerns about suburbanisation, technology, and the networked mind. However, it is a manifestation of the need to be separate and to be collectively part of a "virtuous city" (Groff, 2020)

It is intoxicating and addictive, refuelling my passion to research and write, like a deep and challenging conversation with a trusted mentor. These diverse spaces of informal gathering are modelling for me, and I find these to be *pseudo-mentors* to the work I am trying to build. Jones and Ludhra (2019) wrote of keys and cages which come with success. My positioning as school principal provided the privilege of studying for the PhD in the first instance. As such, this is the latest in a chain of experiences that have taught me about how success provides keys to enter new spaces (Jones and Ludhra, 2019). However, with such success, there can also be a sense of being caged – being pushed back into a marginalised position where others deem you to be more comfortable. The other key which enables access to pseudo-mentoring is the choice to engage in professional learning activities that support and strengthen creativity in your solitude. The informal and open networks of pseudo-mentors provided the framing for the writing project (Markham and Harris, 2021) that laid the seeds for this work. Pseudo-mentors act as sounding boards to question how we continue to work as scholars at this time (Lahiri-Roy et al., 2021). The challenge to locate my work, to be, and to sustain an effort to write, to do, has been greatly impacted by women who create these precious sanctuaries for pseudo-mentoring.

Conclusion

This chapter has discussed the challenges from the disruption of Covid-19 of isolation, opaqueness, and performativity expectations of being an early career researcher, before it highlights the ways in which the pandemic facilitated solitude, sanctuary, and access to pseudo-mentors. Through solitude, there is distance from *noise* that is counter-productive to developing an individual sense of self and identity (Monereo & Liesa, 2020). Sanctuary emerges from the peace, through which safety to work, and to be, is strengthened. Pseudo-mentors provide the inevitable connections to others, not formal roles or obligations, but emerging new belongings, which are purposively multiple and diverse. Through these opportunities for solitude, sanctuary, and pseudo-mentoring, early career researchers, I argue, are able to find and strengthen their identity (Barrow, et al., 2020), research purpose (Boyd & Horstmanshof, 2013), and pathways to success that are more closely aligned to our own values and sense of wellbeing. Is it possible that words like "identity" and "transition" are phantom phobias assigned as diagnosis of ECRs who join the academy only to be met with silence? That's not to say that there must be cheer squads and red carpets, but there must be something more systemic than vague considerations of mentoring from those empowered by professoriate appointments. Meanwhile, positioning ourselves to the silence, the ambiguity, and the carelessness we encounter requires us to choose solitude as a creative practice. Solitude, however we may choose to individually define and shape it, enables us to give ourselves permission to be. When we are safe to be, then we can do, and we can do meaningful and valuable things. We can contribute to the fields, the communities, and the legacies of those who know us as our most authentic selves. Do we continue to generate more research about rampant stress, institutional concerns, or masters and apprentices, all the while knowing that this is the black curtain to the tumultuous collection of ideas and emotions located in the human experiences of ECRs? Christian et al. (2021) challenge us to consider that "[i]t is common vernacular to say that 'ECRs are the future'. If this is factually true, then are we content with how we are shaping this future?" (p. 11).

References

Barrow, M., Grant, B. & Xu, L. (2020). Academic identities research: Mapping the field's theoretical frameworks. *Higher Education Research and Development*, 1–14. https://doi.org/10.1080/07294360.2020.1849036

Bazeley, P. (2003). Defining "early career" in research. *Higher Education*, *45*(3), 257–279. http://www.jstor.org/stable/3447481

Bhopal, K., Brown, H., Jackson, J. (2018). Should I Stay or Should I Go? BME Academics and the Decision to Leave UK Higher Education. In J. Arday & H. Mirza (eds) *Dismantling race in higher education*. Palgrave Macmillan, Cham. https://doi.org/10.1007/978-3-319-60261-5_7

Blackmore, J. (2020). The carelessness of entrepreneurial universities in a world risk society: A feminist reflection on the impact of Covid-19 in Australia. *Higher Education Research and Development*, *39*(7), 1332–1336. https://doi.org/10.1080/07294360.2020.1825348

Boyd, W. & Horstmanshof, L. (2013). Response to Petersen on "'staying or going?': Australian early career researchers' narratives. *The Australian Universities' Review*, *55*(1), 74–79.

Bunnell, T. (2016). Teachers in international schools: A global educational "precariat"? *Globalisation, Societies and Education*, *14*(4), 543–559.

Chopra, D. (2020). *Take hope from the healing cycle*. Soulspring. https://soulspring.org/take-hope-from-the-healing-cycle

Christian, K., Johnstone, C., Larkins, J.A., Wright, W. & Doran, M. R. (2021). A survey of early-career researchers in Australia. *ELife*, *10*, 1–19.

Coplan, R. J. & Bowker, J. C. (2014). *The handbook of solitude*. John Wiley & Sons, Incorporated, Somerset.

Deresiewicz, William. (2009). The end of solitude. *The Chronicle of Higher Education*, *55*(21), B.6.

Ellis, C. (2004). *The ethnographic I: A methodological novel about autoethnography*. Rowman Altamira, Maryland.

Ellis, C., Adams, T. E. & Bochner, A. P. (2011). Autoethnography: An Overview. *Historical Social Research/Historische Sozialforschung*, *36*(4 (138)), 273–290. http://www.jstor.org/stable/23032294

Fisher, A. J., Mendoza-Denton, R., Patt, C., Young, I., Eppig, A., Garrell, R. L., et al. (2019). Structure and belonging: Pathways to success for underrepresented minority and women PhD students in STEM fields. *PLoS ONE* 14(1), e0209279. https://doi.org/10.1371/journal.pone.0209279

Fullan, M. (2013). Realizing Moral Purpose. In P. Hughes (eds) *Achieving quality education for all. Education in the Asia-Pacific region: Issues, concerns and prospects* (vol 20). Springer, Dordrecht. https://doi.org/10.1007/978-94-007-5294-8_5

Garner, J. D., Boynton, V. & Malin, J. (2014). *Herspace: Women, writing, and solitude*. Routledge, Oxfordshire.

Groff, P. S. (2020). Cultivating weeds: The place of solitude in the political philosophies of Ibn Bájja and Nietzsche. *Philosophy East & West*, *70*(3), 699–739. https://doi.org/10.1353/pew.2020.0051

Hayden, Mary. (2011). Transnational spaces of education: The growth of the international school sector. *Globalisation, Societies and Education, 9*(2), 211–224.

Hemmings, B. (2012). Sources of research confidence for early career academics: A qualitative study. *Higher Education Research and Development, 31*(2), 171–184. https://doi.org/10.1080/07294360.2011.559198

Jones, D. & Ludhra, G. (2019). What does it mean to be "successful"? Narratives of British South Asian head teachers and head girls. In P. Miller & C. Callender (eds) *Race, education and educational leadership in England: An integrated analysis* (pp. 237–260). Bloomsbury Academic, London. http://doi.org/10.5040/9781350068629.ch-011

Lahiri-Roy, R. & Belford, N. (2021). "Walk like a chameleon": Gendered diasporic identities and settlement experiences. *South Asian Popular Culture, 19*(1), 47–62.

Lahiri-Roy, R., Belford, N. & Sum, N. (2021). Transnational women academics of colour enacting "pedagogy of discomfort": Positionality against a "pedagogy of rupture." *Pedagogy, Culture & Society*, 1–19.

Long, C. R. & Averill, J. R. (2003). Solitude: An exploration of benefits of being alone. *Journal for the Theory of Social Behaviour, 33*(1), 21–44.

Macho, T. & Rashof, S. (2021). Alone with oneself. *Angelaki: Journal of Theoretical Humanities, 26*(1), 9–21. https://doi.org/10.1080/0969725X.2021.1863587

Markham, A. & Harris, A. (2021). Prompts for making sense of a pandemic: The 21-day autoethnography challenge. *Qualitative Inquiry, 27*(7), 928–941.

McGee, E. O., Botchway, P. K., Naphan-Kingery, D. E., Brockman, A. J., Houston, S. & White, D. T. (2021). Racism camouflaged as impostorism and the impact on black STEM doctoral students. *Race Ethnicity and Education, 2022*(25), 1–21.

Monereo, C & Liesa, E. (2020). Early career researchers' identity positions based on research experiences, *Higher Education Research & Development. 41*(1), 193–210 https://doi.org/10.1080/07294360.2020.1835834

Monk, S. & McKay, L. (2017). Developing identity and agency as an early career academic: Lessons from Alice. *The International Journal for Academic Development, 22*(3), 223–230. https://doi.org/10.1080/1360144X.2017.1306532

Moss-Racusin, C. A., Dovidio, J. F., Brescoll, V. L., Graham, M. J. & Handelsman, J. (2012). Science faculty's subtle gender biases favor male students. *Proceedings of the national academy of sciences, 109*(41), 16474–16479. https://doi.org/10.1073/pnas.1211286109

Noy, S. & Ray, R. (2012). Graduate students' perceptions of their advisors: Is there systematic disadvantage in mentorship? *The Journal of Higher Education* (Columbus), *83*(6), 876–912. https://doi.org/10.1353/jhe.2012.0036

Petersen, E. B. (2006, December). Australian early career researchers negotiating the "culture change" of higher education reform. In *Proceedings of The Australian Sociology Association Annual Conference, Perth* (pp. 4–7).

Petersen, E. B. (2011). Staying or going? Australian early career researchers' narratives of academic work, exit options and coping strategies. *The Australian Universities' Review, 53*(2), 34–42.

Van Langenhove, L. & Harré, R. 1999. Introducing Positioning Theory. In L. Van Langenhove & R. Harré (eds) *Positioning theory: Moral contexts of intentional action* (pp. 14–31). Blackwell, Oxford.

Wear, D. (Ed.). (1993). *Center of the web, the: Women and solitude.* SUNY Press, Albany.

White, K. (2004). The leaking pipeline: Women postgraduate and early career researchers in Australia. *Tertiary Education and Management, 10*(3), 227–241. https://doi.org/10.1080/13583883.2004.9967129

6 Journaling as self–care, journaling for personal and professional development

A visual narrative

Khairunnisa Haji Ibrahim

In mid-2021, amidst the second wave of Covid-19 infections in Brunei Darussalam, I discovered that I have ADHD (Attention Deficit Hyperactive Disorder). I have not been formally diagnosed or assessed by a professional, and much of what I know about ADHD comes from various Internet sources. Nevertheless, this self-diagnosis rang true once I connected ADHD with my ongoing struggles to be productive and happy as an academic and a woman.

I became a lecturer in 2010 and was a highly successful undergraduate and master's student before that. Once I became an academic, however, especially after welcoming my son and beginning my PhD in the UK, I realised that I had been silently struggling the entire time. I faced challenges that impaired my ability to work, teach, write, and even manage my household and family. I have lifelong anxiety and frequent episodes of emotional overwhelm, which are, in fact, traits closely associated with ADHD. In my first iteration of writing this chapter, I began the Introduction with the following:

> "Why is it difficult to just do it?" The words leap out at me from the page. They feel like an accusation, even though I wrote them myself not too long ago. They still sting. "I should like to work hard, but it seems like I lack the capacity for it." Looking back at this page in my journal, filled from edge to edge with such plaintive statements, makes me feel sorry for this version of myself from months ago. That self still wrestled with the realisation that my challenges with work are not merely a matter of a weak work ethic. I cannot simply just discipline myself to do all the things. I am not wired to do so, only able to do a select number of things that interest me. Although I have yet to receive a formal diagnosis, I am confident that I have ADHD.

The passage above highlights the main contributions of this chapter. It illustrates my desperate desire to understand why I could not make myself work in conventional ways, why I felt shame and hurt for not being a productive academic, and how I turned to my journal to vent and self-soothe. This chapter is about my experiences as a woman in academia and the unique challenges of this position. More than that, it is about being a woman in academia who has recognised that her neurological condition affects how she inhabits the roles of academic and of woman, at work and at home. Discovering that I have ADHD was heartbreaking,

DOI: 10.4324/9781003341482-8

but it was also healing. Using journaling, I can now better navigate the world with ADHD lenses on. It has also set me on the path to becoming a better academic, woman, and person.

I describe this journey in this chapter and share the journaling systems and tools that have helped me along my way. I begin with a general description of being in academia and of being a woman in academia. A brief explanation of ADHD follows, along with some insights into how it affects me daily, especially in my career. I then share the journaling strategies I have since developed to manage my ADHD traits, so I can better use my time, energy, and attention.

Academia and the challenges of being a female academic

I joined my alma mater, Universiti Brunei Darussalam, in 2010, four years after graduating with a first-class bachelor's degree in Geography. In those intervening years, I worked as a journalist and editor at a local newspaper. As soon as I had completed my master's studies at the University of Leicester, UK, in 2009, I applied for a lecturer position and was hired almost immediately. As a citizen of Brunei, my employment at the country's premier university comes with automatic tenure. This is a blessing as I do not have to worry about job security. Non-tenured academics have one of the most stressful jobs in the world, constantly having to meet a quota of publications and funding grants to be guaranteed job security. They are embroiled in intense competition in an overcrowded industry for the same limited resources. Consequently, non-tenure-track academics, especially women, have reported that they "worked very hard and slept very little" to secure a permanent position (Fothergill and Feltey 2003).

Furthermore, the academic career is paradoxically malleable and rigid. Flexible working hours allow the academic to take time off for caring duties. At the same time, external and internalised expectations to produce a minimum level of scholarly output can quickly consume the academic's working hours, encroaching even into their free time. For academics with dependents, this results in a delicate balancing act between conducting research that they are passionate about, which can take up a lot of time and energy, and meeting the needs of their families. Brunei, in particular, is a small country with tight-knit family-based communities. While a plus in many ways, it also means plenty of demands on our time from close and extended family.

Having worked in the news industry before joining academia, I find the former very fast-paced but not particularly stressful in the long run. The nature of news meant that my work was done every day as soon as I filed the stories. An academic, however, always has varied tasks with different and much longer timelines. Research is constructed, framed, conducted, and written up entirely by the academic, and this labour can be complex and messy. All of this is business-as-usual in academia, but I am discovering that for one with ADHD, it is also tough to manage.

An academic career is also one of the most intricate and multifaceted professions in the knowledge industry. In an infographic that has gone viral on Twitter, university lecturer Susan Wardell succinctly captured the complexity of a lecturer's portfolio. Titled "An academic's role within the university environment,"[1] the pie chart showcases the three core areas – teaching, research, and service – with each area radiating many splinters of distinct tasks. Each of these three segments is time- and commitment-heavy. Teaching, for instance, is not just about delivering lectures. It also involves many hours of assessing students' work and communicating with them, designing course materials, and undergoing pedagogical training. Research is not merely publishing; it is managing projects, reading, attending conferences, and promoting one's work. Leadership, serving on advisory boards, and conducting peer reviews are just a few examples of service. Outsiders who often mistake us as simply educators and envy us for our long semester breaks do not realise that research and service also make up a substantial amount of our workload.

As if being in academia is not already challenging enough, being a woman in academia comes with its own difficulties. There is extensive scholarly evidence that the costs of being in academia are higher for women than men. For example, only women academics face the "baby penalty." That is, women who have children and prioritise their families are perceived to be less committed and less competent academics, but men in the same positions are not viewed similarly (Mason, Wolfinger, and Goulden 2013). Women in academia also experience comparatively lower productivity, measured in low publication and citation rates, especially compared to their male counterparts (Fox 2005; Lutter and Schröder 2020; Symonds et al. 2006). Rather than from loss of ability or competence, however, declining rates of productive outputs are often due to increased demands on a female academic's time and energy. Nevertheless, women are still promoted less, paid less (Ginther 2003; Ginther and Hayes 1999), and even cited less (Dion, Sumner, and Mitchell 2018; Maliniak, Powers, and Walter 2013).

In my own institution, I personally find that working conditions are similar across genders. Men and women are paid the same according to their rank. Instead, more subtle, silent differences abound, such as the gender-coding of specific tasks. Pastoral duties, such as advising or checking on the welfare of students, are often given to women. Here, women are just as likely, or even more so, to be heads of departments and programmes, but the chain of command and distribution of work remains gendered. An example is the frequency with which female programme members are expected to take meeting minutes, especially when the leader is male. On the other hand, male programme members are still exempt from minute-taking duties even when the programme head is a woman, with female colleagues again filling the same roles.

Defining and embracing ADHD

ADHD stands for Attention Deficit Hyperactive Disorder and is defined as a neurological condition. It is often discussed in relation to children, but there is currently an increasing prevalence of ADHD diagnoses among adults. A paper on adult ADHD describes its symptoms as follows (Gentile, Atiq, and Gillig 2006):

> difficulty getting started on tasks, variable attention to details, difficulties with self-organization and with prioritization, and poor persistence in tasks that require sustained mental effort. Impulsivity and low frustration tolerance may be present to varying degrees.

The diagnosis of ADHD is gendered, as it is often closely associated with hyperactive young males. One of the surprising outcomes of the Covid-19 pandemic has been the rising number of individuals, especially women, who seek diagnosis after prolonged struggles with day-to-day tasks (Sibonney 2021). According to news reports from the UK (Chapple and Collinson 2021) and Singapore (Chia and Chew 2021), many women go for years without realising they have ADHD. Often, it is a crisis – severe depression, frequently missing appointments, or lacking focus in work and relationships, for instance – that spurs them to seek medical help.

My own journey to self-diagnosis was also sparked by the pandemic. The Delta variant came to Brunei in early August, just as the 2021 academic year began. I saw my students only once in person, and we communicated strictly online for the rest of the semester. I was not dealing very well with the movement restriction the second time around, which was longer and more stringent, given how much more contagious Delta was. I spent many days in a cloud of doom and anxiety, unable to adjust to the reality of life confined indoors, yet with the expectation that school and work must continue as usual. Looking for relief and perhaps some answers, I turned to social media to distract myself.

What I found was a plethora of information about ADHD and other mental health issues on various platforms, particularly Instagram. The *New York Times* reported that social media content on ADHD has proliferated in recent years and helped many marginalised individuals in the US, such as women and those from minority groups, seek a diagnosis. "For some people, ADHD content represents a step toward identifying or explaining the ways they have felt different," the article reported (Clark 2021). This was certainly the case for me, as I watched content by mostly women creators and identified with many of the traits and symptoms they described.

Since beginning my academic career, I have had difficulty meeting deadlines, remembering appointments, and finishing tasks. One of the most challenging aspects of academic work is identifying which tasks to prioritise. My strengths are writing and research, but I also have teaching and administrative duties. In an academic year, I teach or co-teach at least four undergraduate courses, contribute a lecture to at least two others, and supervise six or more undergraduate students in their intensive final-year research project, as well as two postgraduate students. I also facilitate the compulsory research methods course for new postgraduates across three faculties. My inability to organise my time and energy made me believe that I was incompetent and lazy, causing a downward spiral of shame and poor performance.

It turns out that the range of skills collectively known as executive functioning, involving planning, focusing attention, remembering instructions, and managing multiple tasks, is poorly developed in those with ADHD (Rodden 2022) – so much so that an ADHD-defining trait is executive *dys*function, along with a propensity for time blindness and the lack of "innate awareness of time and an ability to track its passing" (Read 2020). This makes it very difficult for me to prioritise and then carry out various jobs within the limited hours of my workday. Knowing that this is a common problem for ADHD individuals has made it easier for me to manage my emotions, particularly the shame and stigma around failing to get things done.

I experience shame as an extreme emotion, and I often feel various emotions quite intensely. This is another symptom of ADHD called emotional dysregulation, which includes being "frequently and easily irritated, emotionally excitable or get angry for small reasons … [and having] greater emotional excitability and reactivity" (Retz et al. 2012). Whenever I experience executive dysfunction, my sense of failure and shame is so great that it becomes overwhelming. This is partly due to the numerous, diverse, and complex nature of academic tasks. During the teaching semester, I prepare lectures, deliver them, attend to students' queries and needs, assign them work and then assess it, alongside my retinue of administrative duties.

Overwhelm leads to a related symptom: analysis paralysis. Harvey (2021) describes a more specific condition, *ADHD Paralysis*, akin to "that feeling of the fly buzzing around your head – you know you are meant to do a task, but you find it impossible to make any forward progress with it." In other words, I am so inundated by a crippling fear of failure that I go into stasis, rendering me physically and mentally incapable of taking action. Analysis paralysis inhibits action, yet it is always mentally draining. This is a painful contradiction, and one that happens too often.

Perhaps the most defining trait of ADHD is hyperfocus. Defined as being intensely engaged in matters of interest for prolonged periods (Hupfeld, Abagis, and Shah 2019; Ozel-Kizil et al. 2016), hyperfocus can be a boon or a bane. It becomes a strength or a superpower (Hupfield et al. 2022) when the focus of attention is a priority or something productive. However, ADHD individuals often become immersed in activities that divert their time and energy away from work or other essential tasks. An example is when I am distracted from writing my thesis by a side research project, which sets back my progress towards finishing my doctorate degree. I have always been very interested in very many things and can quickly become an expert on a topic when I hyperfocus. It also means that I get distracted too often. Learning about this particular ADHD trait has helped me better harness my energy towards things that need to be done, although it remains challenging to shift attention to things that matter if they do not spark my interest. This is an ongoing and undoubtedly lifelong challenge, but one I am better positioned to handle now that I know it is part and parcel of my ADHD.

Since my self-diagnosis of ADHD and my journey to learning more about this condition, I have experimented with different strategies to manage my executive functioning, emotional overwhelm, analysis paralysis, and hyperfocus. The fast-paced grind of academia, its "publish or perish" culture, and heavy teaching loads without adequate support or pedagogical guidance, involve feats of organising, focusing, finishing, and task-transitioning, none of which come naturally to me or to ADHD. I wanted some way of keeping my thoughts, emotions, and tasks in order so I could act upon them. Journaling provided precisely the system that I needed.

The structure I need as a woman academic with ADHD: a visual narrative

As a practice, journaling can be considered a feminine hobby, an introspective, inward-looking activity associated with the private sphere, the realm of the feminine. Patriarchy ensures that such spaces and practices, especially when pitted against the dominant masculine ones, become devalued and subject to ridicule. It does not need to be so. In fact, journaling can be activism or at least a form of advocacy for the self. It can also extend to advocacy for the causes the individual fights for, which she has identified and connected with as values dear to herself. As Schiwy (1994: 235) wrote, "the personal journal does hold subversive potential. It can provide a safe channel of thinking and creating one's life beyond the boundaries and terms that society deems appropriate to female selfhood and behaviour in a given historical epoch."

In *The New Diary*, Rainer (1978) wrote that journaling is a feminist strategy of reclaiming the feminine voice, even if the reclamation occurs only in the diary's pages. Nevertheless, she persuasively argues that this act of writing and describing one's life in the journal empowers and is "a gesture against powerlessness." She renders "the 'official' version of reality" – one that caters to and amplifies the voices, wants, and experiences of men and other hegemonic groups – as inconsequential once women weaponise their voices and reclaim personal control through their writing.

The benefits of journaling are many and can be profound. Hiemstra (2001: 19–20) captured them perfectly when he wrote:

> Journaling in its various forms is a means for recording personal thoughts, daily experiences, and evolving insights. The process often evokes conversations with self, another person, or even an imagined other person. In addition, most journaling formats allow reviewing or rereading of earlier reflections leading to a progressive clarification of insights.

Currently, I use several tools in tandem to help manage my attention, time, and energy to get the best outcomes as an academic. Figure 6.1 shows my current journaling system, which comprises several components. It looks elaborate at first glance, but it is the outcome of many long months (and money spent) experimenting to find what works and what does not. Each component serves a specific function and meets a particular need. As the previous section indicated, ADHD individuals thrive on novelty, challenge, and fun, conditions that activate their hyperfocus. Still, at the same time they struggle with poor working memory, weak executive function, low motivation, and emotional overwhelm.

The first component I rely on is the Morning Pages (upper left corner), a journaling practice first espoused by Julie Cameron in *The Artist's Way* (Cameron, 2002). Morning writing is widely recognised as a productivity-enhancing exercise. It has many names – morning pages, freewriting, brain-dumping – and many benefits. These include providing a meditative routine that grounds practitioners to the present and allows the diarist to set intentions for the rest of the day.

Figure 6.1 My journaling system for self-care consists of several notebooks, each with specific functions. I supplement my system with digital tools, such as my smartwatch, to keep me on track.

The Morning Pages has no rules other than to write every morning and to fill three pages. It was difficult in the beginning, but eventually, it became an indispensable practice that allowed me to clarify my goals for the day and cleanse my mind of worries.

I have kept a reflective journal for several years, but its importance and function often change. Currently, I use it to work out complicated emotions, which often manifest as overwhelm. The excerpt in the Introduction, where I lament my inability to "just do it," is an example of how I use this journal. I write about problems I am facing, describe the emotions that swell and surge in intensity and work out what and why I am going through these episodes. I do not often write about what I can do about them, but it usually turns out that I do not have to; I can make better decisions with a clearer mind after I have reflected on my feelings and thoughts. This is also why journaling proves to be beneficial for those dealing with mental health issues, working in stressful jobs, such as nursing (Dimitroff et al. 2017), or facing difficult life phases (Sealy 2012; Ullrich and Lutgendorf 2002). It provides a safe space to explore internal conflicts and difficulties and allows the individual to process and release pent-up feelings.

Recently, I discovered the Traveler's Notebook (TN) journal. This leather-cover system holds several different notebook inserts for various purposes and is highly customisable and adaptable to the user's needs. The TN journal is special because it meets my ADHD needs for novelty and interest-based functions. I have a daily

TN that houses three inserts, as shown in Figure 6.1. The planner houses my monthly, weekly, and daily plans. Having all this information written down provides a structure to my days. An academic wears many hats, with many responsibilities and duties. Keeping track of due dates, meetings, and tasks is essential, but the ADHD mind is weak at this skill, so a robust system that acts as a database or repository must be developed to support it. My TN journal provides this function with the bonus of being narrow and thin enough that it is portable. I carry it wherever I go to store information I can easily access whenever necessary.

Writing things down in notebooks is an analogue form of record-keeping, but this does not guarantee that the information is always put to use. I need to be reminded of upcoming events or things to do. This is where I complement my analogue tools with digital ones. One of the most important is my smartwatch, which serves as a reminder and a tracker. Once I put information in my analogue planner, I also input essential deadlines and events into my digital calendar. I program alerts to remind me two days before the due date and again two hours before. Having the reminders buzz on my wrist is an immediate call to action, and it serves as a challenge for me to get things done. I also use timers on my watch to remind me to take breaks every 20 minutes, like having a Pomodoro system on my wrist.

The weekly tracker keeps a record of things that have happened. I record tasks that I have completed, and I also note progress data: the number of words written in a day, the status of a manuscript, or even how many calories I have burned from exercise. The data help measure progress across several areas, such as writing and exercise. All of this is data, and since research is the bread and butter of academics, recording data comes easily. As a woman with ADHD, I use the data to modify routines or keep me on track and on time when in hyperfocus.

Finally, the Catch-All insert in my TN does precisely as its name implies: it catches everything. Ideas, quotes, observations, or feelings I cannot process at that particular moment are all captured in the Catch-All notebook. As a visual diary, it is another form of tracking my activities and energy levels, all data points I use to continually improve myself. I also use it to take note of administrative tasks and contact details and as a to-do list on the go. As a woman with ADHD whose mind whirs with too many thoughts, and as an academic who generates too many ideas and has a long list of things to do, the Catch-All is where I keep pertinent information, acting again as a safe storage space. Writing things down in the Catch-All helps relieve my mind of worries and reduce mental overwhelm.

Is journaling for you?

Journaling is a very personal, reflexive practice. The circumstances and conditions that lead to its adoption can also be very particular to the individual. A possible barrier to using journaling as a self-care method for the academic is the perception that it has no relevance within the academy. Boundary-work, the process through which a practice or phenomena gains legitimacy (Gieryn 1999), might offer a helpful framework. Rather than think about the journal as a secret diary that only records dreams and dramas, reframing the device as a tool for research may lend it more value in the eyes of an academic. This framework offers two ways of rethinking the journal: as field notes and as autoethnography.

Field-noting is a "sense-making" device whose research purpose is to record and decipher events as they happen, requiring first-hand experiences, many of which are to be communicated later for publication (Cloke et al. 2004). In the case of journaling, publication may not be the end goal. Instead, it is to use and reflect on the content that Parr (2001) notes makes up much of field notes – the raw, unrestrained emotions and feelings of the field-noter, whether it is frustration with the study or "soul-searching, worry-writing" (Cloke et al., 2004). The reader who is inclined toward field observations may think of journaling as a pared-down version of field-noting – the field is the reader's life, the subject the reader's own self, and the events that take place comprise experiences that make up the minutiae of the reader's day.

One's journal can also be autoethnography of one's life. The autoethnographic method challenges enduring beliefs that the doing of science must be detached from the scientist. It counters claims that subjectivity taints and disqualifies research as valid. In this way, Schiwy (1994) considers journaling a form of feminist epistemology because both emphasise "concrete experience as the basis of knowledge."

More pertinently, autoethnography is a suitable framework for thinking about journaling because it emphasises self-understanding. The researcher, or journal writer, is simultaneously the subject and object being observed. The outcome is a better understanding and connection between what is observed, the observer, and the reader (Bochner 2017). In journaling, all three roles are embodied by the academic. Most rewardingly, journaling as autoethnography makes use of observations of what has happened to the self in the past to "reconfigur[e] the self" to move in new directions and, thus, to grow (Freeman 1991). This is an effect of journaling as self-care that I can attest to, especially after discovering I have ADHD. It helps me navigate the dense but exciting maze of academia and provides a greater sense of purpose and growth.

Conclusion

It has been almost a year since I accepted my own diagnosis of ADHD. Understanding that the things I did or did not do were not because of laziness or a lack of ability or care has been healing. Writing down my emotions, experiences, plans for the future, and lessons from the past is a form of reflexive self-care. I can now embrace my quirks, which empower me to get things done my way. I know now that specific tasks or skills are difficult for me with my ADHD; thus, I cannot simply follow conventional or established ways of doing things nor should I feel ashamed about it. Instead, I lean into my strengths – my need for novelty and challenge, my hyperfocus, and my intense curiosity and interest, and use them to leverage my skills and efforts. Journaling, planning, and having tools for tracking progress and reminding me to stay on time have been essential to my progress and growth. I hope this chapter shows that journaling, as a form of self-care and productivity tool, can help us become happier, more productive women in academia.

Note

1 Available to view at https://twitter.com/unlazy_susan/status/1407113654076510230? lang=en

References

Bochner, A. P. (2017). Heart of the matter: A mini-manifesto for autoethnography. *International Review of Qualitative Research*, *10*(1), 67–80. https://doi.org/10.1525/irqr.2017.10.1.67

Cameron, J. (2002). *The complete artist's way*. New York: Penguin.

Chapple, T., & Collinson. A. (2021, October 26). *Why women way wait decades for an ADHD diagnosis*. BBC News. https://www.bbc.com/news/health-59038116

Chia, L., & Chew, Eileen (2021, October 31). These women never knew they had ADHD: A diagnosis changed their lives. *Channel News Asia*. https://www.channelnewsasia.com/cna-insider/adhd-adult-undiagnosed-women-disorder-2277441

Clark, N. (2021, May 24). No one's ever talked to me about this before. *The New York Times*. https://www.nytimes.com/2021/05/24/style/adhd-online-creators-diagnosis.html

Cloke, P., Cook, I., Crang, P., Goodwin, M., Painter, J., & Philo, C. (2004). *Practising human geography*. London: SAGE Publications Ltd.

Dimitroff, L. J., Sliwoski, L., O'Brien, S., & Nichols, L. W. (2017). Change your life through journaling – The benefits of journaling for registered nurses. *Journal of Nursing Education and Practice*, *7*(2), 90–98. https://doi.org/10.5430/jnep.v7n2p90

Dion, M. L., Sumner, J. L., & Mitchell, S. M. (2018). Gendered citation patterns across political science and social science methodology fields. *Political Analysis*, *26*(3), 312–327. https://doi.org/10.1017/pan.2018.12

Fothergill, A., & Feltey, K. (2003). "I've worked very hard and slept very little": Mothers on tenure track in academia. *Journal of the Motherhood Initiative for Research and Community Involvement* *5*(2), 7–19. https://jarm.journals.yorku.ca/index.php/jarm/article/view/1995

Fox, M. F. (2005). Gender, family characteristics, and publication productivity among scientists. *Social Studies of Science*, *35*(1), 131–150. https://doi.org/10.1177/0306312705046630

Freeman, M. (1991). Rewriting the self: Development as moral practice. *New Directions for Child and Adolescent Development*, *1991*(54), 83–102. https://doi.org/10.1002/cd.23219915407

Gentile, J. P., Atiq, R., & Gillig, P. M. (2006). Adult ADHD: Diagnosis, differential diagnosis, and medication management. *Psychiatry (Edgmont)*, *3*(8), 25–30.

Gieryn, T. F. (1999). *Cultural boundaries of science: Credibility on the line*. Chicago: University of Chicago Press.

Ginther, D. K. (2003). Is MIT an exception? Gender pay differences in academic science. *Bulletin of Science, Technology & Society*, *23*(1), 21–26. https://doi.org/10.1177/0270467602239767

Ginther, D. K., & Hayes, K. J. (1999). Gender differences in salary and promotion in the humanities. *American Economic Review*, *89*(2), 397–402. https://doi.org/10.1257/aer.89.2.397

Harvey, A. (2021, June 3). ADHD Paralysis is frustratingly real: Here's how to fix it. *Invisible Illness*. https://medium.com/invisible-illness/adhd-paralysis-is-frustratingly-real-heres-how-to-fix-it-20c630e07c4c

Hiemstra, R. (2001). Uses and benefits of journal writing. *New Directions for Adult and Continuing Education*, 2001(90), 19–26. https://doi.org/10.1002/ace.17

Hupfeld, K. E., Abagis, T. R., & Shah, P. (2019). Living "in the zone": Hyperfocus in adult ADHD. *ADHD Attention Deficit and Hyperactivity Disorders*, 11(2), 191–208. https://doi.org/10.1007/s12402-018-0272-y

Hupfield, K. E., Abagis, T. R., Osborne, J. B., Tran Q.T. & Shah, P. (2022). *Hyperfocus: The ADHD Superpower*. Frontiers for Young Minds. https://kids.frontiersin.org/articles/10.3389/frym.2021.625433

Lutter, M., & Schröder, M. (2020). Is there a motherhood penalty in academia? The gendered effect of children on academic publications in German sociology. *European Sociological Review*, 36(3), 442–459. https://doi.org/10.1093/esr/jcz063

Maliniak, D., Powers, R., & Walter, B. F. (2013). The gender citation gap in international relations. *International Organization*, 67(4), 889–922. https://doi.org/10.1017/S0020818313000209

Mason, M. A., Wolfinger, N. H., & Goulden, M. (2013). *Do babies matter?: Gender and family in the Ivory Tower*. New Jersey: Rutgers University Press.

Ozel-Kizil, E. T., Kokurcan, A., Aksoy, U. M., Kanat, B. B., Sakarya, D., Bastug, G., Colak, B., Altunoz, U., Kirici, S., Demirbas, H., & Oncu, B. (2016). Hyperfocusing as a dimension of adult attention deficit hyperactivity disorder. *Research in Developmental Disabilities*, 59, 351–358. https://doi.org/10.1016/j.ridd.2016.09.016

Parr, H. (2001). Negotiating different ethnographic contexts and building geographical knowledges: Empirical examples from mental health research. In Melanie L. & Claire D. (Eds.), *Qualitative methodologies for geographers* (pp. 181–195). London: Arnold.

Rainer, T. (1978). *The new diary: How to use a journal for self-guidance and expanded creativity*. New York: TarcherPerigee.

Read, B. (2020, April 10). What is "time blindness" and do you have it? *The Cut*. https://www.thecut.com/2020/04/coronavirus-self-isolation-time-blindness.html

Retz, W., Stieglitz, R. D., Corbisiero, S., Retz-Junginger, P., & Rösler, M. (2012). Emotional dysregulation in adult ADHD: What is the empirical evidence?. *Expert Review Of Neurotherapeutics*, 12(10), 1241–1251. https://doi.org/10.1586/ern.12.109

Rodden, J. (2022, February 28). What is executive dysfunction? *ADDitude*. https://www.additudemag.com/what-is-executive-function-disorder/

Schiwy, M. A. (1994). Taking things personally: Women, journal writing and self-creation. *Journal of the National Women's Studies Association*, 6, 234–254. https://www.jstor.org/stable/4316329

Sealy, P. A. (2012). Autoethnography: Reflective journaling and meditation to cope with life-threatening breast cancer. *Clinical Journal of Oncology Nursing*, 16(1), 38–41. https://doi.org/10.1188/12.cjon.38-41

Sibonney, C. (2021, April 7). How the pandemic is helping some women realize they have ADHD. *SELF*. https://www.self.com/story/adhd-diagnosis-pandemic

Symonds, M. R., Gemmell, N. J., Braisher, T. L., Gorringe, K. L., & Elgar, M. A. (2006). Gender differences in publication output: Towards an unbiased metric of research performance. *PloS One*, 1(1), 1–5. https://doi.org/10.1371/journal.pone.0000127

Ullrich, P. M., & Lutgendorf, S. K. (2002). Journaling about stressful events: Effects of cognitive processing and emotional expression. *Annals of Behavioral Medicine*, 24(3), 244–250. https://psycnet.apa.org/doi/10.1207/S15324796ABM2403_10

7 Give me wings, and I will fly

Fareeha Javed

In a patriarchal society, a woman is faced not only by challenges forced upon her by the male members of the society but by the obstacles created by her own kind as well. In such a society, women are not allowed to build their own wings and fly to achieve their dreams. I hail from a similar society where a woman like me who breaks the norms and sets precedence must bear resistance from not only the society but family and friends as well. I hail from Pakistan, where not many girls get a chance to lead their lives the way they want. It is common practice in almost all households to offer more and better opportunities to the male children, be it in education or other life decisions. Luckily, I was born to parents who treated their children equally, irrespective of gender. Rather, in some cases they gave more opportunities to their two daughters to follow their dreams and flap freely when it came to getting educated and choosing careers. My luck further improved when I married a man who was very ambitious for me, who not only supported me in joining academia as a lecturer but also gave me the wings to fly and live my dream. He accompanied me to New Zealand with my three kids, despite this decision putting his career at stake, as I pursued my doctoral studies despite opposition from our families on both sides. In short, I did not receive an encouraging attitude from anyone except my other half. Even my co-workers tried to pull me down by commenting that I was already well settled with a good job, so why would I choose to make the next few years of my life terrible, as a doctoral degree is not an easy road to travel on, especially with three school-going children who needed my full-time attention. It was hard to convince them that I aspired for higher skies to soar in and that for me, there is no limit when it comes to getting a higher education and following my heart. After all, it is all about managing your responsibilities while following your dreams, which I successfully did, and today all three of my children are leading successful lives and are well settled. I believe that simply receiving an education, securing a good job, getting married, and having children should not be the ultimate goal for a woman to be considered well settled and an excuse for putting a full stop to their dreams in life and from aspiring to higher skies to glide in.

Enrolling in a doctoral program in a foreign country and de/reconstructing my identity from a lecturer to a student once again was not a simple thing. I was aware of the hardships it called for, and I chose this thorny path while accepting all these challenges. The decision to leave the comfort of my home country, job position,

DOI: 10.4324/9781003341482-9

societal status, perks, and family and friends and to put my wellbeing at stake took a lot of courage. I am grateful to God that I had the biggest support system available to me, which was my husband, who encouraged me and advised me to never look back and to keep moving forward and flying higher. I accepted the challenges with an open mind and heart, with a strong belief in myself, and I eventually managed to surf successfully with the support and love of my husband and children. I am proud to have become a role model for my children and my students today, who look to me as a source of inspiration and as a mentor to pursue their educational and career goals and to never give in to hardships and challenges.

I have been associated with academia since 1997 and have been teaching in women-only institutions. My students are young women belonging to all sections of Pakistani society who find in me not only a teacher and mentor, but also a guide to help them find answers and solutions for many of their problems, or at least a friend who listens to their issues patiently even if I am not able to solve them. Getting a higher education not only provided a clear career trajectory but also helped me reconstruct my identity and become a better human being who tries to play a positive role as a responsible member of the society because I feel that it is my responsibility to give back to the society and my country with the education, knowledge, and experience I gained through all these years. I think my biggest achievement is that I am now holding a position where I can play a positive role in women's empowerment by instilling courage and confidence in my students and making them productive members of the society. I hope that these young women will play an effective role in reforming the society.

I have been associated with higher education and academia for more than 25 years now. All these years have been full of challenges and hardships and have been a roller coaster of work and family responsibilities, with demands that at times affected my health, both physically and mentally. There were moments when I neglected self-care and pushed myself to meet my goals. I even neglected my health problems and did not receive proper medical treatment for my ailments for almost three years, which in the end took a toll on me and resulted in me going through a major surgery. Women in academia, or any other job role across the globe, are faced with untold challenges like my own. However, in Pakistani society, it is more challenging for a woman to decide to leave the comforts of her home to follow a career and pursue her dreams due to household responsibilities. Working women are expected to manage household chores and look after their children and parents-in-law along with their jobs, which leaves them with no time for self-care. There is also a dearth of existing literature on the topics of burnout, self-care, and wellbeing amongst women in academia in the Pakistani context. It therefore becomes important to study these topics in the Pakistani context, which I will do in this chapter. The aim of the chapter is to identify the experiences I had and the meanings I drew from them (in the past and in the present), and to give other aspiring or present higher-education academics advice on how to manage professional burnout and take care of their selves and wellbeing. In this chapter I will situate the importance of self-care and wellbeing of women in academia with glimpses from my lived experiences, which I learnt quite late in my life and career. I hope my experiences and recommendations for self-care will help aspiring higher-education academics understand the value of self-care and its pivotal role in overall wellbeing.

My pet cats (Frankie is the one on the right and Smokey is the one on the left; see Figure 7.1) are my biggest source of stress relief, in whom I began seeking comfort after a long, tiring workday ever since my three children grew up and moved out of my home around two years ago for their own life pursuits. I talk to them; they are really good listeners and tend to understand what I am saying. When I pet them, I feel an energy being released from their bodies that takes away all the stress and makes me feel relaxed. They act as partners and boosters in my self-care regimen and wellbeing just like a loved one would.

Literature review

In this section, I take a brief review of existing literature on self-care and strategies for self-care.

Self-care

The impact of job demands on occupational burnout has been widely studied in the context of health sciences, medical professions, and education (e.g., Hakanen et al., 2007; Xanthoupoulou et al., 2007; Miller et al., 2018; Tuxford & Bradley, 2015). According to Boogren (2018), the daily practice of being conscious of, and responding to, one's fundamental emotional and physiological needs, which include the structuring of one's daily routine, relationships, and surroundings, is character-ised as self-care. Self-care is a mindful approach in which one prioritises oneself, and it aids in balancing life's duties and commitments. Boogren (2018) reports that a majority of individuals associated with the teaching profession experience high levels of stress. A number of these concerns are caused by compassion fatigue, which is the feeling of being tired by daily emotions. In turn, academics who are stressed have an impact on their students' academic progress and wellbeing. The most suitable way that guarantees that an academician is taking care of and

Figure 7.1 My pet cats, with Frankie on the right and Smokey on the left.

nourishing their health and wellbeing is to develop a daily self-care routine in which one prioritises oneself. When academicians practise good self-care, they are better able to care for others, establish healthy connections, be resilient, and manage personal and professional duties (Lawler, 2020).

The following five stages are proposed and recommended by Lawler (2020) for developing a self-care regimen:

1) Determine what helps you feel centred. It is critical to recognise that self-care cannot be regarded as a one-size-fits-all strategy. Various things provide delight to different individuals, and it is critical to recognise those precise objects when beginning a self-care regimen.

2) Consider how such elements can be incorporated into your day-to-day life. These notions might be things that can be done in the background or things that consume time at a set time of day. If one begins small, this will make it easier to establish habits. Choosing one habit to implement for an entire week is a suggested method.

3) Establish daily objectives for adopting self-care habits. Once you have identified self-care routines that will help your life, set precise objectives for how and when to implement them into your daily routine.

4) Evaluate after seven days. Noting good thoughts and rewards will provide motivation to continue with certain habits.

5) Adjust and fine-tune your strategy as you go. Understanding that one self-care practice at one moment may not be ideal at another is critical. One should expect some hiccups along the road as it is a journey, not a destination.

(Lawler, 2020)

Self-care practices are an example of job resources. They are a complex concept that is seen to be effective in fostering personal as well as professional general wellbeing (Dorociak, Rupert, Bryant, & Zahniser, 2017). Professionals in healthcare and education are expected to manage the emotional pressures of their jobs while also serving the requirements of their customers and pupils. Self-care, according to Lee and Miller (2013), is defined as behaviours that promote and improve the overall wellbeing of an individual. Self-care can prove to be a useful technique for professionals for promoting emotional resilience, taking charge of their overall health and emotional wellbeing, and avoiding occupational burnout (Lee & Miller, 2013). According to research, self-care activities like appropriate sleep, peer and social support, and strategies for increasing self-awareness and emotional resilience all benefit overall health and wellbeing of an individual (Dorociak et al., 2017).

It was found by Bell, Rajendran, and Theiler (2012) that aspects like high work expectations, absence of professional resources, and lack of self-care behaviours are related to occupational burnout among Australian university professors. According to Bell et al. (2012), to lower the potential risk of occupational burnout, both the organisation and the individual should play an equal role to reduce perceived work pressures. In addition to proper supervisory support, executing and enabling useful treatments and programmes to minimise job-related stress and fostering work-life balance would promote professional self-care practices and create emotional resilience among professionals (Bell et al., 2012).

Strategies for self-care

As one goes along practising self-care, one finds out that the more one practises it, the more one becomes self-aware, and eventually discovers more self-love, that in turn will rub off on those one comes in contact with on a daily basis in the shape of deeper kindness, appreciation, and compassion (Lawler, 2020). Self-care is an important technique that has the tendency to be tremendously effective in developing more resilient academicians, resulting in reduced burnout. Resilient people, in turn, hold a positive self-image and are dedicated to taking care of themselves (Lifeworks, 2019). Resilience amongst academicians can be achieved by making sure to practise self-care. These self-care practices include getting enough sleep every night, eating healthier, getting exercise, staying connected with one's loved and dear ones (Alani & Stroink, 2015; Shepell, 2019), and appropriate support. Meanwhile, organisational methods can be: reduced workload or ample administrative assistance (Alani & Stroink, 2015).

According to Bradley, Whisenhut, Adamson, and Kress (2013) and Little (2016), self-care is a professional's capacity to maintain or improve personal wellbeing via the use of multidimensional stress-management approaches whilst creating and maintaining support systems. However, Salloum, Johnco, Kondrat, and Olsen (2015) contend that the techniques adopted and used for this purpose may differ depending on a professional's disciplines of interest and their circumstances. Bloomquist, Wood, Friedmeyer-Trainor, and Kim (2015) and Coaston (2017) posit that individuals and organisational administrators should be deliberate in their adoption of activities directed at self-care.

Self-care strategies are regarded as the best practice for wellbeing, and they demand deliberateness to attain that wellbeing (Lee, 2018). In burnout research studies, higher levels of self-care have been found to be associated with a reduction in the impacts of burnout (Rupert, Miller, & Dorociak, 2015). Mindfulness, spiritual practices (meditation), and physical activities, for instance, are examples of self-care activities (Cacciatore, Thieleman, Killian, & Tavasolli, 2015; Newell & Nelson-Gardell, 2014). Physical activity as noted by Coaston (2017) is a key component of self-care in the development of wellbeing. According to Bloomquist et al. (2015), meditation, for example, is a spiritual activity that may be related to religion. Spiritual self-care techniques and specialised practices, such as dialogue (faith) journaling, may ease the stress that leads to burnout (Dombo & Gray, 2013). Hotchiss and Lesher (2018) maintain that mindfulness activities like meditation, yoga, and tai chi are examples of self-care practices, as are regular activities like exercise, healthy eating habits, and colouring. Individual and organisational initiatives that give organisational support and policy enactment to welcome personal activities are successful self-care practices (Dombo & Gray, 2013).

Reading, family socialising, and vacations are examples of unidimensional self-care activities. Nevertheless, the intensity of such activities is an important aspect in improving wellbeing, as noted by Cardinal and Thomas (2016). Baldschun

(2014) argues that individuals may heal via contact with family outside of the job, implying a favourable influence on wellbeing. Self-care can thus be thought of as a multidimensional notion that functions as a continuum and entails treating the personal and professional selves as if a professional handles their stress (Bressi & Vaden, 2017; Little, 2016).

Burnout has been extensively researched by philosophers, human service experts, and medical researchers (Fink, 2017). Burnout causes professionals to become disengaged, resulting in losses at physical and psychological levels, attitude and behavioural changes, and feelings of despair and hopelessness (Travis, Lizano, & Mor Barak, 2016). As a result, organisations lose skilled workers and incur financial losses.

A comprehensive approach and an individual viewpoint are two perspectives of the historical idea of self-care. Members of the holistic approach in the community believe in healing, while the individual perspective includes care in the home. Baldschun (2014) stresses that self-care must be purposeful and persistent to be effective, and it must be supported by agency administration. Self-care methods have proved inconclusive in several circumstances. Lee and Miller (2013) found that despite studies being primarily focused on human services workers, there is a dearth of research conducted on self-care habits amongst academicians in higher education. Miller et al. (2018) discovered that social work professors who practised self-care were more capable of handling job-related stress and assisting their students in an effective manner and were less likely to experience occupational burnout. Miller et al. (2018) also found variations in academics' levels of self-care, with greater levels noted amongst higher-ranking academics and those having more years of academic service. The authors also emphasised the need for professional socialisation, stressing its relevance and early introduction in the academicians' career for avoiding or preventing academic isolation and occupational burnout (Miller et al., 2018).

Methodology

This study employs the qualitative method of autoethnography. The term "autoethnography" does not appear in the *Oxford English Dictionary*. Nonetheless, it is a phrase that defines a specific study technique that has an extensive lineage, particularly in anthropology (Tedlock, 2000). Furthermore, it is a phrase that is increasingly being used in research in a variety of fields. Employing Wendy Bishop's (1999) concept of ethnography as the portrayal of a particular culture's lived experience, autoethnography aids in expressing the core objective of my study. This research thus portrays my own viewpoint as a higher-education academic, taking into consideration my personal struggles, challenges, experiences, connections, ups and downs of life, and celebrations that helped mould and build my own experience. A hermeneutic phenomenological investigation of a higher-education academic's self-reported experience enables the writer and reader to delve into the core and meaning of being an academic (Raudenbush, 1994). At the core of all such investigations are "attention to detail, nuances, subtleties, and contextual awareness," which give the researcher a rigorous and thoughtful mindset. In a personal narrative, there are no defined processes or specific formulae. There are just paths and structures that act as landmarks. First-person descriptions emphasise turning points in life, the openings and closings, as well as individual voices and milestones that imply codified expression (Denzin, 1989) in this study.

Finding my wings

I used to be committed to practising self-care on a regular basis to improve physical fitness when I was younger, specifically during the first 13 years of my entry into higher education as a lecturer. At that time, I didn't realise the real value of self-care. I only recognised it after I had stopped practicing it and became burnt-out and lost my health. As a young academic and a young mother, I used to manage my day in a very systematic manner and never forgot to make time for self-care in the form of exercise, having a good night's sleep, hanging out with family and friends, homemaking, and taking care of my kids' needs and comforts. However, things took a turn when I decided to pursue my doctoral studies abroad at Massey University, New Zealand. The decision was monumental and demanding, which left me exposed to a completely alien culture and a different lifestyle with less sleep and more work. I had to meet academic and research deadlines while looking after my growing kids and giving them time, doing chores, and meeting other everyday demands. The biggest challenge was adjusting in the new culture, to both a new country and a new education system. Although it was easy to adjust in New Zealand as it is a very friendly country, it was a different story at the university. I had acquired all my prior education in my home country, Pakistan, which is why it was initially very challenging for me to understand the New Zealand education system and learn new ways to complete my academic tasks successfully. The professors and administrative staff at the university in New Zealand were very helpful, and within a few weeks I managed to understand the system and its demands. I was eventually successful in managing all the responsibilities in a very apt manner but at the cost of my self-care. I was left with no time for myself. I stopped getting exercise and did not have time for socialisation. This left me with no channels for relieving stress, and eventually I felt burnt-out, and my health also started deteriorating.

Upon the successful completion of my doctoral study, which I did while standing steadfast against all the odds, I returned to my home country and to my job. My responsibilities as an academic also increased manifold after achieving a higher degree (PhD). Prior to doing my PhD, I was responsible for delivering lectures, preparing lessons, setting examination question papers, marking scripts and assignments, and other minor responsibilities. Upon returning to Pakistan from New Zealand after successfully completing my doctoral degree, I faced various challenges in adjusting to the work demands and professional responsibilities, which increased with the achievement of higher qualification. The challenges were of various types such as increased working hours and a wider job scope and job role associated with higher education. After completing my PhD, along with all the aforementioned responsibilities, I had to participate in research-based activities, such as supervising research students and developing the curriculum. I also had to attend, present, and serve as keynote speaker in conferences and seminars and participate in panel discussions. I had to head several boards and committees and departments, examine theses and other assessments, write book chapters and research articles for publication, develop, design, get approved, and launch new study programmes, and much more. All of these required multitasking as well as longer working hours, which ultimately left me little time for self-care and caring for my wellbeing.

However, I consciously made an effort to manage all my responsibilities while finding time for self-care because I could not put my health at risk again. By this time, I had become hypertensive (high blood pressure) and was put on regular medication. I have made it a habit to check my blood pressure twice a day, in the morning and then in the evening, to keep track of it on daily basis. I also use a mobile application for checking my heart rate and the number of steps I walk through the day, as I do not get enough time for regular exercise. I also started following a schedule and took care to get a good night's sleep, eat healthily, and spend quality time with my family and friends. Self-care gave strength to my wings to help me keep flying and soaring higher. However, after a few years, my children started moving out as my daughter got married, my elder son began his job abroad and got married, and my youngest son went abroad for his university education. Suddenly, my initially full house became quiet with only my husband and me to accompany each other. At this stage, my elder son, being very thoughtful, got me a kitten and I couldn't be more grateful for such a wonderful gift. I was so happy to have Frankie (the kitten) in my life, who was just like a little baby to me. Three months after Frankie's arrival, I brought Smokey (my other kitten) home. Both are now my best companions.

In Pakistani society, women, either working or staying at home, must bear greater, and in most cases all, household responsibilities. Not all working women can afford to get domestic help, and thus have to do all the chores themselves, which naturally has an adverse effect on their physical and mental health. I have been one of those lucky women who could afford to get domestic help for most of my household work. Working long hours at the university makes me so tired that sometimes I find it hard to cook or to find time for that. I manage this by doing bulk cooking over the weekend or ordering home-cooked food from food delivery apps. This strategy helps me find time for myself, stay connected to my loved ones, and spend time with my husband. I also find time every day to talk to my children, which is another strategy that helps me to refresh myself after a long and tiring day of work. Last, but not least, I enjoy the company of my two cats. I love and revel in taking care of their needs, grooming them, and taking them for visits to their vet.

My self-care practices are endorsed by existing research too (e.g., Bell et al., 2012; Dorociak et al., 2017; Hoenig, 2020; Lee & Miller, 2013; Miller et al., 2018; Myers et al., 2012), which shows that teaching is a job with a relatively high rate of burnout. Because of the precise attention to detail that an academic must have, the added stress of handling other elements of life, such as being able to exercise for self-care, is frequently compromised as was the case with me. I still don't get time to exercise. Burnout is a fact of the high-stakes work of academia, but there are tools and ways to help academics stay balanced at their workplace. This is significant enough to represent a physiological requirement that academics should pay more attention to, in order to practice greater self-care as I do.

There is a need for a self-care strategy that includes regular, attainable reminders; a daily reminder about how much water an academic should drink each day and how much sleep they should receive each night will assist them in reaching their self-care objectives. A daily reminder to do 20 minutes of exercise every day might help educators accomplish their self-care objectives in a better way. I regret that I am unable to find time for exercise. It has been observed that everyday workplace commitments, along with extracurricular activities, prevent academics from practising self-care, as is the case with me. Children, home chores, and supplementary occupations all take precedence over self-care goals. Incorporating a daily reminder to encourage realistic objectives might assist those academics who are not already practising improved self-care. When educators are encouraged to think more about practising greater self-care, their general mental wellbeing improves. Hence, this would help improve self-care for them.

Academics should understand that self-care is critical for both mental and physical health. Academics encounter several challenges daily and feel stress during the workday, which can be overcome by being resilient. Resilience is referred to as the process of successfully adjusting in the face of adversity, trauma, tragedy, danger, or significant sources of stress. According to Fredrickson (2001), academics who are exposed to more pleasant emotions on a daily basis may be more resilient. Shepell (2019) argues that resilient people have a positive self-image and are dedicated to taking care of themselves.

According to research, academics are overworked and require rest and relaxation time. This is rigorous and unpleasant emotional work, which contributes to teacher burnout and universities' failure to retain academics (Philibert, Soto, & Veon, 2020). One of the most predictive features of higher education academic burnout is emotional weariness. Academics' needs must be satisfied by means of self-care goals. According to research, self-care increases resilience. Teachers who emphasise self-care will be more effective in promoting resilience. Resilient people have a positive self-image and are dedicated to taking care of themselves (Shepell, 2019). High levels of job stress are substantially associated with eventual burnout, although high levels of self-actualisation and resilience serve as an effective barrier between job stress and burnout (Schwarzer & Hallum, 2008). Academics must first fulfil their bottom-tier wants to achieve self-actualisation. In order to accomplish this, they must apply self-care practices. Higher education academics who practise self-care can have an effect on the future of education if they are reminded and encouraged on a regular basis. In short, practicing self-care helps me recover from burnout and weariness and perform my professional responsibilities in a better way.

Conclusion

Self-care is a state in which a person is in tune with their body, listening to it, checking in on it, consciously tuning into their thoughts, and questioning their actions and belief systems if things appear to be off-balance in their life. Academics should eat healthy food, sleep more, and exercise in order to become more resilient. These should be focal themes for academics, and they should be included in any prospective application. To summarise, academics do not have enough time to practise self-care every day. I recommend regular reminders to integrate self-care in modest additions throughout the workday. Researchers believe that this effort may benefit academics who are unaware of resources to assist them in achieving their goals. Teaching is a difficult job with a high risk of burnout, and academics often do not have self-care methods to assist them in coping with a demanding and emotionally draining job. Self-care practices implemented on a daily basis can assist them in developing the abilities required to confront the challenges of the higher-education profession. Academics must create reachable daily objectives in order to effectively serve themselves and others. Incorporating measures to encourage greater self-care, such as through daily reminders and realistic objectives, might assist academics in being prepared for the high demand and stress of their profession.

References

Alani, T., & Stroink, M. (2015). Self-care strategies and barriers among female service providers working with female survivors of intimate partner violence. *Canadian Journal of Counseling and Psychotherapy, 49*(4), 360–378. https://cjc-rcc.ucalgary.ca/

Baldschun, A. (2014). The six dimensions of child welfare employees' occupational wellbeing. *Nordic Journal of Working Life Studies, 4*(4), 69–87. https://doi.org/10.19154/njwls.v4i4.4708

Bell, A. S., Rajendran, D., & Theiler, S. (2012). Job stress, wellbeing, work-life balance and work-life conflict among Australian academics. *Electronic Journal of Applied Psychology, 8*(1), 25–37. https://doi.org/10.7790/ejap.v8i1.320

Bishop, W. (1999). *Ethnographic writing research: Writing it down, writing it up, and reading it.* Portsmouth, NH: Boynton/Cook Publishers.

Bloomquist, K., Wood, L., Friedmeyer-Trainor, K., & Kim, H. (2015). Self-care and professional quality of life: Predictive factors among MSW practitioners. *Advances in Social Work, 16*(2), 292–311. https://doi.org/10.18060/18760

Boogren, T. (2018). *Take time for you: Self-care action plans for educators.* Bloomington, IN: Solution Tree Press.

Bradley, N., Whisenhut, J., Adamson, NB, & Kress, V. (2013). Creative approaches for promoting counselor self-care. *Journal of Creativity in Mental Health, 8,* 456–469. https://doi.org/10.1080/15401383.2013.844656

Bressi, S., & Vaden, E. (2017). Reconsidering self-care. *Clinical Social Work, 45*(1), 33–38. https://doi.org/10.1007/S10615-016-0575-7

Cacciatore, J., Thieleman, K., Killian, M., & Tavasolli, K. (2015). Braving human suffering: Death education and its relationship to empathy and mindfulness. *Social Work Education, 34*(1), 91–109. http://dx.org/10.1080/02615479.2014.940890

Cardinal, B., & Thomas, J. (2016). Self-care strategies for maximizing human potential. *Journal of Physical Education, Recreation, & Dance, 87*(9), 5–7. https://doi.org/10.1080/07303084.2016.1277198

Coaston, S. (2017). Self-care through self-compassion: A balm for burnout. *The Professional Counselor, 7*(3), 285–297. https://doi.org/10.15241/scc.7.3.285

Denzin, N. K. (1989). *Interpretative ethnography.* Thousand Oaks, CA: Sage Publications.

Dombo, E. A., & Gray, C. (2013). Engaging spirituality in addressing vicarious trauma in clinical social workers: A self-care model. *Social Work and Christianity*, *40*(1), 89–104. https://swc.nacsw.org/

Dorociak, K., Rupert, P., Bryant, F., & Zahniser, E. (2017). Development of the professional self-care scale. *Journal of Counseling Psychology*, *64*(3), 325–325. https://doi.org/10.1037/cou0000206

Fink, G. (2017) *Stress: Concepts, cognition, emotion, and behavior: Handbook of stress series, volume 1* (Vol. 1). London: Academic Press.

Fredrickson, B. L. (2001). The role of positive emotions in positive psychology: The broaden-and-build theory of positive emotions. *American Psychologist*, *56*, 218–226. https://doi.org/10.1037/0003-066X.56.3.218

Hakanen, J., Demerouti, E., Xanthopoulou, D., & Bakker, A. (2007). Job resources boost work engagement, particularly when job demands are high. *Journal of Educational Psychology*, *99*(2), 274–284. https://doi.org/0.1037/0022-0663.99.2.274

Hoenig, C.Y. (2020). *Professional self-care practices, emotional work and burnout in Australian psychology academics*. [Honours thesis, Edith Cowan University]. Retrieved November 2, 2021, from https://ro.ecu.edu.au/theses_hons/1543

Hotchiss, J., & Lesher, R. (2018). Factors predicting burnout among chaplains: Compassion satisfaction, organizational factors, and the mediators of mindful self-care and secondary traumatic stress. *The Journal of Pastoral Care & Counseling*, *72*(2), 86–98. https://doi.org/10.1177/1542305018780655

Lawler, M. (2020). *How to start a self-care routine you'll follow: Everyday health*. Retrieved October 10, 2021, from https://www.everydayhealth.com/self-care/start-a-self-care-routine/

Lee, J. (2018). ASC framework for social workers: Build a strong foundation for practice. *Families in Society: The Journey of Contemporary Social Services*, *94*(1), 96–103. https://doi.org/10.1606/1044-3894.4289

Lee, J., & Miller, S. (2013). A self-care framework for social workers: Building a strong foundation for practice. *Families in Society: The Journal of Contemporary Social Sciences*, *94*(2), 96–103. https://doi.org/10.1606/1044-3894.4289

Lifeworks (2019). Annual Report-2019. Retrieved October 11, 2021, from https://lifeworks.com/en/annual-reports

Little, J. (2016). Cultivating human beings, not human doings: Challenging discourses of self-care. *Scottish Journal of Residential Child Care*, *15*(3), 124–138. https://doi.org/10.14334/111.444.ijsp.2017.09

Miller, J., Grise-Owens, E., & Shalash, N. (2018). Investigating the self-care practices of social work faculty: An exploratory study. *Social Work Education*, *37*(8), 1044–1059. https://doi.org/10.1080/02615479.2018.1470618

Myers, S., Sweeney, A., Popick, V., Wesley, K., Bordfeld, A., & Fingerhut, R. (2012). Self-care practices and perceived stress levels among psychology graduate students. *Training and Education in Professional Psychology*, *6*(1), 55–66. https://doi.org/10.1037/a0026534

Newell, J. M., & Nelson-Gardell, D. (2014). A competency-based approach to teaching professional self-care: An ethical consideration for social work educators. *Journal of Social Work Education*, *50*(3), 427–439. https://doi.org/10.1080/10437797.2014.917928

Philibert, C. T., Soto, C., & Veon, L. (2020). *Every day self-care for educators: Tools and strategies for wellbeing*. New York: Routledge, Taylor & Francis Group.

Raudenbush, C. A. (1994). *Improvisation: An autobiography of my first year as an administrator*. [Doctoral dissertation, University of Kansas, Lawrence, Kansas]. ProQuest Dissertations and Theses Global.

Rupert, A., Miller, A., & Dorociak, E. (2015). Preventing burnout: What does the research tell us? *Professional Psychology: Research and Practice, 46*(3), 168–174. http://dx.doi.org/10.1037a0039297

Salloum, A., Johnco, C., Kondrat, D., & Olsen, K. (2015). The role of self-care on compassion satisfaction, burnout, and secondary trauma among child welfare workers. *Children and Youth Services, 49*(C), 54–61. https://doi.org/10.1016/j.childyouth.2014.12.023

Schwarzer, R., & Hallum, S. (2008). Perceived teacher self-efficacy as a predictor of job stress and burnout: Mediation analyses. *Applied Psychology. An International Review, 57,* 152–171. https://doi.org/10.1111/j.1464-0597.2008.00359.x

Shepell, M. (2019). *The importance of self-love, positivity, self-esteem, and resilience.* Retrieved from https://www.lifeworks.com/uk/blog/the-importance-of-self-love-positivity-self-esteem-and-resilience/

Tedlock, B. (2000) Ethnography and ethnographic representation. In Denzin, N.K. & Lincoln, Y.S. *Handbook of qualitative research* (pp. 455–486). London: SAGE Publications, Inc.

Travis, D., Lizano, E., & Mor Barak, M. (2016). "I'm so stressed!": A longitudinal model of stress, burnout and engagement among social workers in child welfare settings. *British Journal of Social Work, 46*(4), 1076–1095. https://doi.org/10.1093/bjsw/bct205

Tuxford, L., & Bradley, G. (2015). Emotional job demands and emotional exhaustion in teachers. *Educational Psychology, 35*(8), 1006–1006. https://doi.org/10.1080/01443410.2014.912260

Xanthopoulou, D., Bakker, A., Demerouti, E., & Schaufeli, W. (2007). The role of personal resources in the job demands-resources model. *International Journal of Stress Management, 14*(2), 121–141. https://doi.org/10.1037/1072-5245.14.2.121

8 Navigating fieldwork amidst my menstrual cycle

Being a female ethnographer in a remote Indian region

Sampurna Das

Remote areas are those geographies that are physically, economically, and politically distant from the centres of power and governance. They perform poorly in terms of development indicators like health, hygiene, education, and transportation, especially in developing countries like India. This chapter is based on my doctoral fieldwork in one such remote region of India. I have conducted ethnographic research in one of the many riverine islands (or char, as locally known) in the northeastern Indian state of Assam. My fieldwork was mediated by the broader questions of my research that sought to understand *the lives and livelihoods in these remote riverine islands.* Pursuing this goal from a university located in the Indian capital of New Delhi, where I witnessed the finest in developmental activities afforded by a developing nation, added further layers of inquiries: How do these riverine islands grapple with their history of under-development under colonial and post-colonial states, while also imagining a developed future for themselves? How does our understanding of remoteness and development change when we are grounded in an ever-shifting riverine island rather than a contiguous static landmass located inland?

These river islands (or chars) are spread along the Brahmaputra River, flowing through the entire breadth of Assam. Geomorphologically, these river islands are shifting in nature − eroding and accreting every year − given their location in the Brahmaputra, one of the world's highest erosion- and accretion-prone rivers (Gogoi, 2018; Islam, 2021). As per the latest land survey of 2004, there are officially 2,251 river islands covering around 5 percent of the total area of Assam (GOA, 2004). The islands are physically, economically, and politically distant from the centres of power and governance. As per a government survey (GOI, 2014 in Kumar and Das, 2019), only 1.4 per cent of households of the overall river island population have sanitary latrine facilities. Medical facilities are stagnant, with only 52 primary health centres across 2,251 river island villages (GOA, 2004). The state always blames the unpredictable erosion and accretion of these riverine landscapes as a reason for the lack of cadastral surveys and thereby the delay in allocation of development projects.

I conducted my doctorate fieldwork in Osthir char,[1] one of these 2,251 river islands, located in the Barpeta district of Western Assam. It takes an about two-hours-long motorboat journey, one way, to reach Osthir char from the nearest

DOI: 10.4324/9781003341482-10

jetty town. The first thing I noticed during my pilot study was the non-existent sanitation facilities. Functional toilets (toilets with septic tanks and proximity to a regular water source) were limited only to the household of the village chief, close kin of the chief, and the primary school (the only educational facility on the island), creating conditions for open defecation. There was also rampant littering in various pockets. Clearly, in places like Osthir char, the state's scheme to eradicate open defecation and waste disposal had fallen flat.[2] This lack of functional toilets and allocated space for waste disposal largely translated into impediments for women using any form of menstrual hygiene product (be it a sanitary napkin or menstrual cups). All they could afford was to wear two underpants, with an added layer of straw or old fabric in between on days with heavier blood flow.

I realised fairly early during my pilot study that it would not be feasible for me to undertake fieldwork during my menstrual cycle. My body needed extra attention during menstruation, something not possible on the island. There was no option but to move out of the "field" every month during my cycles. I was already feeling guilty at the thought of taking these monthly breaks. As I reflect now, this guilt was largely derived from the lack of training or discussion around centering the wellbeing and needs of self-care of the researcher when doing ethnography. Nonetheless, I actively catered to my needs. I used strategies like tracking my menstrual cycle, peer debriefing, journaling, embroidering, and reflecting on fieldnotes. One of these strategies, embroidering, can be seen in Figure 8.1. This chapter will dwell on my experiences and the importance of practising wellbeing and self-care as an ethnographer.

Once, towards the end of my fifteen-month ethnography, I mustered some courage and stayed back in the field for one of my menstrual cycles. This could be

Figure 8.1 Embroidery has been one of the many techniques of self-care I was using during my ethnographic fieldwork. I would embroider every time I was on my menstrual breaks. Given the nature of this artwork, it allowed the simultaneity of thoughts. It allowed my mind to think beyond fieldwork, revel in the creative process, and simply sit back and relax. At other times, it gave me time to reflect on field events of the past weeks, usually impossible when one is continuously noting and observing interlocutors. Together, embroidery refreshed my mind and body, boosting me to keep up with the long-term field negotiation.

seen as an attempt to put me in the shoes of my menstruating interlocutors. It was uncomfortable, to say the least. It required so much planning – from washing my bloody garments sneakily at dusk, to disposing of the sanitary napkins by digging a pit. I am sure I am not the only ethnographer to have faced such challenges, but for reasons (ranging from objectivity to rationality of doing fieldwork) such discussions are often missing from published ethnographic research. In retrospect, I ask – What kind of subjectivities and negotiations are developed by the ethnographer when faced with traumatic conditions? What does it mean for a female researcher to invest in wellbeing and self-care while on fieldwork?

Doing ethnography vis-à-vis the self (care)

The canonical ethnographic research (like Malinowski, 1922; Gluckman, 1954; Turner, 1970) never centered on the ethnographer. These researchers had a penchant for distanced and disembodied fieldwork, where the body of the ethnographer is often unnamed and implicitly male. Such distanced observation was considered necessary to make objective and rational observations.

It was only with the steady rise of feminist ethnographers that we find accounts centering on the ethnographer's experience in the field – ranging from physical to emotional (Abu-Lughod, 2016; Harding, 1987; Behar, 2003). Feminist ethnographers used self-reflection to deepen ethnographic analysis and to highlight the dilemmas of fieldwork. As Nairn (1999) asserts, feminist researchers are "bringing the body back," and thereby addressing and redressing the fear of femininity that had made field research such a disembodied affair. Increasingly, ethnographers are talking about their active and performative bodily role in their research, and thereby the need for wellbeing and self-care (Friederic, 2010; Coles et al., 2014; Branson and Radui, 2018).

They argue that the only way to enable self-care and simultaneously maintain research ethics and rigour is by being well aware, well equipped, and having clear guidance. Doing fieldwork without being aware and prepared of the "vicarious trauma" (Močnik, 2020) will lead to an incomplete knowledge process. Here, the body of the ethnographer becomes an important element of the research – the "locus of politics and praxis" (Giardina and Newman, 2011). These newer forms of ethnography – "embodied ethnography" – place the "researcher" and the "researched" in a reciprocal relation. "Embodied ethnography," developed as a critical framework, conceptualises the role of the researcher's body in the process of participation and looking for meaning in the field. Particularly adopted by feminist researchers navigating difficult terrains of fieldwork, this framework has helped them to establish that the ethnographer's body should not be understood as an unmediated and empty vessel of data collection, but as a form of negotiation and production of knowledge. The body of the ethnographer is a breathing, sweating, and bleeding entity (in my case), that co-produces meanings while interacting with the field. This body thereby needs to be taken care of upfront.

In embodied fieldwork "the body work is inserted into fieldwork just as fieldwork is inserted into body work" (Hopwood, 2015). Adding embodiment allows researchers to extend the current interpretive and ethnographic practices by degree and intentionality. This approach to interpretation is messy but thorough. Loic Wacquant's (1995, 2005, 2009) concept of "carnal sociology" centres on the importance of embodiment, lived experiences, and reflexivity in doing ethnography. Such an embodied position requires careful examination of self (care) that may inform us of our embodiment and such aspects of our being that as ethnographers are taken for granted (Turner, 2000). Wacquant's theorisation coordinated two elements: how the researcher's flesh-and-body was situated in the field and how the researcher negotiates his or her subjectivity within the norms of the field. The researcher's body is used not just to understand the field, but as an element that experiences the field, and how then these experiences become a potential source of knowledge-making. As such, optimum knowledge production can take place only when the body is in a state of relative wellbeing.

This chapter will build on these existing works of embodied ethnography, reflexivity, and self-care, and my experiences of being a menstruating female researcher in remote terrain. The next section will detail my experiences of establishing myself as an ethnographer. In a place lacking sanitation facilities and with a low literacy rate, explaining to someone about graduate research, menstruation, and ethnographic goals is not easy. It also consists of the methodological negotiations I made to understand the dialogic relation between the field and myself. The chapter will critically investigate the concepts of "field" and "ethnography." The final section will look at some of the orchestrations I made each month during my menstrual cycle to undertake fieldwork. It will detail how I managed to create a balance between my fieldwork and self-care: from marking those few days every month to filling up pending fieldnotes, doing archival research, peer debriefing, embroidering, and journaling, to dealing with guilt on missing events in the field. My fieldwork revolved around my bleeding. This section will look at how I unlearned rules of "doing ethnography." I will unpack, based on my experiences, the importance for a researcher to observe and record one's negotiations with the physical and social conditions of the field while producing knowledge.

Situating myself as an ethnographer

Entering the field was stressful. As a female researcher, I faced issues of inclusivity and gender parity in the field. This was something we were not warned about in our training for fieldwork. Given the geographical remoteness, the lack of sanitation facilities, and my medical history of menstrual unease, I had a tough time negotiating with my family to conduct ethnography. For the longest time, my father wanted to accompany me for fieldwork or at least for me to have a female aide. I kept explaining how it was impossible – primarily, how the presence of this additional figure might change the way the field would unfold. At times, the pressure was so overwhelming that I felt that the best bet would be to give up on fieldwork.

This also had to do with my parallel struggles of finding a livable space. I had visited numerous river islands in the hope of zeroing on my geographical field site, only to find most river islands with no functional toilet whatsoever. That was the minimum criteria I had set for finalising on a site. It was only towards the end of my two-month pilot study, when I already was worried about not finding a site, that I traveled to Osthir char. Sanitation facilities there were marginally better than other river islands in the sense that there were a couple of households with functional toilets, even though the toilets themselves were in bad shape owing to scarce usage. Open defecation was preferred over toilets.[3] It is only after landing in the field that one is faced with untoward practicalities of doing ethnography. Such issues of self and self-care rarely feature in the classroom discussions of research methods.

Finally moving into the field with my baggage in September 2019, I became the talk of the island immediately. Initially, they were hesitant to host a female researcher for so long. My primary interlocutor was skeptical about the length of my stay, for he expressed: "There is nothing much to know/write about river islands. I can tell you everything. You need not stay more than a week. One year is too long a period. Why do you want to waste time?" Their underlying concern is that they were not sure if they would be able to provide enough safety and sanitation facilities. Owing to widespread illiteracy,[4] it was difficult for them to understand why some academic degree would require someone from the country's capital, not to mention a female, to live on their remote river island. It was only after lengthy and arduous explanations that I was able to build trust. Meanwhile, my interlocutors too had developed interesting notions around the roles and responsibilities of myself as a researcher. For them, my research work should bring them developmental schemes and jobs. Others too have reported such expectations from their interlocutors (Speed, 2006). In fact, as researchers, we also ponder whether we can bring any immediate benefits, such as developmental schemes, to our interlocutors, often resulting in guilt when we are not able to do so (DeLuca and Maddox, 2016).

Coupled with this was another misconception, albeit more burdensome. Many of my interlocutors went on to doubt the sincerity and rigour of my research because of my menstrual breaks. They would often discuss how my absences would eventually mar their chances of receiving development benefits that ought to come through my contacts. Many times, I have come across people (mostly male interlocutors) saying that instead of me, my university should have sent a male researcher. With a male researcher, they assumed that there was a better chance of information reaching the government and therefore of them getting benefits. Other floating judgements include that because I was a female I can take my career casually – how I can keep taking breaks and jollily extend my study period and not look for a job quickly to support my parents, unlike if I were a male researcher. I wanted to explain to them that my body needs care during menstruation and hence the absence. I tried a few times but talking about menstruation, especially to male interlocutors, was deemed inappropriate. I stopped as I did not want to risk my rapport.

These sharp jibes from my interlocutors, combined with the academic vacuum over issues of wellbeing and self-care during fieldwork, multiplied my guilt. I felt remorseful to be away from the "field" for a week catering to the physical and mental needs of my menstruating self. Eventually, discussion with my supervisor and cohorts helped me understand that ethnography does not just happen when one is physically out in the "field." The "field" is not limited to the geographical site (Gupta and Ferguson, 1997). The field is a complex interplay of site, method, and location. Although complete presence may carry the attraction of generating complete knowledge about the situation, ethnography happens when we take note of how the researcher is navigating the field. So, with or without my physical presence, ethnography would still happen. In a COVID-19 beset world, the discussion around rethinking ethnography is truer than ever, as long-term fieldwork is no longer possible. I agree and endorse the argument that shorter field visits or working remotely from home can equally generate rigorous relationships and data ("A Manifesto for Patchwork Ethnography"; Gunel, Varma, and Watanabe, 2020).[5]

Eventually, I did take up the issue of menstruation with my female interlocutors. Initially hesitant, the women told me their ways (often unhygienic – using unclean cloth or hay to control flow) of dealing with menstruation. We discussed how the lack of water makes them take up these ways. Eventually, I called for a workshop – along the lines of a menstrual awareness camp – where I discussed ways of making simple cloth napkins, and ways of drying and storing those napkins. The workshop was acknowledged. In the following weeks, I could see women drying their cloth napkins in the backyard uncovered. These looked like acts of resistance for a place where women are used to drying their napkins only by covering with other garments and never under direct sunlight.

Later, the village chief showed displeasure with my workshop and the newfound confidence of the women to openly dry their sanitary napkins. Like everywhere else, here the menstrual cycle is something that should not be discussed, let alone to be confronted with its materiality in the yard. I was asked to discontinue my engagements around it and mind my place. I could sense that I had crossed a certain societal norm, and as a repercussion, was immediately warned of my femininity and to not get carried away by all the respect otherwise bestowed by my interlocutors. Nonetheless, I continued talking about menstruation, albeit in alternate ways – making do with smaller, covert discussions in my room. This was to not further jeopardise my rapport. Pettigrew (1981) rightly highlighted the dilemma female researchers face in a male-dominated setting by asking: "How much of self does one sacrifice for the sake of data?" There is a tussle between, on one hand, maintaining personal principles and goals of research, and on the other, the gendered norms of the field that need to be adhered to (at least partially) to be able to access data.

Practicing self-care during ethnography

Doing ethnography in a remote region posed various physical and emotional issues for me as a female researcher. I was not prepared for this side of long-term immersive fieldwork. This is precisely because our pre-field training in graduate school consisted of modules that showed us versions of ethnographies where everything seemed to have gone well for the researchers. These readings treated physical and emotional fatigue resulting from fieldwork as a non-issue – something that need not be placed at the center of research. Wellbeing and self-care were rarely discussed, although that was something I had to invest in heavily while I was on the field.

As a self-care technique, I started journaling right after the initial few weeks of fieldwork, going by advice from seniors and literature (Charles, 2010; Meyer and Willis, 2019). Journaling helped create a space and time for the self. As a reflective and meditative activity, it promotes self-awareness, stabilises thoughts, locates the stressor, and enables curative measures. To write something about emotional and physical anxiety on paper or a laptop is a preliminary step towards solving it. Although there is no clear consensus about the best techniques for journaling, like many, I prefer my journal to be separate from my field notes. Such compartmentalisation serves the purpose of writing out the anxieties at length, which appear in field notes only on the side. These reflexive ideas can then be developed into a finished piece, like this chapter.

I also always planned my fieldwork around my menstrual cycle, as I leave a day or two before my due date. This was because of the poor transportation facility on the island. It is a long way to reach my accommodation in the state capital. This is a journey I cannot take while menstruating. The journey is divided into three parts, stretching four to five hours.[6] As mentioned earlier, such breaks triggered constant guilt, anxiety, and emotional exhaustion. These were clear signs of burn-out, which I ignored in the initial months of fieldwork. Part of it was because no one ever talked about such experiences in the field, and therefore it felt normal to shut these emotions out. However, over time, these emotions were affecting the way I interacted with my interlocutors and my social circle beyond the field. Eventually, I decided that I needed to attend to my emotions and physical discomfort head-on. I explained my situation to my cohorts, who helped me believe that these timeouts taken to attend to my bodily and emotional needs do not in any way mean that I am diluting my ethnographic rigour. Harris and Huntington (2001) had earlier also underlined the importance of thinking through and attending to the emotional and physical anxieties in research. Kleinman and Copp (1993) suggested that not working on these anxieties can negatively impact the quality of the research itself.

I also scheduled my menstruating week in a way that I would check on archives in the state capital, complete my pending fieldnotes and reflect on previous conversations. Sometimes, I would just embroider and not think about research. Nairn (1999) elsewhere highlights the importance of doing away with the fixation on performing and thinking about fieldwork without time off. As such, my time away from the island did not seem like a "break" anymore but very much a part of the fieldwork process. Embroidery, like journaling, is therapeutic and allows for mindfulness (Von Kurthy, 2020). I kept going back to embroidery, seeking refuge from my thoughts throughout the fieldwork. It was a skill I picked up from my mother in middle school. A seemingly mundane and feminine art, embroidery helped me create a balance between fieldwork and self-care. It acted as a booster for the upcoming work weeks after the calmness of the menstrual week.

Another way I practiced self-care during fieldwork was not to entertain misogynistic comments about my menstrual breaks. I would turn any such conversation on its head by pointing out the systemic flaws instead, like how remote regions that lack basic sanitation facilities restrict women's mobility while menstruating and called for the need to demand that the local-level political representatives provide facilities. I would amicably present my point that it is not the women menstruating who are at fault, but the system. I assured my support for any such demands. In a way, I was reinstating the boundaries of conversations. I draw upon an activist-researcher position to practice self-care.

In this process, I also learned to understand the very act of self-care is not an individual issue. As Tokumitsu (2018) also asserted, self-care has increasingly, and dangerously, been pointed out as an individual-only scheme. On the contrary, we require a strong structural network to process physical and emotional exhaustion. Along these lines, I was trying to build a strong support system in the field, which would not mind my monthly absence from the field. To an extent, I was successful. My women interlocutors, being considerate of my breaks, and almost in a manner of compensating for lost data, would update me on any important event that might have taken place during my absence. In addition to my interlocutors, I also depended on my cohorts who were researching different parts of India. This strategy of peer debriefing (Rager, 2005) had also been immensely helpful. We would take the time to talk about respective field experiences and learn from each other various self-care strategies. In one such discussion, I was told that someone was using narcotics and alcohol to deal with fieldwork anxieties. This was to be completely avoided at any costs, as we need to be in complete control to face stressors and find a way out without covering them up. I see this as a shortcoming of our training, which never talked about the ways to deal with the trauma generated from lonely fieldwork. We were just told that "Doing PhD/fieldwork is a lonely journey." But no one talks about changing this. With the toll it takes on the researcher's mind and body, this isolating work schemata cannot be left as a glorified aphorism. I also depended on friends who were not necessarily part of academia but were working professionals located in remote regions. It was they who taught me ways to be firm with interlocutors who were not respectful and at the same time keep maintaining the rapport. Boundaries are important to lessen suffering and not build resentment.

Towards the end of my fieldwork, I understood that an ethnographer should be aware of the physical and emotional tolls of the job. Learning to center oneself early on is key – more so when one is working in areas that are emotionally and physically taxing. Simultaneously, one must identify a "safe space" during the research. "Safe spaces" are not necessarily spatial but can also be found in a person. My cohorts found their safe spaces in locations of their field site where they felt most lively (like a sunset spot) or going back to parents' or to friends' places to eat comfort food. For me, my safe space was my female interlocutors. Discussions around menses – the pain and how I coped with home remedies (like drinking warm water and keeping a hot-water bag around my abdomen) – helped me do so. I also shared my anxieties about my menstruation sabotaging my fieldwork. In return, they shared their dilemmas of menstruating while still managing their lives. Seeing them strive kept me motivated, and more so on days when the bargain between self-care and fieldwork felt a little more stretched. These conversations not only helped build rapport but allowed deeper insights into the local social structure. While starting my doctoral journey, I never imagined that I would be discussing something so corporeally intimate like my menstruation with my interlocutors and that these self-care conversations would become my prime rapport-building method. To trace it backwards, it all began with one of those initial meetings where a curious interlocutor pointed out a hot-water bag lying on my table. I explained that it was to ease pain related to menses. To which one my younger interlocutors quipped that we are alike – "I bleed. And like me, Madam [referring to me] bleeds too". It was good to know that they were able to relate with me, but simultaneously I was aware that there are differences in how my interlocutors deal with their menstruating bodies and how I do. I have the privilege to center my life and fieldwork around my menstrual cycle. I can take a rest and use appropriate hygiene products when needed, unlike them. Most women in my field are severely anemic, pushing them to undergo painful menstruation, but there is nothing they can do. They carry on with their work, fetching water and firewood, and harvesting, with just some hay or extra cloth layer to control the bodily flow. The curious interlocutor, unlike the younger one who saw feminine affinity with me, put my thoughts into words – "While Madam can lie back with a hot water bag, we cannot even drink warm water to ease the pain."

Conclusion

In this chapter, I investigated the complexities of undertaking self-care strategies while on fieldwork. These require constant negotiation and coping with situations, which are often traumatic, more so because of my gender and class position. I had to be absent from the field during my menstruation cycle, which filled me with the guilt of missing events. Added to it were the constant judgements passed by my interlocutors about my absence and perceived lack of seriousness towards my research. This meant that I had to spend considerable time keeping myself emotionally centered. This ranged from making meaningful relations on the field to going back to my old hobbies of journaling and embroidery to build a resilient persona as an ethnographer of the remote region.

The constant negotiation between guilt and fieldwork was central to my fieldwork experience. I was caught unprepared and stumbled a lot in the process. Literature and discussions on this side of ethnography are far and few. Through this chapter, I urge ethnographers to write about their gendered experiences confidently, instead of putting them in the fine print of polished, published work. A primary implication of such writings is that they offer vital and deeply complex insights into works of power in and through ethnography as a mode of knowledge-inquiry and -making, connecting their exclusivity rooted in the bodies of the ethnographer to those in the interlocutors. Such embodied ethnographic work can produce not just theoretical implications but also practical benefits. In the latter vein, female researchers could take up researcher-activist positions and engage in intentional acts of care and resistance for themselves as well as provide solidarity with interlocutors. Such work can puncture notions of sexism, through ideals of care and accountability. Such attempts would be messy, emotional, and often be questioned for lacking objectivity, but ones worth undertaking if we are to truly place wellbeing and self-care at the heart of undertaking academic research.

Notes

1 I have changed name of the river island, on request of anonymity by my interlocutors. Osthir means "moving," in the language spoken by my interlocuters. I am using the local term as pseudonym as it captures very well the shifting nature of the river islands – eroding and accreting each flood cycle.

2 In 2014 the Government of India launched the Swachh Bharat Abhiyan to eliminate open defecation and improve solid waste management. While the urban phase of the scheme had the desired result, the rural phase is struggling behind.

3 Open defecation is related to the idea of familial dominance. Toilets are used only by the women in their reproductive age and those elderly people with restricted mobility – the two demographic dividends lying at the lowest levels of power in a typical Indian household (Coffey et al., 2014).

4 As per the latest data, the literacy rate of the river islands in Barpeta district, to which Osthir char belongs, is marked at abysmally low rate of 17 per cent (GOA, 2004).

5 https://culanth.org/fieldsights/a-manifesto-for-patchwork-ethnography. Accessed on August 18, 2021.

6 Around two hours in the once-a-day-only boat ride from Osthir river island to the nearest jetty town of the district. It is a small country motorboat and hence takes a longer time than if it were a state-sponsored ro-ro or ro-pax boats operating elsewhere in the country. I had to plan my work well as missing the boat ride would mean hiring a private boat that costs a fortune. Plus, these alternate rides are much smaller fishing boats that are technically not suitable to make the two-hour journey on the swift-flowing Brahmaputra to reach the town. The second leg of the journey would be an electric rickshaw to the bus stop. The final stretch is a two-hour or more bus journey to the state capital, which is about 80 km from Osthir char.

References

Abu-Lughod, L. (2016). *Veiled sentiments: Honor and poetry in a Bedouin society*. Oakland: University of California Press.

Behar, R. (2003). *Translated woman: Crossing the border with Esperanza's story*. Boston: Beacon Press.

Branson, D. C., & Radu, M. B. (2018). Do qualitative researchers experience vicarious trauma? And, does it matter?. *Journal of Sociology and Social Work, 6*(1), 12–22.

Charles, J. P. (2010). Journaling: Creating space for "I". *Creative Nursing, 16*(4), 180–184.

Coffey, D., Gupta, A., Hathi, P., Khurana, N., Spears, D., Srivastav, N., & Vyas, S. (2014). Revealed preference for open defecation. *Economic & Political Weekly, 49*(38), 43–55.

Coles, J., Astbury, J., Dartnall, E., & Limjerwala, S. (2014). A qualitative exploration of researcher trauma and researchers' responses to investigating sexual violence. *Violence Against Women, 20*(1), 95–117.

DeLuca, J. R., & Maddox, C. B. (2016). Tales from the ethnographic field: Navigating feelings of guilt and privilege in the research process. *Field Methods, 28*(3), 284–299.

Friederic, K. (2010). Notes from the field: The negotiation of boundaries: Anthropological clichés, witnessing and honest self-work. *Arizona Anthropologist, 20*, 81–88.

Giardina, M. D., & Newman, J. I. (2011). Physical cultural studies and embodied research acts. *Cultural Studies: Critical Methodologies, 11*(6), 523–534.

Gluckman, M. (1954). *Rituals of rebellion in south-east Africa*. Manchester: Manchester University Press.

Gogoi, P. (2018). *Landscape evolution modelling in the large, complex braided river the Brahmaputra: A case study of Majuli Island, North-East India* (Unpublished Doctoral dissertation), University of Nottingham.

Government of Assam. (2004). *Socio-economic survey of char areas, 2002–03*. Directorate of Char Development. Ministry of Minority and Social Welfare.

Gunel, G., Varma, S and Watanabe, C. (2020). A manifesto for patchwork ethnography. Member voices. *Fieldsights*. Retrieved from: https://culanth.org/fieldsights/a-manifesto-for-patchwork-ethnography

Gupta, A., & Ferguson, J. (1997). Discipline and practice: The field's site, method, and location in anthropology. In Ferguson, J. (Ed.), *Anthropological locations: Boundaries and grounds of field science* (pp. 100–147). Oakland: University of California Press.

Harding, S. G. (Ed.). (1987). *Feminism and methodology: Social science issues*. Bloomington: Indiana University Press.

Harris, J., & Huntington, A. (2001). Emotions as analytic tools: Qualitative research, feelings, and psychotherapeutic insight. In K. Gilvert (Ed.), *The Emotional Nature of Qualitative Research* (pp. 129–146).

Hopwood, N. (2015). Relational geometries of the body: Doing ethnographic fieldwork. In Green, B. & Hopwood, N. (Eds.), *The body in professional practice, learning and education. Professional and practice-based learning, vol 11*. Cham: Springer. https://doi.org/10.1007/978-3-319-00140-1_4

Islam, M. (2021). *Studying erosion, sedimentation and flooding pattern of Brahmaputra River using Google Earth Engine*. Retrieved from https://www.narcis.nl/publication/RecordID/oai:cdm21063.contentdm.oclc.org:masters2%2F115310

Kleinman, S., & Copp, M. A. (1993). *Emotions and fieldwork*. Newbury Park, CA: Sage Publications.

Kumar, B., & Das, D. (2019). Livelihood of the char dwellers of western Assam. *Indian Journal of Human Development, 13*(1), 90–101.

Malinowski, B. (1922/1994). *Argonauts of the western Pacific: An account of native enterprise and adventure in the archipelagos of Melanesian New Guinea*. London: Routledge.

Meyer, K., & Willis, R. (2019). Looking back to move forward: The value of reflexive journaling for novice researchers. *Journal of Gerontological Social Work, 62*(5), 578–585.

Močnik, N. (2020). Re-thinking exposure to trauma and self-care in fieldwork-based social research: Introduction to the special issue. *Social Epistemology, 34*(1), 1–11.

Nairn, K. (1999). Embodied fieldwork. *Journal of Geography, 98*(6), 272–282.

Pettigrew, J. (1981). Reminiscence of fieldwork among the Sikhs. In Roberts, H. (Ed.), *Doing feminist research* (pp. 62–82). London: Routledge and Kegan Paul.

Rager, K. B. (2005). Self-care and the qualitative researcher: When collecting data can break your heart. *Educational researcher, 34*(4), 23–27.

Speed, S. (2006). At the crossroads of human rights and anthropology: Toward a critically engaged activist research. *American Anthropologist, 108*(1), 66–76.

Tokumitsu, M. (2018). Tell me it's going to be OK: Self-care and social retreat under neoliberalism. *The Baffler*, (41), 6–11.

Turner, A. (2000). Embodied ethnography. Doing culture. *Social Anthropology, 8*(1), 51–60.

Turner, V. (1970). Symbols in Ndembu ritual. In Emmet, D. & MacIntyre, A. (Eds.), *Sociological theory and philosophical analysis*. London: Palgrave Macmillan. https://doi.org/10.1007/978-1-349-15388-6_8

Von Kurthy, H. (2020). Exploring the potential of embroidering as a therapeutic intervention in occupational therapy (Unpublished Doctoral dissertation) University of Brighton.

Wacquant, L. (2005). Carnal connections: On embodiment, apprenticeship, and membership. *Qualitative sociology, 28*(4), 445–474.

Wacquant, L. (2009). The body, the ghetto and the penal state. *Qualitative Sociology, 32*(1), 101–129.

Wacquant, L. J. (1995). Pugs at work: Bodily capital and bodily labour among professional boxers. *Body & Society, 1*(1), 65–93.

9 Mentoring practices in higher education

Self-care through the lens of the mentee in the era of remote learning

Anisha Kaur Sandhu

The beginning of one's journey in academia is notoriously difficult. Early career academics (ECAs) are recognised as facing numerous workplace stressors and have been categorised as "potentially vulnerable knowledge workers," struggling with anxiety, stress, frustration, and exhaustion due to an increasing workload and expectations. They are pressured to cope with the steep learning curve of stepping into teaching, research, and administrative roles with the expectation of meeting rigorous demands of teaching quality, research performance, stakeholder engagement, and satisfactory student experiences and outcomes (Hollywood et al., 2019). ECAs overwhelmingly struggle with their mental health due to feelings of isolation at work (Belkhir et al., 2019). This is further exacerbated by changes since the pandemic – including the absence of face-to-face interaction through regular modes of education, compulsory adoption of digital technologies, work from home (WFH) practices which often result in unregulated work routines and increased hours, as well as additional administrative responsibilities – have caused significant physical and emotional stress (Aczel et al., 2021; Jakubowski & Sitko-Dominik, 2021). It is necessary to upgrade oneself daily to adapt, evolve, and remain relevant or functional in an ever-changing environment (Strotz et al., 2018). This never-ending competition of an individual with themselves, others, and other workplace pressures or deadlines impacts ECA wellbeing negatively.

Pre-pandemic, employee groups such as ECAs, females, and people of colour or indigenous backgrounds were already known to experience barriers in their academic careers, be it for career progression or promotion to leadership roles (Ellinas et al., 2019; Spencer et al., 2021). This, however, has been further exacerbated during the pandemic, which has had significant professional and personal impact on ECAs, particularly females, who may not have gained as many positive opportunities while potentially enduring gender inequity in division of labour as the boundaries between home and work life blurred (Agarwal et al., 2018; Myers et al., 2020).

I am a female ECA from a minority background, working as an assistant lecturer at the School of Pharmacy in Monash, Malaysia, an international campus belonging to Monash University, which is privately operated in Malaysia. Our curriculums and teaching pedagogy closely mirror those offered by the Faculty of Pharmacy and Pharmaceutical Sciences in Monash, Australia, with a degree of local contextualisation to reflect the healthcare needs prioritised in our unique

DOI: 10.4324/9781003341482-11

geographical setting. At this stage of my career, work challenges are innumerable as I learn how to educate and research while I juggle postgraduate study and continue to upskill in my field.

The role of a mentor in early career academia

The global Covid-19 pandemic has emphasised further the need to stay connected, as colleagues work remotely due to strict social distancing protocols or must embrace flexible work models that allow WFH practices to continue (Aczel et al., 2021). It is crucial to form strong bonds and surround oneself with peers who are friendly, empathetic, and encouraging (Belkhir et al., 2019). In these circumstances, an ECA benefits greatly from a mentor who provides a supportive and protective presence to help their mentees cope more effectively with the ambiguity, perceived uncertainty, and stress of the work environment (Carmel & Paul, 2015). Mentorship assists ECAs in the formation of their academic identity and in finding a sense of belonging in the organisational culture and values of the academic community they have become a part of (Badiozaman, 2021; Shuler et al., 2021). Mentors encourage their mentee to progress in their career journey, guiding with their wisdom and experience while facilitating their mentee's personal development. Having a mentor who supports these qualities allows for mutual respect, providing an environment of ease and approachability so that one can discuss matters openly and unhesitatingly. This helps their mentees feel valued, engaged, and motivated at work. ECAs of female or minority backgrounds have been found to benefit greatly from formalised mentoring schemes or informal mentoring relationships as they are better supported to navigate through the challenges of neoliberal academia while growing into better role models to lead future generations of academics (Kwedi Nolna et al., 2017; Oberhauser & Caretta, 2019; Shuler et al., 2021).

Decoding mentoring theory and relationships

What is mentoring?

Bozeman and Feeny (2007) proposed the following definition of mentoring:

> Mentoring is a process for the informal transmission of knowledge, social capital, and psychosocial support perceived by the recipient as relevant to work, career, or professional development. Mentoring entails informal communication, usually face-to-face and over a sustained period of time, between a person who is perceived to have greater relevant knowledge, wisdom, or experience (the mentor) and a person who is perceived to have less (the protégé/mentee).
>
> (p. 731)

Mentoring is regarded as a pairing or grouping of unequal knowledge where the colleague with more knowledge, experience, or advice (mentor) imparts these to the junior or peer with less experience (mentee) (Bozeman & Feeny, 2007; Carmel & Paul, 2015). If we were to analyse the definition above, mentoring not only allows for the transference of knowledge, permitting a mentee to gain from their mentor's experience and guidance, but is also a means of generating social capital where a mentee can benefit from a mentor's connections to grow their network. More importantly, in relation to self-care, this definition speaks of psychosocial support. While numerous other definitions of mentoring exist in published literature, a predominant theme emerges whereby one of the primary functions of mentoring identified is its ability to provide psychosocial support (Eby, 1997; Kram, 1983; Ismail et al., 2009; Roberts, 2010; Brunsma et al., 2017). This highlights the invaluable role a mentor plays, not only in the mentee's professional and academic growth, but also in their personal development, where a supportive mentor-mentee relationship can potentially foster positive self-image as well as emotional and psychological wellbeing (Crisp & Cruz, 2009; Eby et al., 2007).

Another point to note in the mentoring definition by Bozeman and Feeny (2007) is the nature of mentoring relationships. Mentoring relationships differ from supervisory relationships, where the latter involves a junior staff reporting to a senior, generally borne out of management requirements within the organisational hierarchy of the faculty. However, in the context of academia, mentoring is regarded more as a critical development activity that may be part of a non-incentivised institution or faculty-wide formalised mentoring scheme or a self-selected informal mentoring arrangement (Carmel & Paul, 2015).

Formal versus informal mentoring relationships

According to Dahlberg and Byars-Winston (National Academies of Sciences, Engineering, and Medicine, 2019), formal mentoring traditionally refers to an organisationally structured program where a mentor and mentee are allocated to one another, while informal mentoring "develops spontaneously based on mutual interest and interpersonal comfort" (p. 76). Mentees typically report more successful outcomes in terms of career progression and support from informal mentorship when compared to formal mentoring relationships (Chao et al., 1992; National Academies of Sciences, Engineering, and Medicine, 2019). This is because informal mentoring occurs in a more flexible and organic manner (Bozeman & Feeny, 2007). Informal mentoring relationships also tend to be longer-term as they develop naturally with the mentor and mentee readily identifying with one another (Meschitti & Smith, 2017). It can lead to more positive psychosocial activities such as counselling, role-modelling, and social interactions where a space of trust is created for the mentee to converse about non-work-related skills and matters in addition to work-based discussions (Inzer & Crawford, 2005; Meschitti & Smith, 2017). Informal mentoring is often viewed as "friendship first, learning and career second and third" (Inzer & Crawford, 2005, p. 35). This lends itself heavily to the emotional and social aspects of self-care, which are very important for early career academics.

A mentee has the potential to gain significantly from seeking a balance between formal and informal mentoring; studies find that each form of mentorship provides complementary forms of support (Erickson et al., 2009; Desimone et al., 2014; National Academies of Sciences, Engineering, and Medicine, 2019).

The benefits and significance of mentoring for female early career academics

Research shows that among the interventional activities provided by mentors, emotional and psychological support holds higher value to mentees, particularly women mentees (Athanasiou et al., 2016; Chung & Kowalski, 2012; Cross et al., 2019; Eliott et al., 2010; Simon et al., 2004; Straus et al., 2009; Taylor et al., 2009; Welch et al., 2012). This is attributed to the protection and buffer a mentor provides to their mentees when they face organisational change, assisting them in dealing with uncertainty in their role and workplace dynamics such as politics, conflict, as well as changes in organisational culture (Viator, 2001).

In general, examples of psychosocial support provided by mentoring may include mentors supporting: (1) emotional wellbeing via creating a safe space for open communication and suggestions of coping strategies in periods of stress to cultivate resilience; (2) confidence building via encouragement, guiding better self-awareness, providing feedback and enhancing the mentee's feelings of being valued by affirming their capabilities; and (3) the development of leadership skills through positive role-modelling in skills such as negotiation or conflict resolution (Barber, 2013; Brunsma et al., 2017; Ismail et al., 2009; Kram, 1985; National Academies of Sciences, Engineering, and Medicine, 2019; Ragins & Cotton, 1999; Schockett & Haring-Hidore, 1985; Taylor et al., 2009).

While positive outcomes with respect to transmission of knowledge and skills or career progression remain among the main advantages of mentoring, this chapter intends to focus on the psychosocial aspect by exploring how mentoring can help a mentee build better self-care practices through:

- Confidence building by harnessing the power of positive affirmation
- Guiding better self-awareness through self-reflection techniques
- Promoting emotional wellbeing by creating a safe space for open communication with active listening, highlighting its importance in the remote working environment
- Suggestions of coping strategies to alleviate stress, cultivate resilience, and beat burnout

Case study: Anisha – self-care through the lens of a mentee

Visual narrative: Inviting self-care into the physical or remote workspace

The first strategy is to harness the power of positive affirmation – represented in the form of a "Be Kind" jar that is regularly filled with new and short messages of empowerment. There are additional visual reminders to let go of what cannot be controlled, to practice gratitude, and to start the day with optimism. The second strategy is to have better self-awareness – represented by the stack of journals that promote reflections on wellness, self-identity, gratitude, sleep, and goals. The third strategy is to beat burnout by managing time and energy better through consciously carving out protected periods to digitally detox. This is especially relevant in our remote or hybrid workplaces presently, where we remain hyper-connected all day long through various technological devices (see Figure 9.1).

Building self-care practices through my mentorship journey: "How I met my mentor"

When I joined academia in 2018, I was incredibly nervous. I had been living abroad for a decade and practicing as a pharmacist for six years. I felt unprepared for the sudden switch to a career in education and research. It meant that I would have to start at the bottom of the career ladder again, while dealing with the unfamiliarity of a field that I had no foundational experience in. The workplace dynamics were also new and challenging. I struggled with the silence. I went from working collaboratively in busy pharmacies and hospitals within inter-professional teams to shifting in a university, where independent working styles and quiet time for thinking were often prized; I felt lost. My faculty was also experiencing a period of revitalisation that resulted in three reporting line changes within a year.

Figure 9.1 The image above contains elements of three useful self-care strategies I gained from my mentor that can be placed on a "work-from-home" desk to build a mindful space with visual reminders to cultivate resilience.

Comprehensive staff onboarding programmes were still being built and finalised. So, when I joined, I was not sure whom I could turn to or which doors to knock on. I wanted direction, and I also craved conversation.

I soon started a daily ritual where I would seek comfort and feel centred by popping into the staff kitchen for a mid-morning break to whip up a steaming hot beverage. In my second month as an ECA, I had a chance encounter at the staff kitchen with an esteemed senior professor. We had a spontaneous conversation about the transition from clinical practice to academia, and I noticed that he was very open in giving advice to guide me. For the first time, I felt like I was not alone.

Our first conversation led to more kitchen conversations over the course of the next few months. I gained more pearls of wisdom with each interaction – useful training suggestions, helpful ideas on what research fields to consider, and even a discussion on which highways had less traffic for an easier commute! I did not realise it at the time, but we had begun our first steps into forming an informal mentoring relationship. When a campus-wide mentoring scheme initiative was introduced six months later, I decided to approach my professor to join the scheme together with me so he could formally be appointed as my mentor. He agreed and remains my mentor to this day.

Our mentor-mentee relationship has evolved organically over the past four years, and we have achieved a balance of: (1) sustaining a formal mentorship, where my mentor has provided valuable guidance in strengthening my education knowledge base while growing my network and work-based collaborations in mutual research interests and (2) developing an informal mentoring relationship – where my mentor has played the role of confidante and advisor, helping me to navigate through the social challenges and pressures of academia.

Uniquely, when the formalised campus-wide mentoring scheme was introduced, neither of us were a part of the participant database. It served as the catalyst to our mentoring partnership. This ties in with research that states that female academics may have better access and more opportunities to be mentored via formalised schemes compared to informal mentoring (Meschitti & Smith, 2017; National Academies of Sciences, Engineering, and Medicine, 2019). However, formalised mentoring programmes in academia are not always guaranteed to succeed due to factors such as: (1) lack of time and drive to participate actively in mentoring; (2) mentee stigma and vulnerability in showing and acknowledging weaknesses and areas requiring improvement; and (3) mentor-mentee misalignment in subject/spe-cialty, working style, goals, values, or personality (Carmel & Paul, 2015; Meschitti & Smith, 2017; Zellers et al., 2008). On learning of the scheme, I recognized that our pragmatic demeanour, working and communication styles, as well as fields of expertise and interests aligned. It made sense for us to pair together. Hence, I chose to approach him rather than select a mentor from the available list. Incorporating both formal and informal mentoring could be why our mentor-mentee relation-ship has remained consistent and successful throughout the years.

Strategy (1): Harnessing the power of positive affirmations

Life is full of sudden, unexpected decisions. Academia was not a part of my life plan, but when the opportunity presented itself, I took it and left my comfort zone as a practising pharmacist. What took me by surprise was how overwhelmed I felt by the steep learning curve that presented itself in both education and research. I suffered from "impostor syndrome," feeling a lack of confidence when I realised how much I did not know and how much I needed to learn. I did not know at the time that my feelings were like those of numerous ECAs. Research shows that academia is performance-driven and highly competitive, where academics are expected to excel in multiple ways through teaching, research, and external engagement (Badiozaman, 2021).

Though the initial years were a struggle, I credit my mentor for building my confidence and encouraging my growth as an ECA. Not only was he full of sage advice, but he was very kind. He would offer unbiased opinions and feedback where I required help, and he took the time to ensure that we had regular check-ins where he would comment positively on my progress. I observed how influential his words were in empowering me to cope with the challenges in settling into academia and embraced introducing positive affirmations into my daily life. I felt centered and positive and focused on achieving the necessary goals of the day, week, or month when I look at the motivational quotes and phrases on my desk or in my "Be Kind" jar.

Strategy (2): Creating better self-awareness through self-reflection

I realised the impact of reflection when I began actively self-reflecting to become a better educator and healthcare professional and to grow my career after joining academia. In conversations with my mentor, he would often see strengths or attributes in me that I was unaware of myself. Equally, he would discuss ways in which I could improve when designing educational experiences, building learning material, collaborating in scientific writing, resolving problems or conflicts, and executing research projects. I learnt to become humble and be open to learning and improvement, which was a difficult lesson because as a female ECA from a minority background, being honest about my capabilities made me feel vulnerable.

I began to feel more comfortable in being reflective through journaling. Reflective journals encourage creativity of thought and a better understanding of myself, while gratitude journals make me feel appreciative of small gestures in my daily life that would have otherwise gone unnoticed. Wellness journals give me a chance to reflect on self-care and what I could do for myself, while goal-directed planning journals give me a chance to reflect on and chart my growth as an individual. While reflection was initially a conscious exercise, it is now a subconscious process I practise naturally in everything I do. It has helped my confidence tremendously, improved my performance in many aspects of my life and career and cultivated resilience because I can recognise my strengths and weaknesses, as well as the opportunities and threats within my environment to continually adapt and improve my reaction to the situations I experience.

Strategy (3): Digitally detoxing to alleviate stress in the remote workspace

There is a need to digitally detox and disconnect from the hyperconnectivity of today's remote workplace. When the world was plunged into various stages of lockdown during the pandemic, academia pivoted abruptly to embrace online technology. Online classes and research, tele-meetings, and digital events became the norm. This was the perfect chance for a technologically savvy ECA to step up and engage in opportunities that were no longer constrained to the physicality of needing to meet face-to-face on campus. Myriad options were available for collaboration in education and research with academics in all corners of the world, and I did not know how to say no for fear of missing out on an experience that could be beneficial to my career (Hinton et al., 2020). Unsurprisingly, I began to experience burnout after months of emailing constantly, working weekends and public holidays, and answering student queries or attending conference calls at all hours of the day. I found it hard to relax and sleep because my mind was constantly active and as my family observed, I was always found working, either on my laptop, phone, or iPad.

My mentor supported me through this time by organising regular virtual check-ins and he taught me why it was important to say "no" from time-to-time. He said, "You cannot have your finger in every pie, you know!" and reminded me that health is a priority we cannot take for granted. He advised me to stay more focused on a few tasks rather than spreading myself so thinly. He also suggested that I respect and observe traditional working hours. I now try to: (1) send and respond to student/work-related queries and emails during business hours only; (2) attend meetings that are scheduled during working hours; (3) take time out after work and in the weekends to pursue hobbies; (4) limit digital events on the weekends unless necessary; and (5) limit using my devices before I sleep.

Discussion

Connecting the dots: Building self-care practices from mentoring

For an ECA, establishing an effective mentoring network is the first step in building a community of trust. Mentors act as modelling influences, allowing the ECA to have an academic benchmark to aspire to in terms of competencies, skills, knowledge, or behaviours (Bandura, 1994). A nurturing mentoring relationship is a valuable method to instil self-efficacy for self-regulation and to build confidence to ensure the ECA has stronger self-belief (Bandura, 1994; Diggs-Andrews et al., 2021). Having a strong sense of self-efficacy is important for personal wellbeing as it fosters a positive outlook on difficulties faced (Bandura, 1994). This aids the ECA in viewing demanding tasks as challenges to overcome rather than threats to avoid, and he or she is more likely to be resilient in recovering from setbacks, which can be a helpful buffer to stress and anxiety (Bandura, 1994). Inadvertently, this will also help the ECA progress further in academia, as discovered by Bielczyk et al. (2019), where self-management guidelines for ECAs recommended that they "manage time properly, take care of oneself, surround oneself with positivity, grow one's network, mentor and be mentored, be mindful and understand themselves," among other suggestions.

To surround oneself with positivity, a good first step is to embrace the power of positive affirmation. Researchers have suggested that self-affirmation should be regarded as a wellbeing intervention given its benefits in improving mood and adaptive functioning and cultivating resilience to situations (Howell, 2017). Neurological research has also proven that self-affirmation can restore self-competence and retain motivation and positive self-view while improving problem-solving in times of chronic stress, which is useful for ECAs who need to navigate through the difficult challenges of academia (Cascio et al., 2016; Cresswell et al., 2013). In fact, a study by Goyer et al. (2017) also showed that psychological interventions like self-affirmation and reflective writing translated into positive long-term benefits for minority students along college trajectories. Hence, the benefits of using a self-care strategy like positive affirmation could be useful for female ECAs.

Reflection has often been considered as an essential self-care strategy. Positive reflective writing exercises like journaling have been found to reduce mental distress and increase wellbeing by cultivating resilience and decreasing anxiety (Smyth et al., 2018). Hurd and Singh (2020) detail how powerful exercises in collaborative and critical reflective practice can be used to nurture wellbeing in the context of ECAs. Their experiences in reflecting on and sharing feelings of exhaustion, self-doubt, and isolation led to a shift in the way they incorporated daily wellness into their personal life. It gave them a deeper understanding of the self-care practices that nurtured their wellbeing and the important boundaries that needed to be put in place, like respecting work hours and limiting email notifications after work hours (Hurd & Singh, 2020). This of course leads to how crucial it is to create healthy practices surrounding digital-device use to mitigate the increasing effects of stress and burnout ECAs face, which is especially relevant in current times and in the post-pandemic world. Pandya and Lodha (2021) find that the Covid-19 pandemic has resulted in a drastic increase in screen times, and there is an urgent need to enforce healthy digital habits. Useful self-care tips to incorporate digital boundaries to work-from-home practices are detailed further in this chapter.

Mentoring in the hybrid workplaces of the future

Diversify your mentor portfolio

The pandemic disrupted the frequency of the meetings I had with my mentor, as we both got caught up in juggling numerous responsibilities. Our mentorship had also steadily grown into a mutual collaborative partnership as we worked on the same education research portfolio. During this time, I had also begun to have a clearer understanding of my role and discovered the research fields I was interested in to pursue further. At this point, I started to seek different mentors who could guide me in my other research interests or in furthering my knowledge of education principles. Mentoring literature has often argued that mentoring needs to move beyond being defined as a dyadic relationship (i.e., one mentee to one mentor) between two individuals (Higgins & Kram, 2001). This is because it is impossible for a mentee to develop effectively through the guidance of a single mentor alone, as research has shown that mentees with multiple mentoring relationships often report higher job satisfaction (Baugh & Scandura, 1999, Higgins & Kram, 2001).

Adopting the strategy to diversify and gain additional mentors during this time proved to be beneficial. It prevented my mentors from being overburdened by the time and energy required to guide me. I was also able to rely on each mentor to lend me varied perspectives and expertise, guide me in building new knowledge and skill sets, introduce new social capital, or provide different forms of psychosocial support. Between my different mentors, I had regular virtual check-in sessions that helped me feel supported and less isolated.

Regular virtual check-in sessions

Overall, once my mentors and I adapted to the new normal, we found virtual mentoring sessions to be more convenient due to the flexibility in organising meetings that were no longer constrained to physical meetings on campus. This allowed for more frequent monthly check-ins to take place, which made me feel less isolated as I could receive regular career and wellbeing advice. Regular virtual mentoring sessions are recommended to ensure mentee motivation and success, as well as to show that a mentor cares and is invested in their mentee's wellbeing (McReynolds et al., 2020).

Self-care tips for the hybrid workplaces of the future

Embracing work-from-home as a result of the Covid-19 pandemic has certainly revolutionised, and will no doubt leave a lasting impact on, working patterns post-pandemic. Flexible working practices have brought about a range of benefits, including less time wasted commuting between the home and the office and more opportunities to bond with family (Oakman et al., 2020). However, more reports have arisen of employees succumbing to burnout as they are unable to prevent the blurring of boundaries between their personal and professional life (Oakman et al., 2020). A factor contributing to burnout is that employees are often working extended hours and are hyper-connected digitally, responding to work-based notifications all day long (Oakman et al., 2020; Toniolo-Barrios & Pitt, 2021; Xiao et al., 2021). As a result, they not only suffer from the effects of exhaustion, stress, and screen fatigue, but also find it difficult to mentally disconnect from work (Oakman et al., 2020; Toniolo-Barrios & Pitt, 2021; Xiao et al., 2021). These issues are also widely reported in academia and have been felt deeply by female academics, including ECAs (Johnson et al., 2021).

While this points to the importance of organisations recognising their role in implementing policy changes by creating adequate work-from-home frameworks to ensure employee wellbeing, the following self-care tips, in addition to the strategies mentioned above, can go a long way in nurturing a better, healthier online working environment for ECAs:

Creating a mindful workspace

(1) **Design a home-based workspace**
   Creating a designated workspace at home increases your concentration on work tasks by reducing distractions (Kaushik & Guleria, 2020). If a separate

room is unavailable, try to work in a quiet corner and request cooperation from family or flatmates to minimise disruptions during work hours. This translates to greater productivity and better job satisfaction as your workspace is designed to support your work-from-home needs (Abdulaali et al., 2020; Samani, 2015).

(2) *Invest in ergonomic furniture*

Studies show that employees do not tend to take into consideration the ergonomics of their workspace while WFH which can result in new health issues such as body and neck pain, lower productivity, and job dissatisfaction (Messenger et al. 2017; Xiao et al. 2021). Taking the time to invest and learn how to adjust ergonomic furniture for your home-based workspace can improve wellbeing and job satisfaction.

(3) *Declutter for a happier you!*

The state of your workspace (whether physical or online) has the potential to impact your focus and productivity, emotions, and behaviour (Sanders, 2019). Research has shown that cluttered environments may cause stress or anxiety and may affect decision-making (Roster & Ferrari, 2019). An easy solution is simply to regularly tidy and systematically declutter your workspace (Sanders, 2019). Also, consider streamlining all paperless e-documentation and files to prevent feeling overwhelmed from dealing with messy, disorganised folder storage on your computer and devices. Organising your emails using the labels function in your inbox will also prevent the added stress of retrieving important messages. Embracing task or project planning applications is also a good way of prioritising tasks and goals clearly while allowing for seamless tracking of your progress, projects, and other responsibilities. Having clarity in all these aspects translates into self-care by reducing potential stress triggers.

Scheduling wellness into your workday

(4) *Schedule breaks*

Scheduling breaks is a useful way to incorporate self-care into your workday as it helps increase focus to tasks and combat screen fatigue (Toniolo-Barrios & Pitt, 2021). These are some options to incorporate quick breaks while working:

- Do some light stretches
- Practice a mindfulness technique, for example, deep breathing or doing a body scan
- Take the opportunity to fit in some steps so you can hit a healthy daily target, for example, pacing around your living area
- Head over to the kitchen to make yourself a nourishing mid-morning or mid-afternoon warm beverage

(5) *Limit productivity interruptions and create a distraction-free environment*

Limiting productivity interruptions and doing your best to create a distraction-free environment is essential to ensure your wellbeing and continued success while working from home (Oakman et al., 2020). The following tips can be included into your daily routine:

- If your environment is noisy, consider noise-cancelling headphones or earbuds
- A soothing background sound can help some ECAs focus better on their work tasks
- Allocate specific periods in the day where you respond to emails
- Limit device notifications

(6) **Block a "focus and creativity" stretch in your weekly calendar**
In our present day, our work calendars often fill up very quickly with numerous meetings whether in person or on technological platforms. To ensure that you are functioning optimally and completing tasks to your best ability, try to set aside a few hours or one day a week without meetings. This will help you free your mind for high-focus activities like writing or to indulge in long-term strategic thinking (e.g., to map career growth).

Nurturing supportive collegial relationships

(7) **Organise digital social networking events or catch-ups**
To combat feelings of isolation and increase collegial rapport, create your own virtual community where you can organise digital events with your colleagues. This could range from fun events like online Zumba, thought-provoking book clubs, and relaxed online quizzes using gamification applications to one-on-one coffee meetings or networking events to grow your connections.

Valuing yourself, your health, and your energy

(8) **Learn to say "no" and be kind to yourself**
It is natural for ECAs to feel competitive when comparing their career journeys with their peers or fear missing out on important opportunities that may accelerate their career growth. As a result, ECAs tend to say "yes" to too many duties, resulting in being overstretched and overwhelmed (Hinton et al., 2020). Learning to say "no" when needed is essential for self-care and sustained productivity. The best way to learn this is to observe how your mentor or senior colleague limits their engagement in a task.

Above all, be kind to yourself. Try not to race to a career goal if you end up experiencing burnout or stress. You are on your own journey; enjoy it!

(9) **Use mindfulness techniques to combat stress**
Mindfulness techniques are useful ways to stop anxiety and reactionary behaviour to stressful situations (Toniolo-Barrios & Pitt, 2021). Some useful techniques to use are meditation and the body-scan exercise (Toniolo-Barrios & Pitt, 2021). Meditation involves sitting silently and anchoring your attention to the present moment, while the body scan exercise involves closing your eyes and taking long breaths as you slowly feel the awareness of different physical sensations from the top to the bottom of your body (Toniolo-Barrios & Pitt, 2021).

If you feel overwhelmed, paying attention to your breath (e.g., How does your stomach rise and fall? Does your breath feel warm or cold? What are the sensations in your nostrils?) is a simple mindfulness technique that can help to anchor your attention to the present in order to centre your thoughts (Toniolo-Barrios & Pitt, 2021).

(10) ***Celebrate your wins!***

Celebrating progress or achievement of goals, whether big or small, can boost employee engagement with work, happiness, motivation, creativity, and productivity, as was studied in a *Harvard Business Review* article by Amabile and Kramer (2011). They alluded to the "progress principle," where they found that making progress in meaningful work contributes most to an employee's inner work life, which is a combination of emotions, motivations, and performance-based perceptions (Amabile & Kramer, 2011). Take the time to appreciate and reward yourselves for all the positive steps you are making in your growth as an ECA. This is a powerful form of self-care, and you deserve it!

Conclusion

This chapter highlights the importance of the psychosocial support provided by nurturing mentoring connections that have a crucial role in ensuring early career academic wellbeing and self-care. A variety of self-care strategies are also discussed to help early career academics adapt to online workplaces.

References

Abdulaali, H. S., Usman, I. M. S., Hanafiah, M. M., Abdulhasan, M. J., Hamzah, M. T., & Nazal, A. A. (2020). Impact of poor Indoor Environmental Quality (IEQ) to inhabitants' health, wellbeing and satisfaction. *International Journal of Advanced Science and Technology*, *29*, 1284–1296.

Aczel, B., Kovacs, M., van der Lippe, T., & Szaszi, B. (2021). Researchers working from home: Benefits and challenges. *PLoS ONE*, *16*(3). doi:10.1371/journal.pone.0249127

Agarwal, S., Spiekerkoetter, E., Austin, E. D., de Jesus Perez, V. A., Dezfulian, C., Maron, B. A., … Perman, S. (2018). Career development of young physician-scientists in the cardiovascular sciences: Perspective and advice from the early career committee of the Cardiopulmonary, Critical Care, and Resuscitation Council of the American Heart Association. *Circulation Research*, *122*(10), 1330–1333.

Amabile, T. M., & Kramer, S. J. (2011). The power of small wins [online]. Retrieved from https://hbr.org/2011/05/the-power-of-small-wins

Athanasiou, T., Patel, V., Garas, G., Ashrafian, H., Shetty, K., Sevdalis, N., … Paroutis, S. (2016). Mentoring perception and academic performance: An academic health science centre survey. *Postgraduate Medical Journal*, *92*(1092), 581–86.

Badiozaman, I. (2021). Early career academics' identity development in a changing HE landscape: Insights from a Malaysian private university. *Asia Pacific Journal of Education*, *41*(3), 424–439. doi:10.1080/02188791.2020.1793732

Bandura, A. (1994). Self-efficacy. In Ramachaudran, V. S. (Ed.), *Encyclopedia of human behaviour*, *4*, 71–81. New York: Academic Press. (Reprinted in Friedman, H. [Ed.], *Encyclopedia of mental health*. San Diego: Academic Press.

Barber, Lisa A. (2013). The impact on career women of mentoring, role models, and defining moments during college student leadership experiences. *Master of Arts in Higher Education Theses, 96.* Retrieved from https://pillars.taylor.edu/mahe/96

Baugh, S. G., & Scandura, T. A. (1999). The effect of multiple mentors on protégé attitudes in the work setting. *Journal of Social Behavior and Personality, 14*(4) 503–522.

Belkhir, M., Brouard, M., Brunk, K. H., Dalmoro, M., Ferreira, M. C., Figueiredo, B., … Smith, A. N. (2019). Isolation in globalizing academic fields: A collaborative autoethnography of early career researchers. *Academy of Management Learning & Education, 18*(2), 261–285, doi:10.5465/amle.2017.0329

Bielczyk, N. Z., Ando, A., Badhwar, A., Caldinelli, C., Gao, M., Haugg, A., … (2019). Effective self-management for early career researchers in the natural sciences. *Neuron, 106*(2), 212–217. doi:10.1016/j.neuron.2020.03.015

Bozeman, B. & Feeny, M. K. (2007). Toward a useful theory of mentoring. *Administration & Society, 39*(6), 719–739. doi:10.1177/0095399707304119

Brunsma, D. L., Embrick, D. G., & Shin, J. H. (2017). Graduate students of color: Race, racism, and mentoring in the white waters of academia. *Sociology of Race and Ethnicity, 3*(1), 1–13 doi:10.1177/2332649216681565

Carmel, R. G. & Paul, M. W. (2015). Mentoring and coaching in academia: Reflections on a mentoring/coaching relationship. *Policy Futures in Education, 13*(4), 479–491. doi:10.1177/1478210315578562

Cascio, C. N., O'Donnell, M. B., Tinney, F. J., Lieberman, M. D., Taylor, S. E., Strecher, V. J., & Falk, E. B. (2016). Self-affirmation activates brain systems associated with self-related processing and reward and is reinforced by future orientation. *Social Cognitive and Affective Neuroscience, 11*(4), 621–629. doi:10.1093/scan/nsv136

Chao, G. T., Walz, P. M., & Gardner, P. D. (1992). Formal and informal mentorships: A comparison on mentoring functions and contrast with non-mentored counterparts. *Personnel Psychology, 45*(3), 619–637.

Chung, C. E., & Kowalski, S. (2012). Job stress, mentoring, psychological empowerment, and job satisfaction among nursing faculty. *Journal of Nursing Education, 51*(7), 381–88.

Cresswell, J. D., Dutcher, J. M., Klein, W. M. P., Harris, P. R., & Levine, J. M. (2013). Self-affirmation improves problem-solving under stress. *PLoS ONE, 8*(5), e62593. doi:10.1371/journal.pone.0062593

Crisp, G., & Cruz, I. (2009). Mentoring college students: A critical review of the literature between 1990 and 2007. *Research in Higher Education, 50*(6), 525–545. doi:10.1007/s11162-009-9130-2

Cross, M., Lee, S., Bridgman, H., Thapa, D. K., Cleary, M., & Kornhaber, R. (2019). Benefits, barriers and enablers of mentoring female health academics: An integrative review. *PLoS ONE, 14*(4). e0215319. dpi10.1371/journal.pone.0215319

Desimone, L. M., Hochberg, E. D., Porter, A. C., Polikoff, M. S., Schwartz, R., & Johnson, L. J. (2014). Formal and informal mentoring: Complementary, compensatory, or consistent? *Journal of Teacher Education, 65*(2), 88–110.

Diggs-Andrews, K. A., Ghislaine Mayer, D. C., & Riggs, B. (2012). Introduction to effective mentorship for early-career research scientists. *BMC Proceedings, 15*(7), 1–7. doi:10.1186/s12919-021-00212-9

Eby, L. T. (1997). Alternative forms of mentoring in changing organizational environments: A conceptual extension of the mentoring literature. *Journal of Vocational Behavior, 51*(1), 125–144.

Eby, L. T., Rhodes, J. E., & Allen, T. D. (2007). Definition and evolution of mentoring. In T. D. Allen & L. T. Eby (Eds.), *The Blackwell handbook of mentoring: A multiple perspectives approach*, 7–20. Blackwell Publishing.

Ellinas E. H., Kaljo, K., Patitucci, T. N., Novalija, J., Byars-Winston, A., & Fouad, N. A. (2019). No room to "lean in": A qualitative study on gendered barriers to promotion and leadership. *Journal of Women's Health*, *28*(3), 393–402. doi: 10.1089/jwh.2018.7252

Elliott, B. A., Dorscher, J., Wirta, A. & Hill, D. L. (2010). Staying connected: Native American women faculty members on experiencing success. *Academic Medicine*, *85*(4), 675–79.

Erickson, L. D., McDonald, S., & Elder Jr. G. H. (2009). Informal mentors and education: Complementary or compensatory resources?. *Sociology of Education*, *82*(4), 344–367.

Goyer, J. P., Garcia, J., Purdie-Vaughns, V., Binning, K. R., Cook, J. E., Reeves, S. L., … Cohen, G. L. (2017). Self-affirmation facilitates minority middle schoolers' progress along college trajectories. *Proceedings of the National Academy of Sciences of the United States of America*, *114*(29), 7594–7599. doi:10/1073/pnas.1617923114

Higgins, M. C., & Kram, K. E. (2001). Reconceptualizing mentoring at work: A developmental network perspective. *Academy of Management Review*, *26*(2), 264–288.

Hinton, A. O., McReynolds, M. R., Martinez, D., Shuler, H. D., & Termini, C. M. (2020). The power of saying no. *EMBO Reports*, *21*. doi:10.15252/embr.202050918

Hollywood, A., McCarthy, D., Spencely, C., & Winstone, N. (2019). 'Overwhelmed at first': The experience of career development in early career academics. *Journal of Further and Higher Education*, *44*(7), 998–1012. doi:10.1080/0309877X.2019.1636213

Howell, A. J. (2017). Self-affirmation theory and the science of well-being. *Journal of Happiness Studies*, *18*(1), 293–311.

Hurd, F. & Singh, S. (2020). "Something has to change": A collaborative journey towards academic well-being through critical reflexive practice. *Management Learning*, *52*(3), 347–363. doi:10.1177/1350507620970723

Inzer, L. D., & Crawford, C. B. (2005). A review of formal and informal mentoring: Processes, problems, and design. *Journal of Leadership Education*, *4*(1), 31–50.

Ismail, A., Abdullah, M. M., & Francis, S. K. (2009). Mentoring program and its impact on individuals' advancement in the Malaysian context. *Journal of Industrial Engineering and Management*, *2*(3), 592–615. doi:10.3926/jiem.2009.v2n3.p592-615

Jakubowski, T. D., & Sitko-Dominik, M. M. (2021). Teachers' mental health during the first two waves of the COVID-19 pandemic in Poland. *PloS one*, *16*(9), e0257252. doi:10.1371/journal.pone.0257252

Johnson, T. P., Feeney, M. K., Jung, H., Frandell, A., Caldaduro, M., Michalegko, L., … Welch, E. W. (2021). COVID-19 and the academy: Opinions and experiences of university-based scientists in the US. *Humanities and Social Sciences Communications*, *8*(146). doi:10.1057/s41599-021-00823-9

Kaushik, M., & Guleria, N. (2020). The impact of pandemic COVID-19 in the workplace. *European Journal of Business and Management*, *12* (15), 1–10.

Kram, K. E. (1983). Phases of the mentor relationship. *The Academy of Management Journal*, *26*(4), 608–625.

Kram, K. E. (1985). *Mentoring at work: Developmental relationships in organizational life.* Glenview, IL: Scott, Foresman.

Kwedi Nolna, S. K., Essama Mekongo, P. E., & Leke, R. (2017). Mentoring for early-career women in health research: The HIGHER women consortium approach. *Global Health, Epidemiology and Genomics*, *2*, e3. doi:10.1017/gheg.2016.20

McReynolds, M. R., Termini, C. M., Hinton, A. O. Taylor, B. L., Vue, Z., Huang, S. C., … Carter, C. S. (2020). The art of virtual mentoring in the twenty-first century for STEM majors and beyond. *Nature Biotechnology*, *38* (12), 1477–1482. doi:10.1038/s41587-020-00758-7

Meschitti, V. & Smith, H. L. (2017). Does mentoring make a difference for women academics? Evidence from the literature and a guide for future research. *Journal of Research in Gender Studies*, 7(1), 166–199. doi:10.22381/JRGS7120176

Messenger, J., Vargas Llave, O., Gschwind, L., Boehmer, S., Vermeylen, G., & Wilkens, M. (2017). Working anytime, anywhere: The effects on the world of work. [Eurofound and the International Labour Office (2017)]. Retrieved from: http://eurofound.link/ef1658

Myers, K. R., Tham, W. Y., Yin, Y., Cohodes, N., Thursby, J. G., Thursby, M. C., … Wang, D. (2020). Unequal effects of the COVID-19 pandemic on scientists. *Nature Human Behaviour*, 4(9), 880–883. doi:10.1038/s41562-020-0921-y

National Academies of Sciences, Engineering, and Medicine. (2019). *The science of effective mentorship in STEMM*. Washington, DC: The National Academies Press. doi:10.17226/25568

Oakman, J., Kinsman, N., Stuckey, R., Graham, M., & Weale, V. (2020). A rapid review of mental and physical health effects of working at home: How do we optimise health?. *BMC Public Health*, 20(1825), 1–13. doi:10.1186/s12889-020-09875-z

Oberhauser, A. M., & Caretta, M. A. (2019). Mentoring early career women geographers in the neoliberal academy: Dialogue, reflexivity, and ethics of care. *Geografiska Annaler: Series B, Human Geography*, 101(1), 56–67. doi:10.1080/04353684.2018.1556566

Pandya, A., & Lodha, P. (2021). Social connectedness, excessive screen time during COVID-19 and mental health: A review of current evidence. *Frontiers in Human Dynamics*, 3, e684137. doi:10.3389/fhumd.2021.684137

Ragins, B. R., & Cotton, J. L. (1999). Mentor functions and outcomes: A comparison of men and women in formal and informal mentoring relationships. *Journal of Applied Psychology*, 84, 529–550.

Roberts, A. (2010). Mentoring revisited: A phenomenological reading of the literature. *Mentoring & Tutoring: Partnership in Learning*, 8(2), 145–170. doi:10.1080/713685524

Roster, C. A., & Ferrari, J. R. (2019). Does work stress lead to office clutter, and how? Mediating influences of emotional exhaustion and indecision. *Environment and Behaviour*, 52(9). doi:10.1177/0013916518823041

Samani, S. A. (2015). The impact of personal control over office workspace on environmental satisfaction and performance. *Journal of Social Science and Humanities*, 1(3), 163–172.

Sanders, L. (2019). The case for finally cleaning your desk [online]. Retrieved from https://hbr.org/2019/03/the-case-for-finally-cleaning-your-desk

Schockett, M. R., & Haring-Hidore, M. (1985). Factor analytic support for psychosocial and vocational mentoring functions. *Psychological Reports*, 57(2). doi:10.2466/pr0.1985.57.2.627

Shuler, H., Cazares, V., Marshall, A., Garza-Lopez, E., Hultman, R., Francis, T. K., … Hinton, A. (2021). Intentional mentoring: Maximizing the impact of underrepresented future scientists in the 21st century. *Pathogens and Disease*, 79(6), ftab038. doi:10.1093/femspd/ftab038

Simon, C. E., Bowles, D. D., King, S. W. & Roff, L. L. (2004). Mentoring in the careers of African American women in social work education. *Affilia*, 19(2), 134–45.

Smyth, J. M., Johnson, J. A., Auer, B. J., Lehman, E., Talamo, G. & Sciamanna, C. N. (2018). Online positive affect journaling in the improvement of mental distress and well-being in general medical patients with elevated anxiety symptoms: A preliminary randomized controlled trial. *JMIR Mental Health*, 5(4), e11290. doi:10.2196/11290

Spencer, S., Burrows, C., Lacher, S. E., Macheledt, K. C., Berge, J. M. & Ghebre, R. G. (2021). Framework for advancing equity in academic medicine and science: Perspectives from early career female faculty during the COVID-19 pandemic. *Preventive Medicine Reports, 24*, 1–9. doi:10.1016/j.pmedr.2021.101576

Straus, S. E., Chatur, F., & Taylor, M. (2009). Issues in the mentor-mentee relationship in academic medicine: A qualitative study. *Academic Medicine, 84*(1), 135–39.

Strotz, L. C., Simoes, M., Girard, M. G., Breitkreuz, L., Kimmig, J., & Lieberman, B. S. (2018). Getting somewhere with the Red Queen: Chasing a biologically modern definition of the hypothesis. *Biology Letters, 14*(5), 1–7. doi:10.1098/rsbl.2017.0734

Taylor, C. A., Taylor, J. C., & Stoller, J. K. (2009). The influence of mentorship and role modeling on developing physician-leaders views of aspiring and established physician-leaders. *Journal of General Internal Medicine, 24*(10), 1130–1134. doi:10.1007/s11606-009-1091-9

Toniolo-Barrios, M., & Pitt, L. (2021). Mindfulness and the challenges of working from home in times of crisis. *Elsevier Public Health Emergency Collection, 64*(2), 189–197. doi:10.1016/j.bushor.2020.09.004

Viator, R. E. (2001). The relevance of transformational leadership to non-traditional accounting services: Information systems and assurance and business consulting. *Journal of Information Service, 15*(2), 99–125.

Welch, J. L., Jimenez, H. L., Walthall, J., & Allen, S. E. (2012). The women in emergency medicine mentoring program: An innovative approach to mentoring. *Journal of Graduate Medical Education, 4*(3), 362–6.

Xiao, Y., Becerik-Gerber, B., Lucas, G. & Roll, S. C. (2021). Impacts of working from home during COVID-19 pandemic on physical and mental well-being of office workstation users. *Journal of Occupational and Environmental Medicine, 63*(3), 181–190. doi:10.1097/JOM.00000000000002097

Zellers, D. F., Howard, V. M., & Barcic, M. A. (2008). Faculty mentoring programs: Reenvisioning rather than reinventing the wheel. *Review of Educational Research, 78*(3), 552–588.

Part III

Of well-being and self-care in academia

10 A polyvagal pathway

Implications of pursuing it all

Deena Kara Shaffer

That pole, the pace, those pursuits

In the first week of October 2021, I walked forehead-first into a pole. It was a Saturday morning, luminous with sunshine and southern Ontario's orange and golden autumn leaves. I had my two children, eight and six, and our not-quite-year-old puppy, all on our way to my daughters' dance class. That morning had already held: an early wake-up to do the week's budgeting and credit card clearing, grading artefacts from my first-year Sociology course, a cardio routine, a best attempt at meditative thought-quieting, walking the dog, cleaning the dishwasher, the setting up, then eating, then cleaning up breakfast, readying my kids, mental planning and quiet to-do's all the way through, grading portfolios of my third-year Psychology class, and replies to two editors regarding upcoming publications.

When my temple met the pole, we had been going full tilt. My elder cherub had asked moments before, "Mama, can we slow down a little?" My answer, evidenced not with words but my body hustling as quickly as possible, was "no." I continued to race, forcing all four of us to race. As we did, we passed our local park. In the open field, fall morning sunshine streaming in our Toronto neighbourhood, I saw an old neighbourhood acquaintance, a yoga teacher. She had had to close her local studio amid the ongoing Covid pandemic. Hers had been a simple, wood panelled, candle-and-crystal-displaying spot nestled residentially, and that morning had been the first time I had seen her since the closing. She was teaching on the still-green grass surrounded by 10 or 15 folks atop their yoga mats – outdoor, slow, paced, *leisurely*. As they moved into upward dog, my kids trailing behind me, my thoughts jampacked with my ever-present, insurmountable to-do list, and my envy at the scene to my right, *whack*. I walked with such momentum into the pole that I made it shake. I do not recall if I blacked out momentarily, but I do remember the gash in my ear, my children shocked at the bleeding, and my own deeply ingrained, adrenaline-fuelled, in-shock but shockingly predictable response moments later to *keep going*.

My eldest affirmed, "Mama, we don't need to go to dance class today, truly." My littlest kept asking, "Mama, you're okay, right?" My only response was along the lines of *no problem*, *we've got* this, *I've got this*; my only thought was about all that needed to be done. My only impulse was to keep going where we had been going, and at the same pace. Well, maybe a little faster since we were late. That speed

DOI: 10.4324/9781003341482-13

I brought to the pole is the very speed I bring to the most of my hours and days, just as so many female-identifying academics do. I texted their dance studio: "so sorry, we'll be four minutes late." Many mistakes, many poor choices along the way, and several uncomfortable days later, I was diagnosed with a severe concussion, told I was too late for the stitches I ought to have sought, and put on a more than two-month-long medical leave. The days and weeks since have comprised enforced rest – light-less, screen-less, sound-less – and with movement slowed to the gentlest of dog walks around the block. I was, literally (and laughably one day, I hope), stopped in my tracks. I had been both mesmerised by the sight of enjoyment and ease – so absent in my work striving – and because I was trying to fit it all in that morning, as every morning, as every day. Because, as a mother, as an academic, as an activist, as a scholar-practitioner, I was doing and holding so many things at one moment, I did not see that pole (see Figure 10.1 (a) and (b)). I was struck not just by that pole but by community yoga in a park: the sweetest of activities that I longed to do but never seemed to find, make, or prioritise the time for, captured my attention so fully that I was brought out of body, until I was struck back in.

It will no doubt take me some time to fully understand and make meaning of what happened; perhaps there is no meaning, and it was all just an unfortunate accident. *But* that pace I was travelling at, my disregarding the kind voice urging me to slow down, the craving for leisure, and my unquestioning and uninterrupted insistence on keeping-on-going – these do strike me as meaningful. And also mundane. And also an absolute microcosm. They are day-in, day-out, now-banal features of my personal life, like those of so many others, not to mention the hallmarks of my professional one, again like those of so many: unrelenting pace, no space for ease, and ignoring the body's signals, feedback, and outright demands.

I will share my own journey to a polyvagal approach, investigate this brain-focus and body-denial, including what is at stake, and propose practices in support of reinhabiting our bodies for both reclaimed professional and personal wellbeing.

(a)   (b)

Figure 10.1 (a) Image of *the* pole. (b) My bandaged ear, too late for stitches.

This body, here

Without planning, strategising, or even really meaning to, I have been *pursuing it all*, almost all my life. More and more, I understand that this pursuit is constellated by the outward forces of my achieve-achieve-achieve environment and the inward drive to survive. As for the outer, I was born in Toronto, Canada, in the earliest 1980s: umbrellaed in a time of unwavering faith in the stock market, with an uninterruptible momentum to earn, an insatiable appetite to consume, an unrelenting striving for accomplishment. Political forces, local, national, and global, urged me and us to buy more and do more and undertake more and finish more in order to "be" more. Some critical aspects of my positionality, the outer layers of which have impacted where I have been allowed to go and what I have been allowed to do: I am white, I am cisgender, I am middle-class, and I am able-bodied. In my earliest career years, I was a high school teacher in Toronto for students who struggled with mental health diagnoses, learning disabilities, and addictions, which then led me into higher education, where I served as the lone learning specialist for students with disabilities, from chronic illness to psychiatric conditions to sensory impairments, for our downtown university. During this time, I found my vocational footing as a learning strategist or specialist, supporting the metacognition and academic skill-building of students across disciplines and years. I began to develop multi-wisdomed curriculum and a holistic pedagogical approach that prioritised equity and multi-dimensional wellbeing. Borne from this, I started my formal journey as a lecturer and adjunct faculty, instructing largely first- and upper-year undergraduate courses in learning strategies, student development, and Positive Psychology, while researching, publishing, and speaking about progressive, unsiloed, accessibility-forward learning strategies.

As for the inner context, my life has been shaped by traumatic loss and grief, and bereavement has been my greatest teacher of both dis- and re-embodiment. I was an only child and lost my parents in my mid-twenties, both to ruthlessly swift cancers. My mother, Lithuanian, had been born in an American Red Cross displaced persons camp in 1945 Germany, immigrated to Canada, and struggled all her life to find her footing, understand her identity/ies, and feel connected. My father, a rebellious writer, had grown up Jewish in a charged, French-Canadian, Catholic context, and over the years had cast aside all religion and ideology in hopes of less friction. Their journeys were the stories I was raised amidst. Their relationships with their bodies – addiction, under-tending, tragic passings – shaped my own. Their traumas, upbringings, and contexts fuelled a pedestalising of all things accomplishment and achievement – markers of making it, and of survival.

Even after the intensity of caregiving, and their deaths just a couple of years apart from each other, I just *kept going*. Not a bad approach. In so many ways, a terrifically adaptive move. I continued to "achieve" at full-tilt: a teaching career, a graduate degree, publications, a family, a doctorate, conferences, a business, more publications, "thought leadership." A blurry whirlwind of keeping as many plates spinning as I could at any one time, each being praised as a "success." All the while, however, I could not feel my body. Nor did I *know* or *sense* that I could not. I *could* work out hard, take on any high-intensity interval training class, greet each day as a marathon of kid-care, spouse-care, career-care, financial-care, friend-care, community-care, but I could not for the life of me actually, genuinely, deeply feel my feet or my hands or my legs. Not *really*. I could not feel my braced stomach, at the ready for any additional gut-punch. I could not feel that my jaw was so tight my teeth were being ground down, so much so I was surprised when my dentist suggested a night-time mouthguard to prevent further small cracks from forming from the pressure of all-night clenching. I could not feel when I was tired, nor could I feel when I was actually full at the end of a meal. It is not that I was feeling-less; not at all. I am sensitive, I am empathic, enormously so, and I can put words to what emotions I sense. But I was not fully inhabiting the body in which I lived, and often still struggle to.

It was not until I was instructed in a restorative movement class to put my legs on a chair—a posture literally referred to as *constructive rest*—that I could physically feel my body. All my life, I could certainly *think* about my body, comment about my body, and I could ruthlessly judge it for being not enough this or too much that. In that restful pose, I took a literal load off, and started on my path (back) to embodiment.

These bodies pursuing it all

The pace I brought to the pole that morning, and the pace I continued with afterwards for the next 48 hours until my body forced me into stillness, has been the pace by which I have navigated my career journey, and how I have experienced the "given-ness" or "of-course-ness" of how it is all supposed to go. Academic striving is first and foremost characterised as tireless. Relentless. Unforgiving. The route to "get there," "get somewhere," "get ahead," "get *tenure*," implies putting most else on hold or jamming it all in. To brace, to grip on tight, and to ride the 60-to-70-hour weeks – until, one hopes, that one, eventually, in time, *arrives*. Somewhere. And maybe, the hope goes, that perhaps at that somewhere, *then* one can finally exhale, loosen the clench, or at the very least, shift into maintenance mode in place of more-more-more.

It is important to name and centre that this academic long-haul sprint is not balanced across its demands. Michelle Rodino-Colocino writes, reflecting upon Audre Lorde's oft-turned-to insights of self-care as a political interruption and intervention (1988), that:

> As publishing deadlines, promotions, conferences, and grading for 100 students approached, hours grew. Research on faculty workloads and my conversations with colleagues suggest that my baseline and maximum workweeks as a white, cis, tenured faculty are exceeded by those of my colleagues of color, non-binary and trans faculty, and faculty with disabilities.
>
> (Rodino-Colocino, 2021, p. 316)

Lorde, battling cancer and systemic inequities, articulated the gravity of overextending (1988). This very overextension is at the heart of academic professional pursuits:

Professors work long days, on weekends, on and off campus, and largely alone. Responsible for a growing number of administrative tasks, they also do research more on their own time than during the traditional work week. The biggest chunk of their time is spent teaching. …. On average, faculty participants reported working 61 hours per week – more than 50 percent over the traditional 40-hour work week. They worked 10 hours per day Monday to Friday and about that much on Saturday and Sunday combined.

(Flaherty, 2014)

And alongside this breakneck journey in academia, there are all the way along even more pressing plates to keep spinning – little ones, elder ones, the ones to whom we are partnered, the ones to whom we commit to care, and most of all our own selves. And while the "majority of faculty are experiencing elevated levels of frustration, anxiety, and stress" (On the Verge of Burnout, 2020, p. 2), these spinning plates are also not shared equally; indeed "[m] ore than two-thirds of survey respondents are struggling with increased workloads and a deterioration of work-life balance – particularly female faculty members" (On the Verge of Burnout, 2020, p. 2).

To add, there is keeping our own bodies well, active, and cared for. There is keeping our spirits tended to – a kind of contemplative practice. There is keeping our relationships nurtured. There is loving our communities and justice work. There is keeping up with whatever we call our homes, keeping finances from precarity, and keeping ourselves and our beloveds fed.

To live this way, at this pace, within these demands – what does it feel like for you? To even *read* them, and only some of them, posed here, what can you sense? In my body, writing them, I can sense breathlessness, a tightened gut, a clenched jaw, a humming panic in my skull. Our bodies know when we overextend, take on too much, live on the edge of burnout. My project is to listen and heed, interrupt, and nourish, *much* more often.

This chapter will explore what belies "pursuing it all," as we women in academia so often do, through a polyvagal lens. In our bodies, we have what's called a vagus nerve: vagus, as derived from *vagabond*, because this nerve wanders and branches. This nerve ties our brains to our sense organs, and our guts. It is quite literally the brain-body connection. The vagus nerve is how we perceive danger, how we experience safety, and how we intuit our next steps. It is important to note that this polyvagal proposition is as political and philosophical as it is physiological. When we aim to take it all on – to spin all the plates that we do – we risk disembodying, prioritising the cognitive over the corporeal, disregarding being able to sense bodily feedback.

Our polyvagal bodies

Every other TV, metro, and Facebook ad offers some way through the stress that grips us. The fitness company, Peloton, the walking step tracker FitBit, and the meditation app Calm were amongst the top ten advertisements watched in the 2020 pandemic year (Bharwani, 2021). The advertisements themselves were meant to be stress-relieving. Stress solutions, from nutritional supplements to life coaching to wellbeing retreats to tech gadgets, are sold to us day in day out, as ubiquitous as shampoo and mortgage-rate commercials, and with important critiques about the white-woke-wellness-washing of the radical, disruptive possibilities of self-care (Hamblin, 2018). But what actually helps our bodies deal with the stress we encounter? Our capacity to cope, to "respond to and recover from the challenges of daily living is a marker of wellbeing and depends on the actions of the autonomic nervous system" (Dana, 2020, p. 1).

Many of us might recall learning about the nervous system from high school science class. At its simplest, the nervous system – *autonomic* nervous system, or ANS for short – houses that familiar fight, flight, or freeze response of the sympathetic branch, and the rest-and-digest mode of the parasympathetic. It responds to the difficulties "of daily life by telling us not what we are or who we are but *how* we are. The autonomic nervous system manages risk and creates patterns of connection by changing our physiological state" (Dana, 2018, p. xvii). When we meet what we perceive as dangerous, the sympathetic system becomes fired up, mobilising us to take action or to retreat. When we sense safety in our surroundings, the parasympathetic system enables us to feel becalmed. (It is important for me to mention, if not admit, that these are my own rudimentary understandings and articulations – and though I am scientifically untrained, I am no less keen to access the language and nuance.)

Since those long-ago biology classes, much more has been added to what is known and shared about the ANS. Of particular relevance here in this chapter is Polyvagal Theory, posited by American medical doctor Dr. Stephen Porges in the early 1990s. Polyvagal Theory helps to complicate and layer that sympathetic/parasympathetic description of the ANS. It holds that there are actually three facets to the ANS, each with its own characteristics and functions: the dorsal vagal system, which is the oldest in our evolution, enables immobilisation and shutdown in the face of stress or trauma; the sympathetic system, which when activated compels us to fight or to flee; and, the most recent, evolutionarily, which is the ventral vagal system that promotes safety through connection with others, co-regulation, and engaging in relationships (Dana, 2020).

Put differently, these three underlying, scaffolding states of being are a

> dynamic dance we are each in, every day, between the dorsal vagal state of shut down, the sympathetic state of mobilised and primed to take action, and the ventral vagal state of feeling steady and safe to engage in relationship and integration.
>
> (Shaffer & Brecher, 2021, p. 2)

These three vagal pathways can be understood as a hierarchy: when we are in the throes of stress overload, that is,

> when the autonomic nervous system has moved into a dysregulated dorsal vagal or sympathetic state ... [our] brain [has] been hijacked and [we] are held

in a survival response. When the ventral vagal state is active, body and brain work together, and processing and change are possible.

(Dana, 2020, p. 2)

In terms of development, Polyvagal expert and therapist Deb Dana finds it helps to portray it this way:

> Using images, you can feel the flavor of each autonomic state. Humans evolved from ancient reptiles similar to turtles. The image of the turtle hiding in its shell is an apt one for the dorsal vagal state of disconnection. Continuing to the sympathetic nervous system, imagine the darting movements of a fish reacting in an instant to avoid a predator. Finally, arriving in the uniquely mammalian ventral vagal state picture people talking and smiling in a shared moment of connection.

(2020, p. 4)

As Porges describes it, Polyvagal Theory illuminates the adaptation and growth of our nervous system. In its oldest form, we feign death, we isolate, we cannot function. From there, we evolved the ability to meet the threats we face with those fight-flight responses. Then, we could engage in behaviours like listening, perceiving facial expressions, articulating our needs, and co-soothing those we feel close with (2009).

Most critical for this exploration here is less the exact science of it – myelination, vagal tone, heart rate variability – but more so the starting place that "[e]veryday living is a complex experience of autonomic navigation" (Dana, 2020, p. 7). In other words, Polyvagal Theory is about the "science of safety – the science of feeling safe enough to fall in love with life and take the risks of living" (Dana, 2018, xvii). It can help us understand how work and family, and other day-to-day pressures, can feel so difficult to muddle through, let alone flourish in. Dana (2020, p. 7) writes that "[t]rauma, which might be thought of as 'what happens to a person where there is either too much too soon, too much for too long, or not enough for too long'", creates an autonomic demand that shapes the system away from connection toward protection". The ANS response to trauma is an interruption to that innate safety-sensing network that causes us to become dysregulated and requires resilience to bounce out, back, or forward from (Dana, 2018).

To gain a feel for this, ask yourself, have you ever experienced such mounting stress that you have pulled away from others, hunkering down and isolating? Better asked, perhaps, "What are some of the ordinary difficulties that predictably overwhelm your system? Is there an extraordinary source of distress that is too great a challenge for your system?" (Dana, 2020, p. 15). These feel like important questions to ask of your mind, heart, body, and spirit: are there ordinary demands that alone or combined feel extraordinary to cope with? Dana articulates that, "In a state of protection, survival is the only goal. The system is closed to connection and change" (2020, p. 7). Have you, for instance, experienced financial or professional precarity such that your breathing is high up in your chest, your diaphragm feels tight, your jaw is tight, or your muscles are knotted? These are just tiny examples of the way the stress and outright trauma we experience impact our bodies on the most fundamental levels.

The ANS "responds moment to moment to what are often competing needs to survive and to be social" (Dana, 2020, p. 7). And sometimes, just as the big losses, hurtful setbacks, systemic inequities, and health crossroads can feel too much to bear, so too can the events of our day-to-day be "beyond the capacity of the ventral vagus to regulate the system" (Dana, 2020, p. 15). Further, the elevated and complex challenges that punctuate our lives, not to mention when outright catastrophes befall, make autonomic demands, and can make the daily burdens even harder to weather:

> Illness and traumatic events predictably tax the system, but everyday experiences can also trigger dysregulation. Feeling alone, having too many responsibilities in a day, working in a challenging environment, and being in a distress relationship are just some of the experiences that can overwhelm the ventral vagal system.
>
> (Dana, 2020, p. 15)

For us readers, writers, teachers, researchers encountering each other here in this collection, mothers, grandmothers, sisters, aunties, tenders, activists, and more, why this matters so much is that Polyvagal Theory helps us to understand what is happening underneath. And how to tend to it.

Our academic bodies

As an instructor and staff in higher education, I find such resonance with this phrasing of the pulls and pressures that academics encounter:

> Being a professor is a demanding position that includes managing lab[s], teaching … mentoring …, writing, …research, networking…, reviewing,… serving on committees…. Some of us also have served in administrative roles…. My colleagues had spent decades defining themselves in terms of the structure of academic evaluations … [but] the academic world with its chronic evaluation strategies had triggered the bodies and minds of my colleagues into a chronic state of defense.
>
> (Porges, 2020, xiii–xiv)

My own small life, with its big hurts, is no harder or sadder or more challenged than any other. And in so many ways, innumerable really, the privileges that I do embody have meant that my journey has largely personal complexities, not systemic ones. My socioeconomic class, my mother tongue, my outer body, no matter my sorrow at times, have meant a less structurally challenged path. My gender, however, has ensured, without question, that I was reared to caregive, readied to shoulder more domestic demands, and put upon to endlessly critique my appearance, and I will never forget that as a key team-member supporting students with disabilities, when I told a supervisor I was pregnant, his response was, verbatim, "Oh fuck!" he imagines all that would fall on his plate, which he then quickly rephrased as "Oops, I meant congratulations." Whatever plates I am spinning inside of the workday as an academic multiply with what is required at home – this layered pursuit of it all centres on being a mother, wife, and caregiver.

Unsticking these stressed bodies

Polyvagal Theory is the scaffold for our getting unstuck from the rumination that can accompany stressors – searching for why this or why that or why *not* this or that. A polyvagal pathway – a nervous system–informed approach to self-care – can support our taking pause, unhooking, scanning hyper-vigilantly for more stress, searching for reasons, misplacing blame, and scurrying to make meaning, and give us the language of and insight into each of our most elemental behaviours. No longer do we need to berate ourselves for being somehow inadequate or lacking in our skills of caring for ourself, or not being able to better cope with the professional demands of academia, or not being equipped to keep infinitely at pace with our ambitions, but rather we can compassionately awaken to what is, in us, "automatic and adaptive, generated by the autonomic nervous system well below the level of conscious awareness. This is not the brain making a cognitive choice. These are autonomic energies moving in patterns of protection" (Dana, 2018, p. 6). And, so, the more I come to understand what is happening underneath, or rather that there *is* something happening/sensing/assessing around the clock, the more mystified I am as to how often I override what my body is letting me know, ignoring somatic feedback in order to *keep going*. To keep pursuing it all.

> It is common, and sometimes helpful to survive, to forget our bodies, whether or not a conscious choice. Some of that disconnectedness happens on the micro-local level, while much is systemic, pervasive, and imposed. Body-forgetting can arise from trauma, from never being taught in the first place, from the ever-present Cartesian prioritization of mind over body, from the harms of racialization and hyper-sexualization, from some medical knowledges' mind-body dis-integratedness, or from the innumerable additional, tender permutations of body-dissociation. So many of us—teachers, academics, *humans*—myself unequivocally included, overuse or run them ragged, experience targeted body-violence, float away from the body for survival, or forget the body's presence all together. Yet, here our bodies are. "We are motor creatures before we are thinking creatures", and yet it can still and very much feel a radical act to reinhabit our bodies, let alone even remember them, perhaps particularly so in institutions and systems so focused on cognitive perseverance and achievement. Through generational, institutional, colonial, and traumatic hurts of all kinds, we can become "dissociat[ed] from the lived body". Yet, our bodies are front and centre, taking up space, breathing until they're not, with all of their "brilliantly complex systems that operate in

myriad ways *beneath* the layers of our consciousness and *before* we have rational thoughts. A primary focus on the intellect only scrapes the surface…". Indeed, we cannot just think our bodies, nor can we leave our bodies *out* of the full experience of thinking, knowing, doing, or, of course, being.

(Shaffer, 2021, p. 74)

That our ANS has us, some of the time, isolated and withdrawn, but at other times activated, mobilised, and ready to take action, and at still other times, at rest, eased, and becalmed, has me ever curious about how to ensure, if not insist, upon making space for that becalmed-ness, for the capacity for rest and ease.

Without it, we can get overstretched and overtaxed, with stress as our stasis. Indeed, when we are "[u]nder severe stress or threat, the body experiences a surge in sympathetic discharge" (Grabb & Miller-Karas 2018, p. 76). Yet, our ANS reveals that our beings have an underlying rhythm akin to a pendulum (Levine, 1997), ebbing and flowing. When our stressful pursuits take over without inter-ruption, we can become fixed in high stress overdrive, our inner pendulating pulse stuck. This flow, this fluid back and forth, is called pendulation by trauma expert Dr. Peter Levine (1997) and can be envisioned as a physiological model of resil-ience. When we can pendulate between those vagal states, shift between frozen to connected to withdrawing to integrated, this is the ANS capacity at its best, "mov[ing] between sympathetic and parasympathetic modes in optimal balance" (Bensimon et al., 2012, p. 230). Pendulation is always happening; it is

> naturally always occurring. All experience is in constant movement between polarities. Yet, with trauma, pendulation gets interrupted and attention fixates on the trauma. Without an even flow between the vortices, attention is drawn further into the trauma vortex. This produces an experience of more sensa-tion and emotion than we can remain present with, which leads to feeling overwhelmed. When an even flow of pendulation is reestablished, it regulates the nervous system, creating the resiliency that is necessary to remain present and discharge trauma. This resiliency, or self-regulation, is the ability to allow experience to come and go without becoming fixated in some way.
>
> (Lumiere, 2003, p. 255)

Pendulation allows us to inhabit the activated or becalmed poles of the ANS more fluidly (Bensimon et al., 2012). And when we can interrupt sympathetic activa-tion, when we can awaken to that polyvagal wisdom, when we pendulate, we are attentive to "the rhythmic ebb of being 'on' and active, to the flow of pause and rest. When we rest, we pendulate away from being in stuck stress, overdrive, and out-of-body overwhelm; when we rest, we can remember, reinhabit, and reinte-grate sensate experience and body wisdom" (Shaffer, 2021 p. 73).

This body, each day, practising

Intentionally trying to feel, hear feedback from, and reinhabit my body is part of my daily practice – before my pole-encounter, before bereavement, but certainly intensified since both. To do all that I do – as present parent, as attentive partner, as aspiring academic, as kind neighbour, as awake community member, as loving friend, as committed activist, as giving teacher, as home-tender – and to scaffold all that I *want* to do – make professor, finish my book, grow my business, keynote more often, contribute more thoughtfully, and create next-level-excellent programs/curricula/offerings/things in the world – I am made to understand, over and over and over again, I cannot simply barrel through, live in go-go-go mode, or function for too long, let alone *at* full throttle. Reminded by the accidents I have had when I have left my body alone, by hypervigilance waking me up too often in the night, and by my stress or fatigue or burnout that leads me to hide or shut down, what I long for most is that which is sustainable: sustainable energy, sustainable contentment, sustainable production, sustainable parenting, sustainable career-tending, sustainable success. To support this intention of sustainability, ever aware that my "autonomic nervous system is constantly scanning both our external and internal environments" (Rosenberg, 2017, p. 193), I aim to punctuate each day with polyvagal practices, exercises that give my ANS the opportunity to experience that pendulation, to experience unsticking.

Morning

To nourish my own vagal health, every morning I now practise what's considered the most fundamental and basic vagal stimulation exercises. It involves the eyeballs and the cervical spine, or topmost section of the vertebrae. "There is a direct neurological connection between the eight suboccipital muscles and the muscles that move our eyeballs. We can directly experience this connection between eye movement and changes in tension of the suboccipital muscles if we place a finger across the back of the head" (Rosenberg, 2017, p. 193). I am consistently amazed by how a seemingly indirect and brief engagement of my eyes can send a cascade of safety messaging throughout my body (see Figure 10.2).

The practice:

- Lie down on a comfortable surface
- Bend your knees, placing the soles of the feet hip-width from each other, and let your knees fall inward to rest against each other
- Cradle your head in your hands
- Inhale, and on your exhale, look to the right without moving your skull
- Keep your eyes gazing right for at least a count of 20, inhaling and exhaling fully, until your body gives a physical cue of vagal nerve activation, for example a yawn or sigh
- Reset by looking straight ahead, then look to the left, again for a count of 20, and following another cue, look straight ahead, breathing in and out

Evening

In earlier decades, I "pushed" myself in yoga, sometimes over-focusing on its acrobatics and powerful strength, rather than the equanimity of breath, mind, and

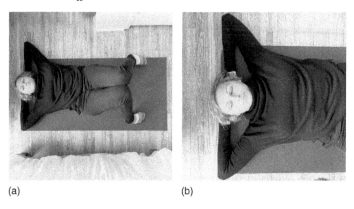

Figure 10.2 (a) Lying on a yoga mat/floor, knees resting on each other, clasped hands behind head, looking all the way to one side before switching to other side. (b) Close-up of gazing to the right.

being that it can invoke. I still love vigorous movement, and the more that I come to learn about the nervous system, the more dedicated I am to postures and practices that restore.

There is ample and increasing data about the physiological and psychological impacts of yoga. In its myriad forms, it is "correlated with both improvement in measures of psychological resilience and improved vagal regulation." (Sullivan, Erb, Schmalzl, Moonaz, Noggle Taylor, & Porges, 2018, p. 67). Yoga supports what can be thought of as "optimal homeostasis" (Streeter, Gerbarg, Saper, Ciraulo, Brown, 2012, p. 571). Restorative yoga, in specific, invites me into this homeostatic, restful state, in which I am held by the floor, putting aside to-do's and demands, and prioritising my breath and body (Lasater, 1995) (see Figure 10.3).

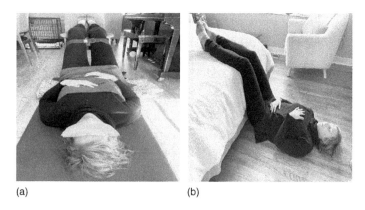

Figure 10.3 (a) Legs-on-chair pose with mat, blankets, yoga strap, and eye pillow. (b) Legs-on-bed, no props.

The practise:

- Lie down on a mat, blanket, or floor, and settle into the natural rhythm of your breath
- Rest your calves on a chair or bed
- Elevate your sacrum slightly with a folded blanket
- With a scarf or yoga strap, wrap your mid-thighs to eliminate effort to hold your legs in position
- If available, use an eye pillow, a blanket for warmth, and any other comforts
- Your hands can rest at your side or on your body
- Rest for 10 minutes

These polyvagal bodies that pendulate, together

This collective Covid-context work has come with

> unprecedented psychological pressure on the population. The adverse, some-times long-lasting, psychological impact of the lockdown restrictions, stay-at-home orders, quarantine, and other repercussions range from anxiety, post-traumatic stress symptoms, psychological distress, confusion, panic disor-der, anger, depression, insomnia, to emotional exhaustion.
>
> (Jelińska & Paradowski, 2021, p. 1)

With this acknowledgement of across-the-board stress, it must be mentioned that the burnout experienced is neither profession-neutral nor gender-neutral (Aldossari & Chaudhry, 2021).

It turns out that of *all* of us, of *all* the ways, that have been jostled and squeezed and overwhelmed by work during the pandemic, teachers are some of those who are most impacted (Jelińska & Paradowski, 2021). There is no question that those in healthcare professions, those with civic care responsibilities, and those support-ing the delivery of goods have borne the brunt. But what is also clear is that

> "educators were thrust into the provision of alternative modes of delivery, or "emergency remote teaching" that for most was an entirely novel form of work. Often, the anxieties were exacerbated by job uncertainty, especially for faculty on precarious contracts. … The combined effect of lockdowns and the transition to online delivery have severely affected teacher … coping and well-being.
>
> (Jelińska & Paradowski, 2021, pp. 1–2)

Even pre-pandemic, the work of teachers was identified as being high stress, asso-ciated with challenged mental and physical health, and incurring lower career satisfaction, all of which makes burnout more likely (Jelińska & Paradowski, 2021).

Add to this, as teachers, and in all professions, women experience more sexual harassment and discrimination than men, are not promoted as often, continue to earn less, struggle to attain positions of management, and shoulder more family responsibilities, each of these being key components of overwhelming work stress (Aldossari & Chaudhry, 2021). Put concisely, "women's work experiences and stresses are higher than their male counterparts and crucially extend this reasoning to argue that this results in a highly gendered experience of burnout" (Aldossari & Chaudhry, 2021, p. 828). In the pandemic, the workload has risen as have departmental demands, all the while promotions have paused and so too have conferences and Professional Development (Aldossari & Chaudhry, 2021). Amidst these, so too have home life pressures intensified.

> Cooking is only me. Cleaning is only me. Home schooling is me. I'm responsible for overseeing that my son has done his homework or he doesn't bother. Women have to do more cooking anyway, the division of housework in my case is not equal anyway. But since the pandemic we are more at house, so there is more cooking, no deliveries, takeaways, not buying ready-made food. So, much more cooking and much more cleaning. I always did most of the housework, I always prepared the breakfast, I always did the cooking, so nothing has changed. But just because of the pandemic it's so much more work that is needed, and we don't go out. We used to go out for breakfast on Saturdays, but now this has changed and this has brought more work [for me].
>
> (Aldossari & Chaudhry, 2021, p. 830)

I wonder then what work might feel like if each of us held not just closely, but as a guiding star, Rodino-Colocino's provocation: "faculty should help each other prioritise self-care over productivity. It is not simply that the former is a precondition for the latter. Ending overextension of our bodies and minds is a radical and therefore profoundly productive act" (2021, p. 317). Perhaps more prudently, what might work feel like if the structures and systems in which we teach, write, research, mentor, grade, and *pursue it all* gave a language to and outright supported a culture shift to interrupt overextension. This wondering feels particularly important to hold *now*, mid-pandemic, when already hyper-pressurised lives feel even more so (Jelińska & Paradowski, 2021).

These wonderings embolden me to commit to my minuscule, for now, practices, my polyvagal micro-moments that punctuate the day, make the day more doable, and make all that I have to do and all that I want to do more manageable. Polyvagal Theory has given me a way to understand and articulate what is happening at the finest, most elemental level that, with practice, I can more frequently sense. When I pendulate, when I feel into what vagal state I inhabit, when I intervene in my own shutdown or stress-stuck responses, when I remember that I have a body, and when I listen to its feedback, I am more sustainably poised to pursue, if not "it" all *at once*, then perhaps all *over time*. And, with practice, I hope to need those external reminders and interventions – my daughter's plea to slow down, my envious gaze at leisure, my skull's brutal pole encounter – less and less, instead turning to, and tuning *in* to, my own vagal cues.

References

Aldossari, M., & Chaudhry, S. (2021). Women and burnout in the context of a pandemic. *Gender, Work & Organization, 28*(2), 826–834.

Bensimon, M., Amir, D., & Wolf, Y. (2012). A pendulum between trauma and life: Group music therapy with post-traumatized soldiers. *The Arts in Psychotherapy, 39*(4), 223–233. https://doi.org/10.1016/j.aip.2012.03.005

Bharwani, S. (2021, January 14). How wellness brands inspired pandemic-weary consumers) *Adage.* Retrieved from: https://adage.com/article/acuity/wellness-brands-inspire-consumers-cope-pandemic/2304421

Dana, D. (2018). *The Polyvagal theory in therapy: Engaging the rhythm of regulation (Norton series on interpersonal neurobiology).* New York, NY: WW Norton & Company.

Dana, D. (2020). *Polyvagal exercises for safety and connection: 50 client-centered practices (Norton Series on Interpersonal Neurobiology).* New York, NY: WW Norton & Company.

Flaherty, C. (2014, April 9). So much to do, so little time. *Inside Higher Ed.* Retrieved from: https://www.insidehighered.com/news/2014/04/09/research-shows-professors-work-long-hours-andspend-much-day-meetings

Grabbe, L., & Miller-Karas, E. (2018). The trauma resiliency model: A "Bottom-up" intervention for trauma psychotherapy. *Journal of the American Psychiatric Nurses Association, 24*(1), 76–84. https://doi.org/10.1177/1078390317745133

Hamblin, J. (2018, November 19). The art of woke wellness. *The Atlantic.* Retrieved from: https://www.theatlantic.com/health/archive/2018/11/wellspring-festival-woke-wellness/576103/

Jelińska, M., & Paradowski, M. B. (2021). The impact of demographics, life and work circumstances on college and university instructors' well-being during quaranteaching. *Frontiers in Psychology, 12,* https://doi.org/10.3389/fpsyg.2021.643229

Lasater, J.H. (1995). *Relax and renew: Restful yoga for stressful times.* Berkeley, CA: Rodmell Press.

Levine, P. A. (1997). *Healing trauma: Waking the tiger.* Berkeley, CA: North Atlantic Books.

Lorde, A. ([1988] 2017). *A burst of light: And other essays.* Mineola, NY: Ixia Press.

Lumiere, L. M. (2003). Healing trauma in the eternal now. In Prendergast, J., Fenner, P., & Krystal, S. (Eds.), *The sacred mirror: Nondual wisdom and psychotherapy,* (pp. 249–268). Minnesota: Paragon House.

On the verge of burnout. (2020). COVID-19's impact on faculty well-being and career plans. *The Chronicle of Higher Education.* Retrieved from https://connect.chronicle.com/rs/931-EKA-218/images/Covid%26FacultyCareerPaths_Fidelity_ResearchBrief_v3%20%281%29.pdf

Porges, S. (2020). Polyvagal exercises for safety and connection: 50 client-centered practices. In Dana, D. (Ed.), *Norton series on interpersonal neurobiology.* (pp. xii–xviii). New York, NY: WW Norton & Company.

Porges S. W. (2009). The polyvagal theory: New insights into adaptive reactions of the autonomic nervous system. *Cleveland Clinic Journal of Medicine, 76* (Suppl 2), S86–S90. https://doi.org/10.3949/ccjm.76.s2.17

Rodino-Colocino, M. (2021). A pand(acad)emic plea for self-care and shorter hours. *Communication, Culture & Critique, 14*(2), 315–319.

Rosenberg, S. (2017). *Accessing the healing power of the vagus nerve: Self-help exercises for anxiety, depression, trauma, and autism.* Berkeley: North Atlantic Books.

Shaffer, D., & Brecher, D. (2021). Inwards, together: An inner-resourcing U-turn. *Journal of Learning Development in Higher Education, 22.* https://doi.org/10.47408/jldhe.vi22.721

Shaffer, D. K. (2021). Pendulation: Awakening to rest. In *Creating a place for self-care and wellbeing in higher education (N. Lemon, Ed.)* (pp. 72–86). Sydney, Australia: Routledge.

Streeter, C. C., Gerbarg, P. L., Saper, R. B., Ciraulo, D. A., & Brown, R. P. (2012). Effects of yoga on the autonomic nervous system, gamma-aminobutyric-acid, and allostasis in epilepsy, depression, and post-traumatic stress disorder. *Medical Hypotheses, 78*(5), 571–579. https://doi.org/10.1016/j.mehy.2012.01.021

Sullivan, M. B., Erb, M., Schmalzl, L., Moonaz, S., Noggle Taylor, J., & Porges, S. W. (2018). Yoga therapy and polyvagal theory: The convergence of traditional wisdom and contemporary neuroscience for self-regulation and resilience. *Frontiers in Human Neuroscience, 12*, 67.

11 Carving your destiny in academia as a "lecturer" and a "mother"

Soubakeavathi A/P Rethinasamy

A review of literature indicates that there are a variety of career tactics and distinct strategies that can enhance or may be critical for career advancement. Studies have reported that those who can identify and implement cohesive and strategic career advancement tactics over time will gain and sustain an edge (Arokiasamy et al., 2017; He et al., 2020; Laud & Johnson, 2012). Nevertheless, the answers to challenges experienced by women academics while balancing family and career are scarce. Undeniably, as in most work environments, women academics face greater and different challenges, especially those with families to manage. In this autoethnography, I provide an illustration of how I endeavoured to maintain a harmonious balance between work and family while carving my career trajectory in academia.

Opportunities and initiatives: schoolteacher to university teacher

I graduated with a bachelor's degree in arts and science, majoring in Biology and English, from University Science of Malaysia (USM) in 1993. Upon completing my degree, I was posted to a secondary school in the outskirts of Sarawak. While teaching at school, I came across an advertisement for a language teacher position at USM. I playfully applied for the position, but a few months later to my surprise, I received a telegram calling for an interview. Although I knew my chances were slim, as I had only one year of teaching experience, I grabbed the opportunity and attended the interview. A few months later, again to my surprise, I received a letter of offer. I was elated, as you can imagine, that at the age of 25 I got to teach in a university. I grabbed the offer and taught the medical and nursing students scientific English at USM's Medical Campus in Kelantan. After a few months of teaching, I realised that I really liked teaching in university. Being surrounded by people who are highly qualified and experts in their fields fuelled my desire to further my studies. One day, I saw an advertisement in the local newspaper for a Master's in English as a Second Language at University Malaya. Again, I decided to try my luck, although I knew that I only had 1.5 years of teaching experience. Again, to my surprise, my application was successful. However, it was a tough decision. Nonetheless, my desire to continue my studies got the better of me, and I resigned from USM and pursued my master's as a full-time postgraduate at UM's Language Centre (now known as the Faculty of Languages and Linguistics – FLL). In my class, I was the youngest, studying together with course-mates with vastly more

DOI: 10.4324/9781003341482-14

experience. After completing my coursework, and before starting on my dissertation, I was offered the position of English language teacher at FLL. I took up the offer and at the same time completed my master's. As the saying goes, "Life offers many opportunities, but it's up to the individual to grab the chance," and I held this philosophy close to my heart as I started the journey of my career. The role of opportunities and personal initiatives lays a strong foundation for career prospects (Robitschek et al., 2012).

Knowledge and action: university teacher to lecturer

As I was entering my fourth year of service in FLL, I got married, and since my husband was working in Universiti Malaysia Sarawak (UNIMAS), I applied to work at UNIMAS. With a master's degree in ESL and five years of teaching experience, I was offered the position of lecturer at the Centre for Language Studies (now Faculty of Language and Communication), UNIMAS. I moved from UM to UNIMAS with my one-and-a-half-month-old baby and joined UNIMAS on 1 December 1999.

While in UM, I only taught English proficiency courses, but in UNIMAS I started teaching TESL (Teaching of English as a Second Language) undergraduates in addition to English proficiency courses. Although it was challenging, I was happy because I got to utilize more of the knowledge I gained from my master's, and at the same time, update my knowledge in ESL. The class size was small, and the online support system, Lotus QuickPlace, provided a luxurious and exciting teaching-learning experience (see Figure 11.1). As I was getting familiar with the teaching-learning environment, I was asked if I would like to join a team going to Bario (an isolated remote highland on the Borneo Island) to conduct educational research. Being passionate about making learning meaningful for students, I agreed, despite being clueless about what lay ahead.

On 1 October 2000, leaving behind my barely one-year-old baby in the capable hands of my husband, I headed to Bario with the eBario research team. The team boarded a plane from the capital city, Kuching, to a small town named Miri and later boarded a twin otter flight to Bario. It was my first time travelling in a small plane, seated near livestock, and I could see the cockpit. The weather was rough, and thus it was indeed a bumpy ride all the way from Miri to Bario. I felt dizzy and nauseous. When we finally landed, I clumsily got out of the plane and headed towards the tiny Bario Airport – it was hardly an airport in the eyes of an urban girl. A group of people greeted us at the airport. Their smiles and warm welcome made my dizziness and nausea vanish into the cool, fresh air of Bario. We headed to the Labang Longhouse Lodge. Surprisingly, the thinness of the mattress, the freezing cold showers, and the lack of basic infrastructure did not bother me at all. The hospitality of the Bario community and the friendliness of the team filled the humble wooden abode with a warm and welcoming atmosphere. It made our accommodation a cosy and comfortable place to stay. The next day, after a good night's sleep and a hearty fresh breakfast, we headed to the school to start our research. Cool and calm, with her beautiful smile, the principal of Bario Secondary School welcomed us and introduced us to the teachers and students. We did not feel as if

Figure 11.1 My Students and I.

we were doing research at all – it was like being with our family. The following year, I made my second trip to Bario with computing staff, this time to set up the Pentium 5s in the Bario Primary School. As we were setting up the PCs, the curious schoolchildren peeped through the "actual" windows of the wooden block. No words can describe the children's anxiety and excitement when they were given the opportunity to "play" with the PCs – I wish I had taken a snapshot to capture that moment. Nonetheless, the image is still fresh in my memory. Imagine remote rural school having Pentium 5 PCs at the outset of the 21st century. All this was made possible through community-driven research. The research conducted in the Bario school resulted in my first journal paper – a high-impact journal paper. And that is how my research endeavours started. As highlighted by Wallerstein and Duran (2010), combining knowledge and action for positive social change to improve the livelihood of communities is rewarding, despite the challenges faced.

Broadening the horizon: pursuing my PhD in the UK

With the teaching experience and confidence gained from being part of the eBario research team, I gathered the courage to pursue my PhD. Together with my husband, I started to plan to pursue my degree overseas. In 2002, my husband was accepted into Oxford University, and I, Reading University. My husband left three months ahead of me to find suitable accommodation and settle the essentials. Then, I flew down to the UK with our 2.5-year-old child and joined him at Oxford University's Wolfson College family accommodation. It was a beautiful family accommodation with neighbours who were postgraduate families from various parts of the world, including Portugal, Sweden, Brazil, South Africa, and the United States of America. We became friends, and our children had a wonderful time playing in the little "global village" right in the middle of the courtyard. While it was exciting to study in a four-season country with a scholarship, it was a great challenge for both husband and wife to pursue PhDs at the same time, and that too with a small child. Since my husband was doing a lab-based study and had to go to the lab every day, and I needed to see my supervisor once every two to three weeks, we decided to live in Oxford. To go to Reading University from my accommodation, I had to walk to the bus stop, take a bus to the train station, then board a train to Reading. From Reading train station, I had to take another bus to the university and walk about one kilometre to my department. In total, it took about two hours to get from my accommodation in Oxford to my department in Reading University.

After successfully defending my PhD thesis towards the end of my first year, my supervisor informed me that he was moving to Roehampton University in Greater London. Initially I was devastated, but then after being assured by my supervisor, Professor Dr. Barry O'Sullivan, that he was happy to "take" me over to his new university, I was slightly relieved. However, I had to write to my funding university, UNIMAS, seeking permission to transfer my PhD to Roehampton University. The uncertainty while waiting for approval was torturous, but I continued to work on my study. A few months later, I was granted permission to transfer my degree to Roehampton University as a second-year PhD student. While this ended the dilemma and anxiety, the move meant that I would now have to travel to London on another mode of public transport, the underground tube, with an additional two to three hours of travelling, bringing the total travel time to and from Oxford to London to almost eight hours. Not to forget, I had to carry a haversack containing my laptop while I wore a thick jacket, gloves, muffler, and toque.

Just imagine, from having a comfortable life as a lecturer, travelling around in an air-conditioned car, to being a postgraduate student – having to walk and take several forms of public transport in a foreign land! Nevertheless, travelling on public transportation in the UK offered an interesting experience. I was mesmerised by the bulbs with beautiful flowers on the ground and the sprouting of the leaves on plants above the land during spring. Contrary to the common description of summer, the English summer was cold, especially for a Malaysian. The multi-coloured hue of the autumn leaves was breathtaking. Although winter was cold and limited our outdoor activities, the little snow that fell in Oxford was exciting, and even the bare trees with leaf-less branches looked exquisite. The quiet and comfortable ambience on the train enabled me to read journal articles. When my eyes needed a break, all I had to do was glance out of the window – the captivating sceneries offered a feast for the eyes and helped me relax during the long travel on public transport. Although window gazing may be viewed as a non-productive activity (Singleton, 2020), it did contribute towards active use of my travel time.

Rain or shine, on average I spent at least eight to ten hours a day working on my thesis. When I did not travel to London, I would send my child to school and then head to the little cosy carrel room provided for postgraduate students in the Wolfson College Library. I would head back to school at about 2:00 p.m. to pick up my child using the tag-along bike with an attachment for her to cycle along with me. While this activity developed my child's cycling ability, it also provided a break from study and helped me keep my mind and body healthy. This in turn contributed immensely towards my active thesis writing. Previous research by Wollseiffen et al. (2016) has also highlighted the positive effect of short exercises on neuro-cognitive performance.

As highlighted by Lirio et al. (2007), family support plays a crucial role in women's career success. In the last eight months of study, while my husband and I were intensely finishing the write-up of our theses, my parents kindly offered assistance. They came and stayed with us to help take care of our child. With my parents' timely assistance and my determination to complete the study, I submitted my thesis in December 2005 and had my viva voce in January 2006. After successfully passing my viva voce, I returned to join UNIMAS on 28 February 2006. My experiences studying in the UK with my husband and being a mother of a young child were extremely challenging, but it formed one of the most beautiful, unforgettable memories of my life. It also enhanced my ability to balance work and family.

Administrative academic: being the dean

Just a year after returning from completing my PhD, with my second child barely a year old, I was appointed as the dean on 1 June 2007. While still in my mid-30s, with two young children and little administrative experience, I faced many challenges in shouldering the responsibility. However, the experiences I gained from working on my PhD and caring for my family in the UK enabled me to multitask quite efficiently. My everyday routine was to leave home by 6:50 a.m., drop my elder child at school, and then head straight to the office. While at work, I focused on administrative and teaching responsibilities. After reaching home, I usually spent some time taking my children to the playground, settling dinner, and tucking them into bed. Then, at about 10:30 p.m., I would start on my research and writing till past midnight. On average, I only got about five to six hours of sleep a day. This was my intense work routine while holding an administrative position. Nevertheless, I survived four years as the dean with strong support from my husband, and I was very lucky to be blessed with a loving and caring babysitter. She took good care of my little one while my husband and I were at work, and this gave me the much-needed peace of mind and enabled me to concentrate while at work. Whenever we were not able to pick up the elder one from school, she offered a helping hand. A full-time live-in helper was also employed to help with the housework. This enabled me to spend more quality time with my family when I get back home from the office. The role of a good babysitter and domestic help for a woman administrate lecturer in managing an upper-management position is crucial (Marlow et al., 1995).

Multipurpose study room at home

Learning together with children is key for children's overall development (Sanchez, 2020). I set up a multi-purpose study room in the house. In the study room, I placed tables for the children as well as for myself with a desktop and a whiteboard. I love working with double PC monitors, so both at home and in my office, I set up two monitors. This enabled me to be with my children, with me doing my work at home and the children doing their schoolwork. Seeing parents do their work in the study room, to some extent, acts as motivation for the children to head to the study room too. As the children advanced in their schooling years, we spent quite a lot of time in the study room together, supporting each other. Whenever they needed assistance, together we headed towards the white board. The children also offered help with the latest computer applications, especially social media, and added creativity to my presentation slides. At the same time, I took on the nomination to be a member of school's Parent-Teacher Association in the school the children were studying at. This helped me stay connected with the teachers and happenings in their school, as well as have better access to my children's progress at school. Since the teachers knew the school board members, the children became a little more careful and committed. It also provided an opportunity for me as an educator to contribute towards the school community.

Being the director of international office

Being a "young" and inexperienced dean, I faced many challenges while shouldering my responsibilities as the dean. Nevertheless, I learnt that "anything that does not kill you makes you stronger." My ability in managing, teaching, supervision, research, and administrative responsibilities paid off; in October 2011, I was promoted from senior lecturer to Associate Professor. Four years after serving as the dean, I was relieved to get back to "normal" academic life. However, it was short-lived. In June 2014, I was appointed as the Deputy Director of International Affairs Division, and then, six months later, as the Director (see Figure 11.2). I managed international students, students' inbound and outbound mobility, international relations, and other internationalization-related matters. During the quarterly International Directors' Committee meetings, I had the opportunity to visit several universities in Malaysia, including Universiti Utara Malaysia (UUM), Universiti Teknologi Malaysia (UTM), Universiti Malaysia Sabah (UMS), and Universiti Malaysia Terengganu (UMT). The visit to UMT allowed me to visit the only state in Malaysia that I had not yet visited. I also had the opportunity to travel to several countries, including Brunei, Mauritius, and Sri Lanka. Serving as the director of the international division not only provided a great learning experience, but also allowed me to meet some wonderful colleagues from other universities in Malaysia and abroad. Despite returning to "full" academic positions, we remain as friends and stay connected via social media.

Studies have shown that administrative responsibilities distract lecturers' research productivity (Nygaard, 2017; Truong et al., 2021). Undoubtedly, administrative responsibilities deprive an academic of time for doing research and making a

Figure 11.2 Director of UNIMAS International Office.

significant mark in academe through research publications, but it does increase the visibility of the administrative lecturer. It opens opportunities for networking and future collaborations. The display of commitment and endurance increases the visibility of the administrative lecturer, strengthens the connections made during the strenuous years, and later bolsters research endeavours, along with adding meaning to life through the strong friendships formed beyond the completion of the administrative tenure.

Turning deprivation into opportunities

An example of a collaboration that had a strong foundation and extended beyond administrative positions is the EduTour programme that I designed with Professor Dr. Tatsuhiro Ohkubo from Utsunomiya University in Japan. EduTour is an international short-term mobility programme aimed at making the students' university life more meaningful and memorable. It offers English-language lessons, visits to the highlights of Kuching, with food and cultural experiences for the Japanese university participants. The UNIMAS participants add a special flavour to the programme by serving as buddies. The experiences students gained from participating in EduTour increase their confidence to take part in other long-term mobility programmes and apply for postgraduate studies overseas. The Japanese students came for a one-year study exchange and internship in UNIMAS, while UNIMAS students started to take part in UU's international seminars and post-graduate opportunities. The collaboration also involved students and teachers from local schools, which opened avenues that established smart partnerships between the local schools in Kuching, Sarawak, and Japanese schools in Utsunomiya, Tochigi. For example, the Lodge Group of Schools and Batu Lintang Secondary School in Kuching established global classroom activities. I was also invited to UU under the scholar visit programme and given a personal tour of Tochigi prefecture by the UU team. The EduTour programme contributes towards the institution's effort in achieving international visibility. Additionally, it paved the path for the creation of ideas worthy of intellectual property and commercialisation while making a significant contribution to the local and international community. The uniqueness of the programme enabled me to claim the copyright for the pro-gramme and it also achieved commercialisation status. The EduTour programme also attracted research grant providers and led to transdisciplinary publications. In short, a complete cycle of research was achieved through the creation of the EduTour programme. This far-reaching effort placed my career at the heart of academia.

Social and recreational strategies: life beyond work

Undoubtedly, the multi-faceted, ever-demanding life as a university lecturer can be strenuous and unending. While being a lecturer emboldens us with multiple responsibilities, we need to take time-outs, do things that we enjoy, and live our life to the fullest. As the saying goes, we need to "stop and smell the roses." As my children grew older, my full-time live-in helper became redundant. I purchased electronic devices that help with routine cleaning tasks such as sweeping, vacuum-ing, and mopping. In fact, these devices can be controlled remotely using my mobile phone. While the machine does the cleaning, I do my work on the PC and take time out to do other activities. When required, hiring part-time home clean-ers can be worthwhile. This helps in reducing physical burdens and frees time for other activities. During my younger days, I remember conversations in which my friends and I boasted about our mother's special dishes. I want my children to have such memories too, so I ventured deeper into baking cakes and bread. Sometimes the children offer a helping hand, enhancing our bonding. Seeing my children and other family members enjoying my creations and getting compliments from the children is rewarding. It also combats the stigma that career women are not good at cooking. I love gardening; watching my plants grow, bear fruits, and bloom in my garden connects me with nature and gives me a special kind of satisfaction. I also adopted a pet dog from SSPCA named Olaf. He grew from a little puppy into a gorgeous young lad. Every time I return from work, Olaf would be the first to greet me with his wagging tail expressing his happiness. Having a pet gives an extra meaning to life. Regular exercises keep the body and mind healthy. When I have time, I take a walk in the Samajaya Reserve Forest and go hiking. When time is limited, I take a walk in my housing area's walk path. Maintaining a healthy social life makes life interesting. Participating in my local Rotary Club activities provides a special meaning beyond work. Social media such as Facebook, Instagram, and WhatsApp enable me to stay in touch with family members and reconnect with old friends. Visiting family members and attending gatherings with school and university mates from time to time makes my life more complete. These activities provide me with self-therapy. At the same time, stepping out of work-related activities gives me fresh ideas for when I return to work.

The friendship I formed with my neighbours at the Wolfson College Family Accommodation in UK has also been maintained. My former neighbours have also completed their study and are living in various parts of the globe, but we continue to stay in touch via social media. They have come to visit us in Kuching, and our visits to their countries became more meaningful with their presence and our catch-up gatherings. It's inspiring to see how they have progressed in their careers and how their children have grown over the years. We spent much time reminiscing on our time spent together at the Wolfson College's Family Accommodation. I also kept in touch with my supervisor, Professor Dr. Barry O'Sullivan. He comes down to Malaysia and my university as a keynote speaker in conferences and conducts workshops from time to time. Maintaining a good relationship with my supervisor helps me to stay in touch with the latest developments and contribute towards building my prominence in my area of expertise. Through my supervisor, I was invited as plenary speaker at the 2014 Curriculum and Assessment Conference, organised by British Council Indonesia, and at the 2018 New Directions Conference, organised by British Council Malaysia.

Now in my early fifties, I am back to being a "normal" lecturer. In my last years of being an academic, I aspire to focus fully on teaching, learning, research, publication, and making meaningful contribution towards my students' learning and the community. The journey continues…

References

Arokiasamy, L., Mansouri, N., Balaraman, R. A., & Kassim, N. M. (2017). A literature review of competence development on academic career advancement: A human resource development perspective. *Global Business and Management Research, 9*(1s), 403–414. http://0-eds.b.ebscohost.com.oasis.lib.tamuk.edu/eds/pdfviewer/pdfviewer?vid=10& sid=1e5480f7-22cc-403d-b836-1f6e2ef4bdc9%40sessionmgr104

He, H., Gao, J., & Yan, L. (2020). Understanding career advancement of newcomers from perspective of organizational socialization: A moderated mediating model. *Chinese Management Studies, 14*(3), 789–809. https://doi.org/10.1108/CMS-03-2019-0116

Laud, R. L., & Johnson, M. (2012). Upward mobility: A typology of tactics and strategies for career advancement. *Career Development International, 17*(3), 231–254. https://doi.org/10.1108/13620431211241072

Lirio, P., Lituchy, T. R., Monserrat, S. I., Olivas-Lujan, M. R., Duffy, J. A., Fox, S., … & Santos, N. (2007). Exploring career-life success and family social support of successful women in Canada, Argentina and Mexico. *Career Development International, 12*(1), 28–50. https://doi.org/10.1108/13620430710724811

Marlow, N. D., Marlow, E. K., & Arnold, V. A. (1995). Career development and women managers: Does "one size fit all"? *Human Resource Planning, 18*(2), 38–49.

Nygaard, L. P. (2017). Publishing and perishing: An academic literacies framework for investigating research productivity. *Studies in Higher Education, 42*(3), 519–532. https://doi.org/10.1080/03075079.2015.1058351

Robitschek, C., Ashton, M. W., Spering, C. C., Geiger, N., Byers, D., Schotts, G. C., & Thoen, M. A. (2012). Development and psychometric evaluation of the Personal Growth Initiative Scale–II. *Journal of Counseling Psychology, 59*(2), 274. https://doi.org/10.1037/a0027310

Sanchez, M. C. (2020). *Learning Together- The importance of parental involvement in their children's education. Capstone Projects and Master's Theses.* 924. https://digitalcommons.csumb.edu/caps_thes_all/924

Singleton, P. A. (2020). Multimodal travel-based multitasking during the commute: Who does what? *International Journal of Sustainable Transportation, 14*(2), 150–162. https://doi.org/10.1080/15568318.2018.1536237

Truong, H. T., Le, H. M., Do, D. A., Le, D. A., Nguyen, H. T., & Nguyen, T. K. (2021). Impact of governance factors over lecturers' scientific research output: An empirical evidence. *Education Sciences, 11*(553), 1–21. https://doi.org/10.3390/educsci11090553

Wallerstein, N., & Duran, B. (2010). Community-based participatory research contributions to intervention research: The intersection of science and practice to improve health equity. *American Journal of Public Health, 100*(S1), S40–S46. https://doi.org/10.2105/AJPH.2009.184036

Wollseiffen, P., Ghadiri, A., Scholz, A., Strüder, H. K., Herpers, R., Peters, T., & Schneider, S. (2016). Short bouts of intensive exercise during the workday have a positive effect on neuro-cognitive performance. *Stress and Health, 32*(5), 514–523. https://doi.org/10.1002/smi.2654

12 Navigating and building resilience in academia

Dual perspectives

Betty Exintaris, Nilushi Karunaratne, and Anisha Kaur Sandhu

Navigating an academic career is a complex process. The modern-day academic faces unique challenges, including administrative overload, large student cohorts, time constraints, and unrealistic workload demands (Hoffman, 2016). The increased bureaucracy of higher education has also negatively impacted academics' work and emotions (Bahia, Freire, Estrela, Amaral, & Espírito Santo, 2017). There are also growing concerns about the constant state of flux in the university work environment as institutions strive to address demands for increased efficiency, accountability, and quality (Behari-Leak, 2017). In the context of these organisational changes, as well as the demand for academics to demonstrate high-level administrative, managerial, scholarly, and entrepreneurial skills (Zábrodská et al., 2018), academic workload is increasingly associated with distress and burnout (Watts & Robertson, 2011). The accumulation of these experiences may not only hinder the wellbeing of the individual but negatively hinder the quality of their teaching as academic staff can feel burdened by having to manage their wellbeing while also providing pastoral care to ever-increasing numbers of students (Tham & Holland, 2018).

Early career academics often feel pulled in multiple directions as they struggle to adjust and balance their new roles. They may consequently become overwhelmed, overburdened, stressed out, isolated, and unmotivated. It is important for those who have successfully navigated the path of academia to assist others such that the prospect of surviving in academia might seem less mysterious and more manageable. For the experienced academic, resilience is challenged through balancing academic advancement with business effectiveness (Lee et al., 2022). Increasing workloads, in combination with decreasing financial resources, funding, and administrative support, place academics at increased risk of burnout. The senior academic often also grapples with the notion of "publish or perish." Within this culture, academic researchers are often deemed "successful" based on the number of publications they have or the prestige of the journals they are featured in. At times, the continual rejection of grant applications and journal articles can potentially lead to feelings of discouragement, social isolation, and avoidance of research projects (Chan, Mazzucchelli, & Rees, 2021).

The critical role of resilience for academic staff is advocated by Gu & Day (2013), who highlight that to teach at one's best over time requires resilience and,

DOI: 10.4324/9781003341482-15

furthermore, that staff need to role-model resilience (Holdsworth, Turner, & Scott-Young, 2018). In the field of social science, resilience describes the ability to withstand and rebound from adversity. Individual characteristics such as self-efficacy, confidence, and coping strategies are important in overcoming challenging situations or recurring setbacks (Castro, Kelly, & Shih, 2010). But rather than thinking of resilience as an inherent personal trait, both internal factors and external resources can help individuals manage difficulties and bounce back quickly and efficiently to persevere and thrive (Bobek, 2002; Day, 2008). This type of successful adaptation ensures that personal wellbeing is maintained (Howard & Johnson, 2004) and is mutually supported by positive personal, professional, and peer relationships (Sammons et al., 2007). The outcome is that teachers maintain job satisfaction and commitment to their profession (Brunetti, 2006).

Overall, the unique pressures of academia can constantly challenge the resilience of academic staff. Our views on cultivating resilience in academia stem from two unique viewpoints – from that of a female researcher and educator with over 20 years of experience of tackling and navigating the world of academia and from two early career academics establishing themselves in the profession. All three academics work at the world-leading Faculty or School of Pharmacy and Pharmaceutical Sciences across Monash, Australia, and Malaysia. The senior academic holds a doctorate in Physiology (Medicine) and is currently employed as a senior lecturer. The early-mid-career academic from Monash University Australia holds a doctorate in Pharmacology (Pharmacy/Pharmaceutical Sciences) and is currently employed as a lecturer. The early-mid career academic from Monash Malaysia holds a degree in Pharmacy and is currently employed as an assistant lecturer. All three academics undertake the scholarship of teaching and learning, often collaborating on numerous education research areas. All three academics have a high engagement profile at their respective institutions. The challenges and obstacles faced by all three academics are not unique to academia, and the challenges and obstacles are, in fact, discipline agnostic, especially in relation to the "glass ceiling" that separates the career progression of female academics in comparison to their male counterparts.

Both lenses reveal unique but often overlapping perspectives on individual and collaborative strategies to overcome obstacles and difficulties while developing and strengthening resilience. The strategies discussed in this chapter provide practical ways to achieve and sustain resilience in academia, allowing them to thrive, rather than just survive, in the profession.

As depicted in our visual narrative, our strategies include:

- Being a mentor/sponsor
- Forming formal/informal partnerships
- Combining resources
- Catching up on a daily basis for coffee
- Finding your voice
- Making time for family/friends/sport/hobbies
- Reflective practice
- Being a champion of other women

Visual narrative: dual academic perspectives on building resilience and self-care (Figure 12.1)

Discussion

From our experience, as two early career academics and one experienced senior academic, we have been able to articulate our recipe for self-care. In addition, we have discovered that cultivating positive relationships, such as mentor/mentee relationships or supportive collegial relationships in academia, is essential for wellbeing by providing emotional sounding boards, orienting us in the workplace, or providing networking opportunities. In this section, we discuss the significance of each of these strategies in the context of our academic journey.

Strategy 1: Create opportunities and embrace mentorship and sponsorship

Traditionally, mentoring has been defined as a relationship between an older, more experienced person (mentor) who helps and enables career development in the younger, less-experienced person (mentee) (Ragins & Kram, 2007). Mentoring relates mainly to the identification and nurturing of potential in the mentee, where the mentor's role is pivotal for providing useful insights for enhancing the mentee's self-awareness (Lancer, Clutterbuck, & Megginson, 2016). Sponsorship, on the other hand, goes to the next level of advocacy.

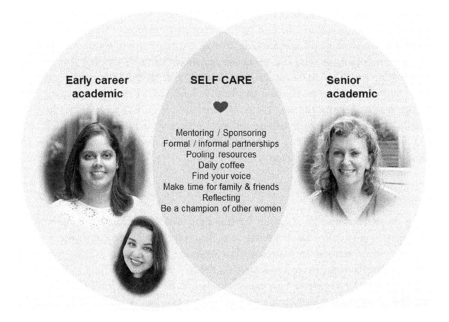

Figure 12.1 The authors, connected by mentorship.

There is much personal reward and personal growth gained from being a mentor and sponsor. Resilience can be supported by mentors, sponsors, and professional support systems. Having the right support system can help individuals reflect on their setbacks and learn from them (Billett, 2003). Having the right mentor can allow an individual to see failures and setbacks as learning experiences.

A mentor's perspective

Mentoring is also a way of "giving back" to the profession. There is enormous personal satisfaction in moulding a mentee's personal and professional development, and in watching early career researchers grow as educators and researchers. More experienced academics can provide advice based on their experiences, with the benefit of hindsight. The more experienced academic has mentored more than 20 undergraduate, Honours, and PhD students in her time. She has provided advice on ways to navigate academia, career advice, and how to tackle different stressful situations, provided support, and has often acted as a sounding board. Another real benefit of mentorship is that life-long friendships can be formed, and we know how important support networks are to building resilience! For mentors, developing one-on-one relationships can be a means of broadening their own professional networks with those in the earlier stages of their academic career progression. This can provide them with renewed insight and understanding of the day-to-day challenges and impact of academic pressures in current times. For the mentor, these relationships often also allow them an opportunity to reflect on their own career choices and encounters with adversity whilst in academia.

The more experienced academic has also acted as a sponsor, for example, stepping down from an invited presentation or to chair a session at a conference and suggesting that an early career researcher stand in her place. Other ways that a mentor can act as a sponsor include having a conversation about the order of authors on papers, grants, and postgraduate supervision. Changing the order of authorship, such that the early career academic is first, can allow the mentee to build confidence. For example, if the mentee hasn't supervised postgraduate candidates before, having the mentor as an associate supervisor to help navigate the intricacies of PhD supervision is invaluable. In this way, the mentee feels supported and the PhD candidate feels supported, all while simultaneously facilitating the growth of the mentee's reputation.

A mentee's perspective

From an early career perspective, having a mentor is invaluable. Academia is a rewarding career with much variety and flexibility, but with that come a lot of stressors, some unique to academia. For example, there is no official handover. New academics are expected to learn "on the fly," while establishing themselves as researchers and educators. The expectations can be overwhelming. However, it certainly does help to build resilience! A mentor can help with building networks and provides invaluable advice on navigating professional challenges and setting and achieving career goals as well as providing a strong sense of emotional support to deal with factors like managing stress, burnout, or other personal difficulties. Interestingly, in our example, the pairing of the more experienced academic with the early career academic has led to a powerful collaboration, which has resulted in grants, awards, and publications in an area new to both parties: education research. The mentorship provided by the experienced senior academic also allows them to function as a protector and a role model who instils confidence and helps the mentee effectively deal with the obstacles and challenges of academia.

For the mentee in a competitive academic setting, the challenge is often to find opportunities to demonstrate their capabilities and skill sets in different ways. Having a sponsor who actively creates opportunities for the mentee to be involved in professional committees, presentation opportunities, or postgraduate supervision allows the mentee to gain experience in these areas while also allowing them to recognise how their skill sets can be utilised and applied in various professional settings. Often, mentors and sponsors are the people who can see greater things in you than you see in yourself. You need to listen to these people, take on their advice and, when they try to offer you opportunities, not shy away from them just because you can't see it for yourself.

Strategy 2: Develop supportive collegial relationships and collaborative partnerships

There is much to be gained by forming informal collegial and supportive collaborative partnerships. Social support suggests that a positive relationship with a significant person is integral to resilience outcomes (Garcia-Dia, DiNapoli, Garcia-Ona, Jakubowski, & O'Flaherty, 2013). These relationships also contribute to general feelings of positivity, which are important in resilience theory (Borucka & Ostaszewski, 2008). Embracing positivity can enhance confidence and self-esteem and contribute to professional satisfaction and transition experience, especially for the early career academic.

We have already discussed that the landscape in the 21st century is changing in terms of gender bias. The academic landscape is also changing in terms of academia being an autonomous career. An academic can no longer afford to be insular, focusing on their research project and teaching load only. Grants, however small, benefit from multiple collaborators and diverse viewpoints (e.g., genders and cultures). Teaching is often conducted in teams. The importance of forming informal collegial and supportive collaborative partnerships in academia is invaluable. By connecting with colleagues within and beyond the faculty, school, or institutions (informally or formally), ideas, grants, and research can be advanced further.

A great example is that the three authors have collaborated on multiple successful education innovation grants. Another example is that our collaboration has also benefited our students. We have run various global student networking events throughout the pandemic, spanning Australia, Malaysia, and Europe. What a fantastic opportunity it has been for our students to connect with their peers nationally and internationally, sparking connections and a sense of community. Our collaboration has also translated to running an annual virtual education symposium with presentations from students and academics across the world.

A mentor's perspective

For the experienced academic, this form of partnership provides them with an alternative point of view, energy, and enthusiasm, and an emotional sounding board. Developing supportive collegial relationships and collaborative partnerships can provide support, guidance, and motivation and allow early career academics to engage and observe experienced academics to assist them in developing skills and knowledge. This strategy also demonstrates to young academics how to navigate and perhaps overcome gender biases, which have historically hindered career progression for females, especially in STEM (Science, Technology, Engineering, and Maths) fields. In this way, the mentor can act as a role model and advocate for female academics.

A mentee's perspective

There are numerous positive benefits from effective partnerships between an experienced and early career academic partnership that can help alleviate feelings of frustration and unrealistic expectations and allow the early career academic to understand and develop pre-emptive strategies to build resilience. For the early career academic, actively engaging with colleagues that have demonstrated their own personal resilience through successful careers provides her with role models who give social support. Seeing the more experienced academic as a role-model also teaches her how to navigate academia, at times in male-dominated settings. For the mentee, observing such interactions, especially in team settings, can be eye-opening and educational at times in terms of how best to approach male-dominated settings to build collegial relationships.

Strategy 3: Find your emotional sounding board

A mentor's perspective

Supportive networks can also be used as an emotional sounding board both within and outside of the university. One significant facet of building resilience is support; having a network of friends, family, and colleagues provides a foundation of trust and perhaps different levels of connection.

A mentee's perspective

Early career academics may have strong support networks outside of the university, but may need to build new networks within the university system, where they can express their ideas and concerns and clarify misunderstandings in a safe and positive environment. In this way, partnering with a more senior academic or having a more formal mentor can be beneficial as a support person or a person who can help you expand your network. For example, the less experienced academic was asked to take on numerous leadership roles and felt that she lacked the experience and necessary skills to be an effective leader in those roles. In contrast, the more experienced academic highlighted the opportunity and the skills and attributes that she had observed in the less experienced academic that made her, in fact, a perfect candidate for those positions she initially doubted herself for.

Strategy 4: Pool your resources

The more senior academic and early career academics have reaped the rewards of pooling their resources. Small contributions from individuals can lead to exponential increases in output/productivity. In this way, partnering early career academics with senior academics can work well. Senior academics bring experience, corporate knowledge, and ideas to the table, whereas early career academics bring the enthusiasm, technical expertise, and drive to enact projects. Diversity is also key. A great example here is a recent joint grant that the three authors collaborated on between the Malaysian and Australian campuses of their university.

Importantly, each academic brought a different perspective: senior versus early career academic, Malaysian background versus Australian background. Each academic enthusiastically contributed to the grant, culminating in the entire grant being completed within a fortnight. It is worth mentioning that the three authors have previously collaborated on multiple grants, forming a cohesive team, and have achieved many successful outcomes. It is also important to remember that unfortunately not all partnerships are successful!

Strategy 5: Create positive daily rituals

Prioritising positivity in psychology relates to the behaviour of using positive states such as contentment and joy as key criteria to structure daily life (Catalino, Algoe, & Fredrickson, 2014). The senior academic and early career academic based in Melbourne, Australia, always begin the day with a coffee and a chat. Our daily ritual provides structure and focus to each day. In lieu of a physical list, most mornings, one of the early career academics and more senior academic would catch up for an early morning coffee at a coffeeshop located close to the workplace. Importantly, the ritual was mutually beneficial. Prioritising positivity is linked with traits that reflect intentionality (e.g., conscientiousness) and emotionally intelligent tendencies (e.g., resilience), which have been shown to predict wellbeing (Catalino & Boulton, 2021). Ritualistic behaviour such as a meeting for a daily coffee can also improve social bonding (Ratcliffe, Baxter, & Martin, 2019).

A mentor's perspective

Coffee was a great way to wake up, to share daily plans, and verbalise what we wanted to accomplish on that day. This strategy was useful to deal with daily stressors, provide accountability, and provide a positive start to the day. While relaying the tasks for the day, sometimes it even became obvious that the aims for the day were unrealistic. Other times, by verbalising what we wanted to achieve, we realised that we could help each other. An alternative strategy could be a walk at the end of the day to share accomplishments, talk about the stressors of the day, and ensure that we're not taking the burden of the day home.

A mentee's perspective

For the mentee, this time brought a degree of consistency and predictability to the uncertain future of what the day might hold. It was an opportunity to slow down and spend time exchanging plans for the day, focusing on how best to prioritise tasks, with the input of the mentor helping to alleviate anxiety about the high pressure needs of the day.

Strategy 6: find your voice

In cultivating your own resilience, your inner voice can be your most helpful companion. It can motivate you to take on challenges, give you comfort when disappointment arises, and encourage you to keep trying (Kumar Pradhan & Kumar, 2020; Olson, 2022). Even though it may be daunting, it's important to learn to find your voice. The literature shows that younger, early career (and particularly female) academics are more likely to have feelings of self-doubt and lack confidence, often culminating in "impostor syndrome," where individuals question their abilities and sense of belonging (Parkman, 2016). Interestingly, and perhaps paradoxically, such individuals are likely to be highly intelligent and accomplished.

A mentor's perspective

Partnering with a more experienced academic can help with feelings of self-doubt and help normalise such negative feelings. For example, they might share personal stories of how the experienced academic felt when first becoming an academic, errors they made, and the like. Conversations such as this can help overcome self-doubt and help the less experienced academic find their voice. Just like the classroom, where less confident students can struggle to contribute to discussion, despite being very capable students, early career academics can find it difficult to speak up. This is not surprising. As academia is not an industry that has a high turnover of staff, new appointments, especially females, often have to navigate established friendships between colleagues who are perhaps already allies and have discussions with more senior people, often in male-dominated environments. Diversity can also play a role here. For example, in many cultures, "speaking up" or speaking when you're not asked a question can be considered impolite or disrespectful behaviour. In this way, having a more senior academic to partner with can help resolve some of these feelings and help build confidence. Recently, the more experienced academic advised the early career academic that expressing an idea or an opinion is important and, in a sense, that the outcome is irrelevant. This has led to the less experienced academic contributing to discussions in meetings and having the knowledge and confidence that if the group doesn't take your suggestion onboard, it doesn't mean that it wasn't a good suggestion. While the more senior academic can still experience some of the feelings described above, the main difference is that with experience come the tools and support networks to overcome feelings of self-doubt.

A mentee's perspective

Being relatively new to academia, in the face of increasing challenges and pressures in academia, younger academics grapple with faltering self-confidence, internalisation of failures, and too much focus on mistakes made. As a result, the mentee might often work longer and harder to seek perfection (Parkman, 2016). Feelings of impostor syndrome result in the younger academic feeling like working harder and longer are the only tools they have to meet expectations of a demanding academic environment. This can at times lead to unrealistic expectations and goals. An experienced mentor can help counter these unrealistic expectations and challenge the negative self-talk and aid the younger academic in finding their unique inner voice that is not influenced by outer pressures.

Strategy 7: Make emotional self-care a priority

It is important to recognise the signs of overload, which can involve changes in health or even attitude and behaviours (McEwen, 2011). Importantly, overload can look very different to different people. By recognising the signs of overload and investing in emotional self-care early, changes to physical and mental health can be avoided. In fact, perhaps counterintuitively, when feeling overloaded and overwhelmed, emotional self-care is often not a priority. Emotional self-care can involve investing time in friends and family, hobbies, sports, meditation, yoga, massages. Below we describe some of the common strategies that the senior and early career academics use to practise emotional self-care.

A mentor and mentee's perspective

Emotional self-care is important. In many ways, academia is a lifestyle. Academia is not a 9 a.m.–5 p.m. career, and as such the work/life model can look very different for academics. Academics need to set their own boundaries, which can be difficult at the best of times, let alone during the global pandemic, when working hours increased exponentially, with the added pressure on the academics to plan online activities, ensure that the activities were interactive, cater to the different needs of diverse student cohorts, respond to student emails ASAP in order to alleviate anxiety and stress, and so forth. Of course, educational activities also needed to be balanced with research and engagement activities. How does the academic achieve everything and still maintain a semblance of a healthy balance of work and home life? The answer is emotional self-care, which is imperative to prevent burnout. In order to achieve this, it's important to deliberately make time to spend with family and friends and to continue with recreational activities, even during the busiest time of the semester. In this way, you're looking after yourself and, importantly, bringing your "best self" to your work. Institutions can also play a role in supporting academics by providing a positive and healthy workplace culture. For example, encouraging academics to take leave, organising social activities, providing workshops on wellbeing and mental health, and explicitly promoting support services available to academics such as counselling and female support groups. A great example of an initiative to support female academics at any stage of their academic career is "Her Research Matters" at the Faculty of Pharmacy and Pharmaceutical Sciences, which promotes, sponsors, and fosters an inclusive and equitable leadership environment to enable all women in research to reach their full potential.

Strategy 8: Reflect, reflect, reflect!

Reflection can lead to positive change (Horton-Deutsch & Sherwood, 2008) and can serve as an additional tool for building resilience (Jackson, Firtko, & Edenborough, 2007) and lead to transformative growth. Through reflection, we have the opportunity for self-discovery, as well as to reframe situations that allow us to learn and grow. Reframing scenarios is particularly powerful as it can help alleviate the impact of highly stressful environments such as those seen in academia.

A mentor and mentee's perspective

At any stage of a career, reflective practice is an important and powerful tool. Reflective practice is essential in all aspects of academia, whether it's thinking about improving a class that didn't go according to plan, or reworking (yet another!) grant that was unsuccessful or having a promotion application rejected and thinking about "where to next?" Strategies such as the "one door closes, one door opens" exercise, where if an opportunity passes by, it is crucial to take stock of the situation and consider what other opportunities are available to participate in and can provide "positive reframing" of a negative situation. If we consider the three examples again, noting that all of the examples have been experienced by at least one of the authors:

- *The class didn't go according to plan.* You may have tried a new technology that didn't work as well as anticipated or the students were disengaged. Positive reframing of the example could be "At least I gave the technology a go. I might try it one more time. Otherwise, I'll try something else."
- *The grant was unsuccessful.* The grant might have taken a month to write and you prioritised the grant over writing papers. Positive reframing of the example could be "I will rework the grant; at least I don't have to start from scratch and I may be successful next time. Moreover, by writing the grant, I'm more on top of the literature, which will help with my next conference presentation."
- *The promotion application was rejected.* This can be quite disheartening, and it's important to remember that this doesn't mean that you're not worthy; it just means that you're not ready to take that next step. Positive reframing of the

example could be "I'll allow myself to be disappointed today and then I'll go and speak to my supervisor about what I need to do to be successful next time."

Strategy 9: Remember to recognise and celebrate your successes

Celebrating successes and victories is a form of self-care. Purposeful acknowledgement of successes can help build resilience and confidence and help restore yourself mentally (Berkman, 2018; Duckworth, Eichstaedt, & Ungar, 2015). When you allow yourself the time to celebrate your victories, and relish all that you accomplished (whatever that may be!), you show yourself appreciation. Celebrating successes is also closely linked to reflection (Aarts, Elliot, & Ebooks, 2012). Sometimes we can get caught up in the cycle of academic life with the idea that when something significant is achieved, for example, a grant or a paper is published, it's a box-ticking exercise and we then quickly move onto "what's next?" In this sense, pairing an early career academic with a more senior academic works well.

A mentor and mentee's perspective

The more senior academic can remind the early career academic to "stop and smell the roses," as it were, and to celebrate the significant achievement. The early career academic can also remind the more senior academic to reflect on positive achievements and celebrate them.

Strategy 10: Be a champion of other women

A mentor's perspective

It is important to be supportive of female academics. Women are uniquely placed to form the supportive networks required to build and support their colleagues and be "Champions of Other Women." From an experienced educator perspective, the challenge is that women have often struggled to progress to senior positions within the academic landscape, which can also cultivate biased attitudes. In a sense there is potential for bias both ways, with the bias experienced by the female academic to progress to leadership positions and, in turn, a biased attitude from the female academic towards other female academics: "I had it tough and that's the way it is for female academics." Women need to be champions of other women by being mentors and nurturing the development of early career academics so there is a cultural shift in such biased gender-based attitudes.

A mentee's perspective

From an early career academic perspective, it is important to strive for success and not be disheartened by previous stories of struggles and difficulties, thereby also learning to be a champion of women. Support groups such as HRM (mentioned above) are crucial for breaking down gender biases and providing females with the tools to work towards promotion, leadership, and management positions.

Our strategies below explicitly link to our visual narrative for self-care, and our discussion has unpacked each of the points below.

- Create opportunities and embrace mentorship and sponsorship
- Form formal, informal, and collaborative partnerships
- Find your emotional sounding board
- Combine resources to increase output and impact
- Catch up on a daily basis for coffee/walk/chat
- Find your voice
- Make time for family/friends/sport/hobbies. This is essential!
- Reflect on positive achievements and opportunities for self-improvement
- Remember to recognise and celebrate your victories
- Don't forget to be a champion of other women

We hope that some, or all, of our strategies work for you!

Conclusion

Resilience in academia is multi-faceted. Resilience evolves and develops as a direct interaction between the academic and their environment. Academics demonstrate their resilience in their willingness to make changes, work in creative ways and achieve positive outcomes despite, at times, insufficient resources. Furthermore, academics should be encouraged to access other types of support, in addition to institutional and governmental support, to sustain their resilience. For instance, professional and community networks go a long way to support academic resilience during times of adversity. The strategies discussed in this chapter provide practical ways to achieve and sustain resilience in academia.

Our views on cultivating resilience in academia stem from those of an experienced female researcher and educator and from two early career academics establishing themselves in the profession. While the dual lenses reveal unique perspectives on individual and collaborative strategies to overcome obstacles and difficulties, thereby developing and strengthening resilience, our strategies and advice for self-care are common. Importantly, the senior academic initially mentored the early career academics, which evolved into extremely fruitful partnerships and lifelong friendships.

References

Aarts, H., Elliot, A. J., & Ebooks, C. (2012). *Goal-directed behavior.* New York: Psychology Press.

Bahia, S., Freire, I. P., Estrela, M. T., Amaral, A., & Espírito Santo, J. A. (2017). The Bologna process and the search for excellence: Between rhetoric and reality, the emotional reactions of teachers. *Teaching in Higher Education, 22*(4), 467–482. doi:10.1080/13562517.2017.1303471

Behari-Leak, K. (2017). New academics, new higher education contexts: A critical perspective on professional development. *Teaching in Higher Education, 22*(5), 485–500. doi:10.1080/13562517.2016.1273215

Berkman, E. T. (2018). The neuroscience of goals and behavior change. *Consulting Psychology Journal: Practice and Research, 70*(1), 28–44. doi:10.1037/cpb0000094

Billett, S. (2003). Workplace mentors demands and benefits. *The Journal of Workplace Learning, 15*(3), 105–113. doi:10.1108/13665620310468441

Bobek, B. L. (2002). Teacher resiliency: A key to career longevity. *The Clearing House, 75*(4), 202–205. doi:10.1080/00098650209604932

Borucka, A., & Ostaszewski, K. (2008). Theory of resilience: Key conceptual constructs and chosen issues. *Medycyna Wieku Rozwojowego, 12*(2 Pt 1), 587–597.

Brunetti, G. (2006). Resilience under fire: Perspectives on the work of experienced, inner city high school teachers in the United States. *Teaching and Teacher Education, 22*, 812–825. doi:10.1016/j.tate.2006.04.027

Castro, A. J., Kelly, J., & Shih, M. (2010). Resilience strategies for new teachers in high-needs areas. *Teaching and Teacher Education, 26*(3), 622–629. doi:10.1016/j.tate.2009.09.010

Catalino, L. I., Algoe, S. B., & Fredrickson, B. L. (2014). Prioritizing positivity: An effective approach to pursuing happiness? *Emotion, 14*(6), 1155–1161. doi:10.1037/a0038029

Catalino, L. I., & Boulton, A. J. (2021). The psychometric properties of the prioritizing positivity scale. *Journal of Personality Assessment, 103*(5), 705–715. doi:10.1080/00223891.2020.1828433

Chan, H., Mazzucchelli, T. G., & Rees, C. S. (2021). The battle-hardened academic: An exploration of the resilience of university academics in the face of ongoing criticism and rejection of their research. *Higher Education Research & Development, 40*(3), 446–460. doi:10.1080/07294360.2020.1765743

Lancer, N., Clutterbuck, D., & Megginson, D. (2016). *Techniques for coaching and mentoring.* London: Routledge.

Day, C. (2008). Committed for life? Variations in teachers' work, lives and effectiveness. *Journal of Educational Change, 9*(3), 243–260. doi:10.1007/s10833-007-9054-6

Duckworth, A. L., Eichstaedt, J. C., & Ungar, L. H. (2015). The mechanics of human achievement. *Social and Personality Psychology Compass, 9*(7), 359–369. doi:10.1111/spc3.12178

Garcia-Dia, M. J., DiNapoli, J. M., Garcia-Ona, L., Jakubowski, R., & O'Flaherty, D. (2013). Concept analysis: Resilience. *Archives of Psychiatric Nursing, 27*(6), 264–270. doi:10.1016/j.apnu.2013.07.003

Gu, Q., & Day, C. (2013). Challenges to teacher resilience: Conditions count. *British Educational Research Journal, 39*(1), 22–44. doi:10.1080/01411926.2011.623152

Hoffman, A. J. (2016). Reflections: Academia's emerging crisis of relevance and the consequent role of the engaged scholar. *Journal of Change Management, 16*(2), 77–96. doi:10.1080/14697017.2015.1128168

Holdsworth, S., Turner, M., & Scott-Young, C. M. (2018). … Not drowning, waving. Resilience and university: A student perspective. *Studies in Higher Education, 43*(11), 1837–1853. doi:10.1080/03075079.2017.1284193

Horton-Deutsch, S., & Sherwood, G. (2008). Reflection: An educational strategy to develop emotionally-competent nurse leaders. *Journal of Nursing Management, 16*(8), 946–954. doi:10.1111/j.1365-2834.2008.00957.x

Howard, S., & Johnson, B. (2004). Resilient teachers: Resisting stress and burnout. *Social Psychology of Education, 7*(4), 399–420. doi:10.1007/s11218-004-0975-0

Jackson, D., Firtko, A., & Edenborough, M. (2007). Personal resilience as a strategy for surviving and thriving in the face of workplace adversity: A literature review. *Journal of Advanced Nursing, 60*(1), 1–9. doi:10.1111/j.1365-2648.2007.04412.x

Kumar Pradhan, R., & Kumar, U. (2020). *Emotion, well-being, and resilience: Theoretical perspectives and practical applications.* Milton: Apple Academic Press, Incorporated.

Lee, M., Coutts, R., Fielden, J., Hutchinson, M., Lakeman, R., Mathisen, B., ... Phillips, N. (2022). Occupational stress in University academics in Australia and New Zealand. *Journal of Higher Education Policy and Management, 44*(1), 57–71. doi:10.1080/1360080X. 2021.1934246

McEwen, K. (2011). *Building resilience at work*. Bowen Hills, Australia: Australian Academic Press.

Olson, S. A. (2022). *Creating wellbeing and building resilience in the veterinary profession: A call to life*. Milton: CRC Press.

Parkman, A. (2016). The imposter phenomenon in higher education: Incidence and impact. *Journal of Higher Education Theory & Practice, 16*(1), 51–60.

Ragins, B. R., & Kram, K. E. (2007). *The handbook of mentoring at work: Theory, research, and practice*. London: Sage Publications.

Ratcliffe, E., Baxter, W. L., & Martin, N. (2019). Consumption rituals relating to food and drink: A review and research agenda. *Appetite, 134*, 86–93. doi:10.1016/j.appet. 2018.12.021

Sammons, P., Day, C., Kington, A., Gu, Q., Stobart, G., & Smees, R. (2007). Exploring variations in teachers' work, lives and their effects on pupils: Key findings and implications from a longitudinal mixed-method study. *British Educational Research Journal, 33*(5), 681–701. doi:10.1080/01411920701582264

Tham, T. L., & Holland, P. (2018). What do business school academics want? Reflections from the national survey on workplace climate and well-being: Australia and New Zealand. *Journal of Management and Organization, 24*(4), 492–499. doi:10.1017/jmo.2018.3

Watts, J., & Robertson, N. (2011). Burnout in university teaching staff: A systematic literature review. *Educational Research, 53*(1), 33–50. doi:10.1080/00131881.2011.552235

Zábrodská, K., Mudrák, J., Šolcová, I., Květon, P., Blatný, M., & Machovcová, K. (2018). Burnout among university faculty: The central role of work–family conflict. *Educational Psychology, 38*(6), 800–819. doi:10.1080/01443410.2017.1340590

13 A great escape for my survival as a female academic in Japan

My story, my career trajectory

Akiko Nanami

When I look back …

Many already know that Japan is one of the most advanced nations in the world on various fronts, such as economy and technology. "Fenix" is the name given to Japan for its strong recovery from the ashes of its loss in World War Two. Although the fenix's neighboring states are catching up, and its strength is weakening gradually as time goes by, no one doubts that it is still one of the most advanced nations in the world. When it comes to academia, and especially women in academia, I suppose not many people, including the Japanese themselves, know what is really going on. Yes, the Japanese education system is well known for its neat organization, and yes, the Japanese government has been generous to international students by providing them with a series of good scholarships – but they are all superficial. The reality of Japanese academia is hidden well behind a closed curtain that not many are interested in opening. Those who are interested in opening or peeping through will see its strong, ever-changing, male-centred world in which women are not expected to pursue their academic career further, despite being "academics," as they could threaten men, or rather "men's jobs" or "men's positions." It is already the second decade of the 21st century but Japan still has the strong societal expectation that the male wins bread and honor while the female stays home and supports his going out. This has been applied to academia as well, and still is.

I was brave enough to enter this world of Japanese academia at the age of 22. With much hope, and probably overconfidence, from my international upbringings (I completed my education in New Zealand), I was sure that I could maneuver the tough waves, but in reality, I could not swim over to the goal and took shelter in my good old New Zealand home ground. But later, I made a comeback to Japanese academia, and I am still surviving all right. A good question arose from inside me: "How have I done that?" Well, to answer it, let's go back to my time as a postgraduate student when I started my academic career.

Postgraduate school time

In Japan, young people start their first jobs at the age of 22, and many domestic companies expect new recruits to be that age, no younger or older. That's the golden rule, and anyone who did not follow the age-set job hunting trail would

DOI: 10.4324/9781003341482-16

lose their golden ticket to start a good career. Japanese society is a so-called age-dominant society. Japanese people are expected to follow certain life events in accordance with their age. At 7, you will start your primary school, at 13, junior high school, at 16, high school, at 18, university, at 22, start a job – everything is decided by your age. By that I mean that people who decide to continue to study after university are going off of the beaten path of society and will be out of the mainstream for the rest of their lives unless they succeed in academia. Was I aware of the pressure I experienced at the age of 22? Certainly not. I was a naïve young student, who only wanted to study further and not think too much about my own future, not knowing what was waiting before me.

Joining the old boys' club – not

Soon after I was accepted into a master's course by a Japanese postgraduate school, one of the most prestigious ones in Japan, I was allocated to an old professor who already had three senior students. The professor did not supervise me much throughout my master's course, but he did these senior students. That was how the Japanese traditional postgraduate schools were back then. Therefore, having a good relationship with them was essential to my success in my master's course. The result was – I barely managed to obtain my master's degree but decided to leave the Japanese university as well as the country itself. I had had enough during my master's.

The three senior students – all males – had already formed an old boys' club long before my joining. I could tell that they did not welcome having female students join their comfortable club from the very start as they had grown up in Japan's traditional male-oriented culture and obviously perceived prestigious professor-ships as a strictly "male thing." A female student with an international background and strong language ability like myself was seen as a threat to their comfortable environment. Naturally, they ignored me or even bullied me so that I would leave their club and leave them alone.

As mentioned above, Japanese professors did not supervise their students at that time.[1] This was particularly so when they were old. Their main jobs were just to sit quietly while students made their research presentations and said something nasty or unconstructive after the presentation. Of course, not all professors were like that, and there were some who were very much hands-on with their students, but it seemed that professors in Japan saw their jobs as not supervising but breaking their students' confidence in research only to secure their positions by crushing young, rising researchers.

My supervisor professor did not try to supervise me in all two years of the course – in fact, he read my research paper only once, said, "That's not good enough," and did not give any advice for improvement then and throughout my entire master's course – so his three senior students were supposed to supervise my research. However, it did not happen. On the other hand, a totally different situation was prepared for the two male junior students who were allocated to the same professor after me. The three men supervised them well, by reading their papers in detail and giving advice, and even took them drinking, which I was never invited to. I tried to make contact with them many times, but each time my questions were replied with, "You can look it up in books at the library, and that's what you should do." Well, I felt that I was not included in their club at all, while the two younger students had no problems fitting in. In the first year of my master's at the Japanese university, I was already distancing myself from the club and the research. Looking back at how I felt at that time, I never thought that it was because I was female that they did not include me in the club, but instead because I was not good enough for them. I never thought that the academic world, which is supposed to value freedom and equality more than anything, had fallen into such machoism. Yes, I was young and naïve.

The situation did not improve in my second year, and I soon made up my mind to quit my studies at the end of my master's and not proceed to a doctorate under the same professor, which was essential to get a job in academia in the country. By this time, I had already lost my golden ticket to start a career at a good company, so I was not quite sure where I was heading.

If the lack of supervision by the senior students was the only problem, I could have endured and proceeded to my doctorate because I could study by myself and find a mentor elsewhere (although it was not officially approved, but I knew many students were treated badly by their professors who did this), but my situation worsened. Not only did they not supervise me, but the three senior students started bullying me. For example, one of the three men constantly made fun of my appearance in front of other people. He once said, "You won't be able to find a good husband for yourself because you are too fat. How much do you weigh now?" Totally unacceptable, but other people around him only laughed when I tried to retort. The other student said to me, "I cannot understand why women need a postgraduate study as they are all going to be *sengyoo syuhu* [a non-working full-time housewife] anyway. Their studies will be wasted." It is hard to believe that this man had also made a very similar sexist comment in a group interview for a study abroad programme selection process where he had two female competitors. But what was even harder to believe was that he was the one chosen for the programme. Some possible explanations for this strange selection could be given. Firstly, the selection board did not have a female member, and secondly, the student's father was a well-known politician in Japan.

The final blow that made me want to leave the school came when I learnt that they had no intention of communicating with me or even acknowledging my existence. One day after the research seminar at which all the students under the same professor gathered, I went to the three senior students to say good-bye. An international student was with me, and when the three students greeted us, they started talking in the language of the international student, which I did not understand. For the whole time, they kept talking in the language, and I was left out. The conversation kept on for 10–15 minutes, but I felt like it was forever, and it was then that I decided to leave the university, although I did not know what I would do after that.

Now, I could partly understand why it had happened. First of all, I was a young, female junior student that they looked down on in their male-oriented society.[2] And secondly, I behaved differently to their likings as a woman. In their view, probably I should have behaved more humbly and treated them "very well" as if they had a superior existence over women. Probably it had nothing to do with my research skills or personality, but I was a woman in academia, which wasn't tolerated in their club.

Healing my wounds

After the incident, I stopped trying to communicate with them, and went to the university when only absolutely necessary. I had no supervision or advice on my master's thesis at all, either from the professor or the senior students, but I did not care. I had written my thesis in accordance with the master's programme guidelines, and I knew they would not pay attention to what I wrote as I had already declared that I would leave. I would no longer be a threat to their boys' club, so I knew they would be happy to see me leaving; my thesis would pass regardless. In March 2001, I graduated from the postgraduate school and obtained my master's degree. But I had lost my confidence as a researcher, and also as a woman. The two years of my master's had caused so much damage to me that I needed to heal somewhere in a quiet environment.

"I cannot be here anymore." I wanted to distance myself from not only the nasty old boys' club but also from the country itself. Unconsciously, I was beginning to understand that Japan had a very different culture toward women, compared to New Zealand, where I grew up, and that made me uncomfortable. This feeling was pushing me to go and find a new world where I could feel safe and comfortable. Hence, I decided to go to England.

Although my experience at the Japanese postgraduate school was an unhappy one, I surprisingly did not lose my interest in studying. My family was worried about me when I left the school without any plans but supported my decision to go abroad. I was tempted to go back to New Zealand, but I wanted to challenge a new environment. I applied for some postgraduate schools in England, and one of them offered me a place with a scholarship. In September 2001, I moved to Lancaster, England.

As a matter of fact, I was in England for only four months before I moved to New Zealand. But those four months healed me. I started my second master's degree at Lancaster, where I met many local and international students, male and female. Although the studying was hard, as I did not study much in my first master's course, I enjoyed discussions with other students, who tried to treat each other with respect. Of course, it was not a perfect place, but I felt comfortable being in a mutually respectful environment. I met some great people, including a female lecturer who taught a course on Non-governmental Organisations (NGOs) who left a great impact on my academic career. Only then did I realise that the Japanese university had few female professors, and my research area had none. No wonder I was "different."

The English postgraduate school helped me regain my confidence. There, no one was making sexist comments toward me or being nasty. The course was made up of students of different ages, but no one was a senior or junior. We were all the same master's students and in an equal relationship, which was different from the

Japanese power structure defined by age. We were from different backgrounds of countries and races, so age did not matter.

Three months passed, and my wounds were healing day by day. I was regaining my confidence as a researcher and a woman. With my energy coming back, my motivation for research was rising. I was happy to study in the master's course in England, but my interest was leaning towards the Asia Pacific area, which was far from where I was. Although I was content, I decided to quit my second master's course halfway and go back to New Zealand.

The place where I was reborn

In April 2002, I went back to my good old hometown, Christchurch, New Zealand. The University of Canterbury had accepted me for a PhD course and later awarded me with a PhD scholarship, which helped me financially pursue my career.

The NZ university did not have a system of allocation like the Japanese one, but I did have two supervisors. Later, both were changed as one of them did not share my research interest and the other one went back to his home country at a very early stage of my thesis writing. Then, I met my new supervisor and my mentor, who helped me be reborn and grow as an academician with confidence. Honestly speaking, I was cautious at first, as I had had a terrible, or it might be accurate to say no, experience with "supervision," but he was totally different from my past one. He was quiet but very warm-hearted and gave me clear supervision. As soon as he found out that I did not have many research skills, he got some Kiwi research students to help me, who later became good friends of mine. Not only did he teach me how to research and write a thesis, but he also showed what kind of an academician I should become. Sadly, he passed away in 2019, but my experience with his supervision still guides me all the time.

It took me almost five years to complete my PhD and obtain my degree, but it was a fruitful and precious five years. Throughout the years, I have come to understand that the following three factors are needed for survival as a female academician. Apart from finding a good theme and growing research skills, we need to:

1. Find a good and respectful supervisor
    As I mentioned, I had two supervisors before, but as soon as I found they were not suitable for me, I changed them. To do so, one needs to be familiar with the given PhD guidelines (there was a section in my book called "how to change your supervisors in a nice way") and maneuver the system. By doing this at an early stage of my PhD course, I have grown my own research skills, such as problem finding, scoping, book researching, fieldwork, and taking action. These are all essential to thesis writing skill.
2. Hang around good research mates (friends)
    In Christchurch, I was given a research office in my department that I shared with work mates. They were not horrible to me like the ones in Japan, although most of them were my seniors, like the Japanese ones. What really mattered there was not age but personality. There were, of course, some

horrible students, but they faded away without much notice as they were not welcomed and could not join "the club." Well, this time I was welcomed to join "the club." I had three workmates throughout my PhD, and they all became my friends regardless of their age, gender, and race. There was no power structure among research students. We were all pursuing our own research projects and sharing the research space. No one was bullying anyone, which is the way it should be, but this was not the case where I was in Japan.

The university was like a man-made paradise, where people were treated equally. Having enjoyed the environment, I knew things were quite different outside the university. New Zealand is a good and peaceful country, which is why I immigrated there when I was young, but still there were race-related issues occurring from time to time. I wanted to focus on my PhD study, so I intentionally cut off my personal relationships outside the university, which turned out to be correct. After finishing the PhD, I had a plenty of time to hang around with people outside the university (both good and bad!).

3. Have a balanced life
    Although I sacrificed much of my life to my research during my PhD, I tried to have a good balance of life. But as mentioned above, I did not want to be disturbed much by outside distractions. I spent my non-research time with my old friends from my time at high school in Christchurch. That was a huge advantage, going back to my old hometown to pursue my academic career, where I did not have to meet new people that I would have had to put in extra effort to be friends with. My old friends had been my friends for a long time by then, so I could have a balanced life relatively easily by being with them.

    One mistake that I think I made during my PhD time regarding a balanced was that I fell in love with someone. That someone was not a good person to me, so I poured too much energy into the relationship, which turned out to be wasted. The relationship did not end well, but it also gave me a different type of energy (anger, some people may call it), which became a good driving force for my research. If that someone was a good person, I might have lost my passion for my research as I was too content with my non-research life. It may have been a good life too, but I am happy that my energy from an unhappy relationship has brought me this far in academia.

These three factors were what I found to make me successful in my PhD, and they are still very useful for my academic career in Japan. The next section is about my comeback to the Japanese academic world, from which I once left in bitterness, and my on-going survival.

Going back to the wild jungle – strategy for career trajectory

After obtaining my PhD, I got an academic job in New Zealand in April 2006. Although it was not what I had truly hoped for, it was a good start to my academic career. I was sad to say goodbye to my good, old Christchurch to start the new job, but I could still go back on some weekends. The school I worked for was not a well-structured institution, to be honest, but most of my workmates were great. I also found someone special who was not an academic but tried to understand my career and wanted to share our lives together. I was happy. After a happy three years, however, I was getting my fighting heart back. Well, I had left Japan in such a bad situation, and I did not have a chance to fight back, not only against the terrible environment, but also against myself, who had run away to a safer world. It was no mistake that I chose to run away back then, as I became happy after all, but I wanted to have an opportunity to fight again in Japan. At that time, I was given a job offer at a Japanese university. I thought the time had come for me; I thought I heard the fighting gong ring. I flew back to Japan in March 2009, saying goodbye to all that I loved so much, to a wild jungle.

At the time of writing this chapter, it is May 2021, so a good ten years have passed since I left New Zealand. The Japanese university did not change much, as it is still a male-oriented society, and women are still under the command of men most of the time. It appeared obvious at the time of national crisis (please see my paper, "[T]he rise and fall of women's voice in Japan after the Fukushima nuclear disaster," published in 2016) and other well-known events such as the male chair-person being kicked out of the Tokyo Olympic committee for his sexist remarks in 2020. No wonder the country was ranked 120th in the world in gender balance by the Global Gender Gap Report by the World Economic Forum (WEF) in 2021 and is still falling. As one of the few Japanese women who has obtained a full professorship at a Japanese university, I am fighting hard and still surviving, to my surprise. I thought that I would quickly be returning to Christchurch, as I did not think I would last. My male Japanese colleague even said to me at my welcoming party, "People with a strong international background like yourself would not last here long. They either go back to where they came from or take sick leaves and die eventually." Readers must understand that Japan has not changed much. But I am still surviving strongly. How am I doing that? Here are some tips:

1.   Make maximum use of the legal framework and go to external specialists
     Japan was, and still is, a sexist country and female academicians are not wel-
     comed, as we still seem to threaten men's security in good jobs like university
     professorships. There are a lot of sexual harassment cases that have been
     reported in the Japanese academic world, and I experienced a few harassment
     cases myself. What is different from my past experiences, however, is that
     there are strict laws prohibiting harassment, including sexism. They are called
     the "Guidelines Concerning Measures to be Taken by Employers in Terms of
     Employment Management with Regard to Problems Caused by Sexual
     Harassment in the Workplace," which passed the Japanese parliament in April
     2007. There was a similar guideline in 1999, but it was merely a guideline.
     But the 2007 version comes with punishments under the Power Harassment
     Prevention Law, which forces employers to try very hard to prohibit sexual
     harassment in the workplace. This enforcement came two years before I took
     up my job in Japan, so I had been familiar with the guidelines and used them
     when necessary.[3] That is a powerful support system. Of course, many work-
     places and people do not care about these laws, as they think they write the
     rulebooks and behave selfishly. A lot of workers tend to just endure when they

are harassed, as they are afraid of losing their jobs when they fight back. But the law is the law. In my case, when I felt that their behaviours crossed the line of sexual and academic harassment, I went to a private law firm straightaway to understand my rights. I tried to use the in-university legal framework in vain as they always sided with the employer (the university), and even tried to break confidentiality for the sake of their employers. After all, they do not bite the hands that feed them, and it was good that I learnt that quickly.

2. Do not be afraid of being disliked, as they are never your friends
    After taking the above action, of course I became disliked in the workplace as I was shaking things up. Again, I was not welcomed by "the old boys' club." This time, however, there were some people who sided with me, which did not happen when I was a student. In reality, a job is just a job, so people are content as long as they can make a living. Thus, I had some friends in the workplace who were not threatened by my actions (those who distanced themselves from harassers) and they are now often welcomed by the old boys' club. Therefore, I try to hang around with those who understand my policy and actions to secure my position in the workplace.[4] People who harass you will never be your friends, and they often dig their own grave. So, distance yourself from them and try to show a clear line between you and them by quietly expressing, "here is the line and if you cross it, I will take action against you." I would express this nicely, not aggressively.

3. Always have an exit strategy
    I am still surviving in the jungle of the Japanese academic world at the time of writing and often think of why I could do this. One thing that I can think of is that I always have somewhere to return to – my beloved town and people in New Zealand. I have such lovely memories of the place and people, so they remain my safe shelter even now. They may have become too good to be true in my mind, but it does not matter, as their existence itself is valuable to my survival. I can quit my job tomorrow and go back to Christchurch anytime (although I would have to quarantine as of 2021 due to Covid-19 problems). This thought helps me keep going every day, and it is widely reported that the number of young Japanese that are seeking to live and work abroad is increasing.[5]

    Having received great supervision in the past is also useful. As an academician, it is not a problem that my research is being criticised, but sometimes the criticism is personal and unproductive. On these occasions, I always remember my Kiwi supervisor and his words, which empower me to be objective towards unconstructive criticism. Therefore, having a successful experience is essential for one's own career survival, as these words are truly powerful.

Conclusion – my story

To this point, readers have followed my career trail and my own trajectory. This is no doubt an individual experience that doesn't entirely apply to everyone, if anyone, as everyone has had different experiences. There are some reasons I wanted to tell my own story. Firstly, I gathered survival tips from many aspects of my academic life and presented them to readers in the hopes that they could be of

Figure 13.1 A candid photo of the author, mid-lecture and surviving.

help. Secondly, I wanted to prove to myself that I did survive. Going through the early stages of my academic career was not easy – they bring painful memories – but by writing this chapter, I understood that they were growing pains. It was a healing process for me. Lastly, I wanted to tell the readers from the bottom of my heart that it is totally okay to take a detour at some point in their lives. When you are so focused on your own career, sometimes you do not stop as if you were lost on the trail. Then it is time to take a short break and do something different – meeting new people in a new world. At least, it worked well for me and brought me back to where I started – or even further. I was once lost in my academic career and went off the trail. But I found my way back and am still surviving in the same world thanks to my big detour (see Figure 13.1).

Notes

1 Chikada, "Daigakuin no kenkyuu shido hoohoo ni kansuru kadai to kaizensaku" (A study on various problems and ways to improve on supervisions at postgraduate level in Japan), Nagoya University Press, 2009.
2 Japan has been a traditionally male-oriented society, although it is a member of the G7 summit, which is supposed to be a group of "advanced" states. This social phenomenon has always been one of many social issues and is described in detail in the followings; Katada, *Danson-Jyohi to iu yamai (A social disease called male-prioritized society)*, Gentoo sya, 2015; Minamoto, "Male chauvinism: The male-dominated society in modern Japan," the Institute of Human Rights Kansai University, 2015, to name a few.
3 Yamauchi and Kusu, *Daigaku ni okeru harasumento taioo gaidobukku (A guide to deal with harassment at universities)*, Fukumura Shuppan, 2020.
4 Kishi and Koga, *Kirawareru Yuuki (Braveness to be disliked by others)*, Diamond Press, 2013.
5 S. Kaneto, "Another phase of multiculturalization in modern Japan as seen from the cross-bordering lifestyles of Japanese," Tokyo University of Foreign Studies, 2009.

References

Junko, Minamoto (2015). Male chauvinism: The male-dominated society in modern Japan. *The Institute of Human Rights Kansai University*, 70, 1–48.
Kishi and Koga (2013). *Kirawareru Yuuki (Braveness to be disliked by others)*. Diamond Press.

Masahiro, Chikada (2009). Daigakuin no kenkyuu shido hoohoo ni kansuru kadai to kaizensaku (A study on various problems and ways to improve on supervisions at post-graduate level in Japan). *Nagoya Kotoo Kyooiku Kenkyuu*, 9, 93–111.

Mizuho, Suzuki (2019). *Genba de Yakudatsu! Harasumento wo yurusanai genba ryoku to soshiki ryoku (Useful for actual cases! Organisational capabilities not to let harassment to occur)*. Nihon Keizai Shimbun.

Sachiko, Kaneto (2009). Another phase of multiculturalization in modern Japan as seen from the cross-bordering lifestyles of Japanese. *Tagengo Tabunka – Jissen to Kenkyuu*, 2, 138–165.

Shinzansya Edition Team (2020). *Pawahara boushi hou (Power Harassment Prevention Law)*. Shinzansya.

Tamami, Katada (2015). *Danson-Jyohi to iu yamai (A social disease called male-prioritized society)*. Gentoo sya.

Yamauchi and Kusu (2020). *Daigaku ni okeru harasumento taioo gaidobukku (A guide to deal with harassment at universities)*. Fukumura Shuppan.

14 Uncensored? Writing our resistance as an act of self-care

Michaela Edwards, Louise Oldridge, and Maranda Ridgway

We write as three permanently employed women academics working in a UK business school, at a university established in 1992, where teaching excellence is a primary focus. Research time is applied for and awarded based on publication records and grant capture. In the UK, research outputs in business schools are typically measured against the CABS (Chartered Association of Business Schools) list, which ranks journals from 1 to 4★ with 4★ journals recognised as world leading. This classification informs where you can publish and which publications will be considered valuable and legitimate, leading to pressure to go "above and beyond" to secure the time needed to conduct research.

Often UK universities demonstrate commitment to combating gender inequality via the Athena Swan Award, a framework that awards institutions based on how they manage gender equality. Initiatives like the Athena Swan Award have been critiqued for failing to address intersectionality and attempting to "fix the woman" (Acker, 1990; Ely & Meyerson, 2000; Liff & Cameron, 1997), as well as a "lack of engagement with the structural issues within which gender inequality is rooted" (Tzanakou & Pearce, 2019, 1194). Such initiatives rely on women's work, adversely impacting careers and mental health (Bird et al., 2004; Heijstra et al., 2017; Tzanakou & Pearce, 2019). Academics suffer exclusion and hindered career progression through biased recruitment practices (Husu, 2004; Van den Brink et al., 2010). Although academia is advertised as a neutral space, it produces a "smokescreen of equality" (Bourabain 2021; Dar, Liu, Matinez Dy & Brewis 2021).

In this chapter, firstly, we consider our position within a neoliberal Academy that discourages the writing of emotion into work, outlining how we follow our colleagues in "writing differently" and how this supports a pattern of self-care that we have held since childhood of writing to resist, to be heard, and to emote. Secondly, in writing our frustration and anger in the space of collective support and safety using a "faction" vignette, we hope to create spaces for others to do similar work by contributing to the gradual acceptance of such work in academic spaces. In doing this, we try to engage in a feminist care ethics that seeks to support others in their search for self-care through discussing our strategies as routes forward. In the discussion, we draw on images created as acts of self-care that seek to resist the censorship to which we frequently feel subjected. Finally, we close the chapter with recommendations for self-care, reflecting on our experiences.

DOI: 10.4324/9781003341482-17

Literature

Systemic inequalities are embedded in standards of excellence (van den Brink & Benschop, 2012) and other common bureaucracies of academia (Krishen et al., 2020; Madera et al., 2019), whilst discursive practices of masculinity normalise a single vision of meritocratic achievement (Knights & Richards, 2003). The category of "interloper" in university spaces (Johansson & Jones, 2019) then comes to be occupied by women of diverse backgrounds. This problem is potent in UK management/business schools, where the white, cis-male, single, childless, care-free middle-class patriarch dominates. As Aiston and Kent Fo (2021, 138) highlighted, "The academy is positioned as a 'care-free workplace' that assumes that academics have no other commitments than the devotion of their time to the profession" (Morley, 2007; Morley, 2013). The concept of "fairness" and a belief in the meritocratic academy fails to acknowledge the gendered nature of family life (Nikunen, 2012) and the gender stereotyping that occurs at work (Nikunen, 2012; Aiston & Fo, 2021; Aiston & Jung, 2015; Barrett & Barrett, 2011; Leberman et al., 2016; Kjeldal et al., 2005; Schein, 2007; Morley 2007; Ropers-Huilman 2000; Turner, 2002). Gatekeeping in selection processes and resource allocation hinders women's advancement (Husu, 2004; Van den Brink et al., 2010) and confinement to the "ivory basement" (Fitzgerald, 2012) results in women being allocated underappreciated work in copious quantities.

Pullen and Rhodes (2018) note that control strategies of neoliberal organisations have increased anxiety, leaving employees feeling responsible for issues that they cannot control. Petriglieri et al. (2019) also highlight the exploitation of employees' existential dread. We know that organisations often constrain personal identities whilst providing idealised identities for employees to strive towards (Ashforth et al., 2008). Compounding these difficulties, subtle and everyday micro- and macro-structures of discriminatory practice result in the disempowerment of early career scholars and contribute to a regime of inequality (Acker, 2009) in academia. Often careers that employ a historic apprenticeship model link advancement with the exercise of power or privilege. In academia, gatekeeping typically occurs early on, affecting the development of PhD candidates and post-doctoral scholars. Trevino et al. (2018) have also highlighted challenges at every stage of management scholars' career development (Treviño et al., 2018; van Miegroet et al., 2019). Boncori and Smith (2019) have further lamented the frequent rejection of papers felt to be too personal, and Bourabain's (2021) work illuminated many exclusionary practices. Racism and sexism are often subtle and ambiguous (Bourabain, 2021), they are difficult to speak confidently of, and speaking up is often dangerous (Milliken et al., 2015).

Writing as resistance

Here, we draw from scholarly work on activism in academia (including Suzuki & Mayorga, 2014; Boncori & Smith, 2019; Johansson & Jones, 2019; Dar et al., 2021; Pullen et al., 2020; Liu, 2021; Mackay, 2021). Our ongoing uncensored writing builds on existing knowledge working towards the liberation of those who are marginalised. Recognising injustice and writing together offers a means to sustain our academic sisterhood. This responds to Liu's (2021) framework for scholar-activism, which calls for resistance and the creation of liberatory knowledge and rest, where self-care is an act of warfare. We try to open up spaces in which writing differently can become accepted. In doing this, we nurture our connections and seek to assist in developing opportunities for others to further address the intersections between racism and sexism through self-care practices. Although we do not write about racism here as it does not pertain to our specific experiences, we nevertheless seek to open up spaces for others to decolonise the mind and the land (Liu; 2021).

Collectively and historically, our writing has taken different forms. For example, in the Academy, we engage in scholarship, which challenges and recognises injustices. Still, we continue to write in diverse ways beyond academia, engaging in self-care whilst acknowledging our love of writing. This self-care includes, for example, creative writing and calligraphy.

Whilst we seek to write to create liberatory knowledge (Liu, 2021), we also acknowledge our privilege in being given a voice, where so many have not, and recognise that publications such as this also act as an opportunity to "progress" within a neoliberal academy. Furthermore, although we identify as women, we occupy multiple positionalities and "each carr[ies] various racial, class, and cultural privileges, as well as institutional power" (Tilley & Taylor, 2014:59).

How we enact self-care

Increasingly, academics "write differently," pushing the boundaries of academic writing, infusing it with emotion, embodiment, and affect (Boncori & Smith, 2019; Johansson & Jones, 2019; Pullen et al., 2020). Anger is often a feature, alongside sadness, frustration, and even joy and hope. "Writing differently" allows for expressing feelings in a forum not usually accepting of such emoting, alongside challenging and resisting academic writing conventions. Here we follow a path laid by our brave colleagues who dared to go first. We highlight how we may write into existence new norms and academic conventions (Bayfield et al., 2020) that allow more significant space for other academics to tell their truths in appropriate ways and, importantly, for our careers and others to receive credit for this.

Critiquing the neoliberal promotion of individual responsibility, Gaudet et al. (2022:10) make an essential distinction between self-care and self-help. They note that "self-care identifies the relationship to oneself in the context of a conception of what it means to be human based on interdependence rather than individual independence." Bayfield et al. (2020:421) discuss efforts in "slow scholarship" such as collaborative "innovative scholarship and writing, or unconventional approaches to self-care," helping craft new norms in academia. Indeed, many academics writing in this vein are increasingly drawing on feminist care ethics to enact political practice (Bayfield et al., 2020; Johansson & Edwards, 2021). This relies on "persons as relational and interdependent, morally and epistemologically," rather than independent, self-sufficient actors (Held, 2006:13). Noddings (2003:3) believed caring relations to be "ethically basic." Feminist authors have described care as "a species activity that includes everything that we do to maintain, continue, and repair our 'world' so that we can live in it as well as possible" (Fisher & Tronto, 1990:40).

Feminist care ethics has been considered to contribute to the literature on identity work within organisations (Islam 2013) and to the role of holding/facilitative environments (Petriglieri et al., 2019). Askins and Blazek (2017) critique the individualised and managerialised nature of the Academy "(and beyond)." Their commitment to more caring academia encourages us to explore how we support each other to enact caring practices in our writing and, in doing so, open spaces into which others can write and resist. We wish to diverge from visions of self-care that place the burden of responsibility on individuals, seeking instead to weaponise our individual self-care practices through collective resistance. As Bayfield et al. (2020:421) note, "instead of each individual caring for their wellbeing, we might extend care to others, so it becomes a political act of resistance."

Methodology

Rather than using traditional research questions, we challenge the dichotomy of academic freedom and conformity by drawing upon a reflexive dialogue between the authors. We identify several questions or prompts. For example: Why do I write? How do I conform? How do I resist? How is writing self-care? encouraging each author to prepare an uncensored piece of reflexive free writing. In this way, writing became a discovery method and a creative and analytical process (Richardson, 2000; Castle, 2017).

We were guided by a collaborative feminist reflexive approach (Linabary, Corple & Cooky, 2021). We reviewed each other's writing, discussed, and took notes to extend our accounts, surfacing our similarities and differences. In doing so, we interrogated our challenges and frustrations as women academics. The collaborative approach allowed us to discuss issues and build on each other's ideas while viewing our own experiences in diverse ways (Esposito & Evans-Winters, 2021). Additionally, this approach to reflexivity provided the opportunity for emotion to surface and otherwise hidden intersubjectivities and injustices to become visible.

Extending our accounts, we developed a single vignette into which our three stories and perspectives are interwoven into a single narrative. We accept and acknowledge that detail is lost in this interweaving, but what remains is what unites us and matters most to us. This single narrative is a "faction"; it is both fact and fiction (Bruce, 2019). The fact element is resonant of the vignette emerging from our lived experiences. Yet, it is fictitious in that we present a single vignette that is not the verbatim quotes of any individual author. The vignette was a valuable tool to depict complex issues realistically and engagingly (Leicher & Mulder, 2018).

The use of a faction-based vignette follows Bruce's (2019:2) statement that "academics have not only the right but the responsibility to represent research in multiple formats." Our vignette seeks not to censor our voices, but to protect the authors from individual scrutiny. Denison (2006:338) has also suggested that "we must feel free to write in ways that combine and synthesise a range of voices." To be valid, a faction must emerge from research gathered in "ethical and methodologically rigorous ways" (Bruce, 2019:5). Further, it should be satisfying to read and artistically constructed (Denison & Rinehart, 2000). Faction gives voice to women and othered groups. However, in line with O'Shea's (2019) work, we challenge the idea that writing needs to be "artistically constructed" and instead seek to reflect our complex travels through academia and the ways we resist and employ self-care.

We adopted a two-phase approach to achieve face validity (Leicher and Mulder, 2018). Firstly, the third author compiled a single vignette based on the written accounts and notes taken during a collective discussion by all three authors. Secondly, the first and second authors reviewed the vignette and made amendments to represent each author's experiences and perspectives.

Faction enables us to achieve a degree of anonymity while still allowing our voices to be heard and stories shared. Thus, we are uncensored in articulating ideas and experiences that may feel uncomfortable if expressed individually. This chapter embodies our argument of writing as resistance. We use the medium of writing to express our frustrations while simultaneously using faction as a methodological shield against victimisation. Hooks (1990:126) noted that when we are not permitted to speak, we each become an "absent presence without a voice." Thus, writing can be a form of activism in creating and developing liberatory knowledge (Liu, 2021).

Additionally, we give ourselves an outlet for our understandable anger in choosing a faction. This chapter is a way of engaging in self-care practices. Hooks argued that when we are not permitted to speak, we each become an "absent presence without a voice" (1990:126). "Faction" allows us to give ourselves a voice in such circumstances.

In engaging in faction, we recognise the limitation of erasing specific narratives of marginalised identities and our differences, such as disabilities. Still, we suggest that creating a factional story allows us to "say what might be unsayable in other circumstances" (Richardson, 1994:521). We speak here of what we share, not to homogenise our differences. Instead, we strive to discuss what unites us and, in doing so, further embody our resistance.

Discussion

Our discussion is based on the single faction vignette described in the previous section. This vignette presents our lived experiences as women academics using writing as self-care and resistance. We are uncensored.

Vignette

I have always written to express myself and the injustices I see and feel, whether they affect me directly or others around me. I write to make my world real. Writing allows me to voice my opinions, frustrations and anger whilst simultaneously playing the part I am expected to play. I have been, and remain, angry. Writing is my voice.

Before I entered this world, I put academia on a pedestal, raised high above the corruptions of industry where there is never enough time to think. I saw academia as the pinnacle of ethical behaviour, progressive thought, and inclusivity. This job provides an opportunity where my knowledge is valued. When I started working in academia, focussing on researching and teaching, I felt like I had found my calling and could make a difference; I could "fix" the challenges in my life.

I want to change the system. I want equality, diversity, and inclusion within the academy. I want it to move from its current masculine hegemonic state to accepting and encouraging subjective feelings, emotions, and embodiment. I don't want to feel that I am losing out because I don't conform to a quantitative and positivistic view of the world; I want the craft of my scholarship to be recognised, valued, celebrated, and make a difference.

Writing allows me to navigate spaces where I must conform. Spaces where I must meet standards I do not set. Spaces where I must play by others' rules if I want to progress, if I want to succeed, and even survive. I conform because I must. I don't make a fuss. I do what I am told and deliver my objectives. I play the game. But I also conform by stealth. I conform by omission, by not fully revealing what I think. I play dumb. I don't always object to the system. I don't always innovate. I rarely do. I realise that I frequently do not teach what I feel matters most in my complicity. Instead, I nod and smile and play dumb. I push my anger down, go home, and let it rise in a safe space.

I find ways to resist and write about what is important to me, fitting the institutional agenda. I focus my research and writing to seek greater understanding, recognition, rights, and social justice. This act is my resistance; writing is my power. I resist through the strength of the academic sisterhood. We share these injustices, write together, and resist together.

When I write, I don't have to think about anyone else, worry about domestic chores, or care for others and the other "noise" in my life. Although it is my job, writing is also my escape where I can be alone with my thoughts and express them how I want. Writing reflects my passions and those things about which I care. In doing so, I am caring for myself. I am giving myself space to express, feel legitimate, and feel important. Writing is my therapy. It is a cathartic act. It is a reminder that I have a voice that might be heard, which deserves to be heard as much as any other voice. A voice that has the privilege of position to speak in support of creating new spaces into which a greater diversity of voices can begin to be heard.

Yet, I am angry that I am not good enough to "the institution, which I have internalised into self-perpetuating impostor syndrome. I am also angry that I am so privileged in many ways while so many are disadvantaged. Do I deserve to be angry? I want to fight for those without my privilege, but is writing a way I can do that?

Uncensored. Is it a step too far? I have many types of writing. Firstly, it is an authentic expression of exactly how I feel at times, unguarded, dangerous. It's in my journal and my creative writing; it appears on my pumpkins. Secondly, I submit writing for the consideration of friends and close colleagues, tamed, respectable, but firm in its argumentation. Thirdly, there is the writing the academic community sees published, often censored, deformed, and bearing witness to the loss of my spirit.

In writing this piece, we make a rare move in submitting our collective pain and anger for review. I want to experience academic freedom to do, say, and write what I wish to, to illuminate the disadvantages women face in the Academy, yet I am taking risks, and putting my head above the parapet. To be genuinely uncensored feels dangerous. I fear contempt and retribution. But to be brave, to make a difference, we must first feel afraid.

Progress feels slow, the steps are small, but I will continue to persist and, in doing so, resist. We are interdependent. In writing, I draw on experiences with colleagues and friends, frustrations borne of their experiences, as well as my own. I don't think this is about what I can do but about what we do together.

Drawing on feminist care ethics, our chosen methodology enables us to support each other in our reflexive, resistant practice. Firstly, we consider how our vignette seeks to maintain individual silence and raise our collective voice. Secondly, we consider the practice of literally "writing our resistance" and how we hope this type of practice can open up spaces for other voices to be heard and acknowledged.

Maintaining individual silence about work problems feels safer than voicing them to many employees, particularly where discussing these issues is viewed as criticising management (Detert & Edmondson, 2011). As our vignette highlights, we have experienced a feeling of being censored despite our continued commitment to the act of writing itself and our feelings of freedom in writing. The act of being uncensored is indeed dangerous, as many scholars have noted (Liu, 2021; Rodriguez, 2011), but of equal importance is the negative effect that not speaking up may have on us. Writing allows us to navigate spaces in which we must conform. Morrison and Milliken (2000) discussed the distressing experience of cognitive dissonance when those who feel that they have something vital to communicate think that they must not speak up. Our piece of faction notes the absences in our voice and our moments of silence in public that speak not to acquiescence but resistance. In our silences and through our voices in continuing to write our truths in other spaces, we maintain our places in the Academy and decline to help or provide our labour to solve problems we have not made.

Our vignette reveals informal writing practices occurring within safe critical spaces (Duckworth et al., 2016) shared by colleagues with similar experiences. By sharing our frustrations and anger, we also share coping strategies. We identify commonalities and practices that allow us to navigate and challenge gender inequalities within the Academy to enjoy "some" academic freedom while simultaneously conforming to management expectations and "playing the game." Thus, while our act of academic writing can be used as a cathartic practice for the productive expression of anger and the claiming of career-based rewards, it also seeks to disrupt the managerial and neoliberal Academy. In so doing, while we recognise our privilege and are rewarded for our non-conformist writing, we also use this chapter to extend liberatory knowledge. We seek to advance a feminist care ethic to colleagues through highlighting our experiences and practices to encourage the academic sisterhood to engage with different forms of writing. We offer our ways of navigating academia, a system that prioritises objective career success and

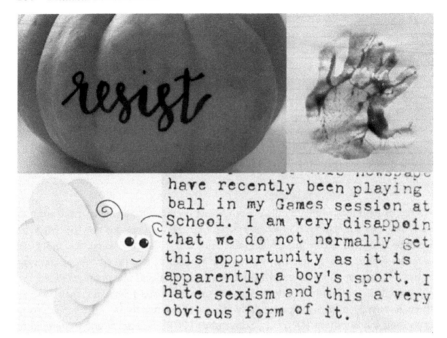

resist

have recently been playing
ball in my Games session at
School. I am very disappoin
that we do not normally get
this oppurtunity as it is
apparently a boy's sport. I
hate sexism and this a very
obvious form of it.

Figure 14.1 From top to bottom, left to right: (a) Output from autumnal lettering workshop October 2021. (b) Child's handprint on a notebook. (c) Picture accompanying creative writing of children's story (which also addresses diversity at an
age-appropriate level). (d) Extract from a family newspaper written aged 12.

conforming career trajectories, as a "political act of resistance" (Bayfield et al.,
2020:421).

Figure 14.1(a–d) shows how our creative work helps us vent our private frustrations, bearing witness to the difficulties we face and acting as another outlet to
highlight and address social justice issues. During a clear-out, one of our mothers
came across a collection of "Family Times," the newspaper we at age 12 had written and distributed among our family. This is one of our first outlets in written
form to highlight the marginalisation faced as a girl at school when wanting to play
football. The butterfly accompanies a children's story, which we are putting into
written form that, whilst entertaining and a creative form of self-care, also seeks to
educate children on difference and inclusion. Indeed, our writing also provides a
therapeutic space away from our responsibilities. We offer output from an online
lettering weekend class in October 2021, written on a pumpkin. Calligraphy is
both writing and art. Organising a weekend course as a self-care act removed us
from teaching, preparing material, and academic writing.

Although this chapter is not an ABS ranked journal, we are passionate about the
topic and have written it around other responsibilities. This reality has been
uniquely highlighted in a child's handprint on our notes as we worked on a draft
at home. It represents the difficulties many women academics face in negotiating
work whilst managing unacknowledged familial responsibilities.

Strategies

In writing this chapter, we have introduced three strategies that we employ. We offer these in the hope that others will benefit.

Firstly, the importance that writing holds – writing is a requirement of our vocation and something that we do for fun and have done for many years. Creative work and writing for fun provide an outlet for our frustrations. Writing, in this sense, is a therapeutic act; it provides a safe space away from our daily responsibilities to express our creativity freely. Writing need not be formalised; the artistic presentation of one word, that is, calligraphy, or storytelling for different audiences, that is, children's books are valuable ways of enacting self-care.

Secondly, in our role as researchers, we call on the sisterhood to embrace methodologies that allow us to support each other in our reflexive and resistant practices in scholarly activism. The call for chapters is an example of one such opportunity to have our voices heard in diverse ways. Collaboration enables us to choose whom we work with, and unique contributions allow us to engage with exciting methodologies that encourage different forms of expression.

Thirdly, we pass on the torch by challenging writing conventions within our field. We use forms of writing and visual expression that we usually keep outside of the academy to write differently and seek institutional credit. We will continue to seek opportunities to write differently and encourage others to do the same. In doing so, we present our lived experiences as women academics as a form of self-care and resistance, contributing to our scholarly activism and, in writing, contributing slowly to a much-needed shift in what constitutes good academic writing.

These strategies amalgamate our friendship in the sending of a greeting card from one to another, with the message "a beautiful thing is never perfect" in calligraphy. This symbolises our collective sisterhood in encouraging each other in the wake of the neoliberal academy and its objective way of measuring success, driving impostor syndrome among us.

Conclusion

In this chapter, we sought to achieve two things. Firstly, we explored our positions within the neoliberal Academy to challenge the discouragement of emotional writing. In doing so, we embraced the notion of "writing differently" as a self-care strategy. Second, while writing as a form of expression is not new, it challenges conventions in the context of academic writing. Thus, we build on our experiences since childhood to mobilise our informal and formal writing as a means of resistance, express our collective voice, and introduce emotion into an otherwise sterile environment.

Secondly, we continue the creation of safe spaces in which the articulation of frustration and anger is encouraged. We employ one such space as a "faction" vignette. This collaborative effort simultaneously enabled our collective voices to be heard whilst protecting our anonymity. It also allowed us to engage in a feminist care ethic in which we sought to support each other and encourage others in their search for self-care.

References

Acker, J. (1990). Jobs, hierarchies, and sexuality: Some further thoughts on gender and organizations. *Gender & Society*, *4*, 139–158. https://doi.org/10.1177/089124390004002002

Acker, J. (2009). From glass ceiling to inequality regimes. *Sociologie du travail*, *51*(2), 199–217. https://doi.org/10.1016/j.soctra.2009.03.004

Aiston, S. J., & Fo, C. K. (2021). The silence/ing of academic women. *Gender and Education*, *33*(2), 138–155. https://doi.org/10.1080/09540253.2020.1716955

Aiston, S. J., & Jung, J. (2015). Women academics and research productivity: An international comparison. *Gender and Education*, *27*(3), 205–220. https://doi.org/10.1080/09540253.2015.1024617

Ashforth, B. E., Harrison, S. H., & Corley, K. G. (2008). Identification in organizations: An examination of four fundamental questions. *Journal of Management*, *34*(3), 325–374. https://doi.org/10.1177/0149206308316059

Askins, K., & Blazek, M. (2017). Feeling our way: Academia, emotions and a politics of care. *Social & Cultural Geography*, *18*(8), 1086–1105. https://doi.org/10.1080/14649365.2016.1240224

Barrett, L., & Barrett, P. (2011). Women and academic workloads: Career slow lane or cul-de-sac? *Higher Education*, *61*(2), 141–155. https://doi.org/10.1007/s10734-010-9329-3

Bayfield, H., Colebrooke, L., Pitt, H., Pugh, R., & Stutter, N. (2020). Awesome women and bad feminists: The role of online social networks and peer support for feminist practice in academia. *Cultural Geographies*, *27*(3), pp. 415–435.

Bird, S., Litt, J., & Wang, Y. (2004). Creating status of women reports: Institutional housekeeping as "Women's Work." *NWSA Journal*, *16*(1), 194–206. https://doi.org/10.2979/nws.2004.16.1.194

Boncori, I., & Smith, C. (2019). I lost my baby today: Embodied writing and learning in organizations. *Management Learning*, *50*(1), 74–86. https://doi.org/10.1177/1350507618784555

Bourabain, D. (2021). Everyday sexism and racism in the ivory tower: The experiences of early career researchers on the intersection of gender and ethnicity in the academic workplace. *Gender, Work & Organization*, *28*(1), 248–267. https://doi.org/10.1111/gwao.12549

Bruce, T. (2019). The case for faction as a potent method for integrating fact and fiction in research. In S. Farquhar & E. Fitzpatrick (Eds.), *Innovations in narrative and metaphor*. (pp 57–72). Singapore: Springer.

Castle, J. (2017). Benefits of freewriting for academic staff engaged in a writing retreat. *South African Journal of Higher Education*, 31(2), 124–137.

Dar, S., Liu, H., Martinez Dy, A., & Brewis, D. N. (2021). The business school is racist: Act up!. *Organization*, *28*(4), 695–706.

Denison, J. (2006). The way we ran: Reimagining research and the self. *Journal of Sport and Social Issues*, *30*(4), 333–339. https://doi.org/10.1177/0193723506292962

Denison, J., & Rinehart, R. (2000). Introduction: Imagining sociological narratives. *Sociology of Sport Journal*, *17*(1), 1–4.

Detert, J. R., & Edmondson, A. C. (2011). Implicit Voice Theories: Taken-for-granted rules of self-censorship at work. *Academy of Management Journal*, *54*(3), 461–488. https://doi.org/10.5465/amj.2011.61967925

Duckworth, V., Lord, J., Dunne L., Atkins, L., & Watmore, S. (2016). Creating feminised critical spaces and co-caring communities of practice outside patriarchal managerial landscapes. *Gender and Education*, *28*(7), 903–917. https://doi.org/10.1080/09540253.2015.1123228

Ely, R. J., & Meyerson, D. E. (2000). Theories of gender in organizations: A new approach to organizational analysis and change. *Research in Organizational Behavior, 22,* 103–151. https://doi.org/10.1016/S0191-3085(00)22004-2

Esposito, J. & Evans-Winters, J. (2021). *Introduction to intersectional qualitative research.* London: SAGE Publications Ltd.

Fisher, B., & Tronto, J. (1990). Toward a feminist theory of caring. In E. K. Abel & M. K. Nelson (Eds.), *Circles of care: Work and identity in women's lives* (pp. 36–54). New York: State University of New York Press.

Fitzgerald, T. (2012). Ivory basements and ivory towers. In T. Fitzgerald, J. White, & H. M. Gunter, *Hard labour? Academic work and the changing landscape of higher education* (pp. 113–135).Emerald: Bingley.

Gaudet, S., Marchand, I., Bujaki, M., & Bourgeault, I. L. (2022). Women and gender equity in academia through the conceptual lens of care. *Journal of Gender Studies, 31*(1), 74–86.

Heijstra, T. M., Steinthorsdóttir, F. S., & Einarsdóttir, T. (2017). Academic career making and the double-edged role of academic housework. *Gender and Education, 29*(6), 764–780. https://doi.org/10.1080/09540253.2016.1171825

Held, V. (2006). *The ethics of care: Personal, political, and global.* Oxford: Oxford University Press. https://doi.org/10.1093/0195180992.001.0001

Hooks, B. (1990). *Yearning: Race, gender, and cultural politics.* Boston, MA: South End Press

Husu, L. (2004). Gate-keeping, gender equality and scientific excellence. In D. Al-Khudhairy, N. Dewandre, & H. Wallace, *Gender and excellence in the making* (pp. 69–76). Brussels: European Commission.

Islam, G. (2013). Recognizing employees: Reification, dignity and promoting care in management. *Cross Cultural Management, 20*(2), 235–250. https://doi.org/10.1108/13527601311313490

Johansson, J., & Edwards, M. (2021). Exploring caring leadership through a feminist ethic of care: The case of a sporty CEO. *Leadership, 17*(3), 318–335. ISSN 1742-7150

Johansson, M., & Jones, S. (2019). Interlopers in class: A duoethnography of working-class women academics. *Gender, Work & Organization, 26*(11), 1527–1545. https://doi.org/10.1111/gwao.12398

Kjeldal, S. E., Rindfleish, J., & Sheridan, A. (2005). Deal-making and rule-breaking: Behind the façade of equity in academia. *Gender and Education, 17*(4), 431–447. https://doi.org/10.1080/09540250500145130

Knights, D., & Richards, W. (2003). Sex discrimination in UK academia. *Gender, Work & Organization, 10*(2), 213–238. https://doi.org/10.1111/1468-0432.t01-1-00012

Krishen, A. S., Lee, M. T., & Raschke, R. L. (2020). The story only few can tell: Exploring the disproportionately gendered professoriate in business schools. *Journal of Marketing Education, 42*(1), 7–22. https://doi.org/10.1177/0273475319879972

Leberman, S. I., Eames, B., & Barnett, S. (2016). Unless you are collaborating with a big name successful professor, you are unlikely to receive funding. *Gender and Education, 28*(5), 644–661. https://doi.org/10.1080/09540253.2015.1093102

Leicher, V., & Mulder, R. H. (2018). Development of vignettes for learning and professional development. *Gerontology & Geriatrics Education, 39*(4), 464–480.

Liff, S., & Cameron, I. (1997). Changing equality cultures to move beyond "women's problems." *Gender, Work & Organization, 4*(1), 35–46. https://doi.org/10.1111/1468-0432.00022

Linabary, J. R., Corple, D. J., & Cooky, C. (2021). Of wine and whiteboards: Enacting feminist reflexivity in collaborative research. *Qualitative Research, 21*(5), 719–735. doi:10.1177/1468794120946988

Liu, H. (2021). *Workshop: Publishing Scholar – Activism, 28 May 2021*. Retrieved from https://disorient.co/publishing-workshop/

Mackay, F. (2021). Dilemmas of an academic feminist as manager in the neoliberal academy: Negotiating institutional authority, oppositional knowledge and change. *Political Studies Review, 19*(1), 75–95.

Madera, J. M., Hebl, M. R., Dial, H., Martin, R., & Valian, V. (2019). Raising doubt in letters of recommendation for academia: Gender differences and their impact. *Journal of Business and Psychology, 34*(3), 287–303. https://doi.org/10.1007/s10869-018-9541-1

Milliken, F. J., Schipani, C. A., Bishara, N. D., & Prado, A. M. (2015). Linking workplace practices to community engagement: The case for encouraging employee voice. *Academy of Management Perspectives, 29*(4), 405–421. https://doi.org/10.5465/amp.2013.0121

Morrison, E. W. & Milliken, F. J. (2000). Organizational silence: A barrier to change and development in a pluralistic world. *The Academy of Management Review, 25*(4), 706–725. https://doi.org/10.2307/259200

Morley, L. (2007). The gendered implications of quality assurance and audit. In P. Cotterill, S. Jackson, & G. Letherby (Eds). *Challenges and negotiations for women in higher education*, (pp. 53–63). Dordrecht: Springer.

Morley, L. (2013). The rules of the game: Women and the leaderist turn in higher education. *Gender and education, 25*(1), 116–131. https://doi.org/10.1080/09540253.2012.740888

Nikunen, M. (2012). Changing university work, freedom, flexibility and family. *Studies in Higher Education, 37*(6), 713–729. https://doi.org/10.1080/03075079.2010.542453

Noddings, N. (2003). *Caring: A feminine approach to ethics and moral education*. Berkeley: University of California Press.

O'Shea, S. C. (2019). My dysphoria blues: Or why I cannot write an autoethnography. *Management Learning, 50*(1), 38–49. https://doi.org/10.1177/1350507618791115

Petriglieri, G., Ashford, S. J., & Wrzesniewski, A. (2019). Agony and ecstasy in the gig economy: Cultivating holding environments for precarious and personalized work identities. *Administrative Science Quarterly, 64*(1), 124–170. https://doi.org/10.1177/0001839218759646

Pullen, A., Helin, J., & Harding, N. (Eds.). (2020). *Writing differently*. Emerald Publishing Limited. https://doi.org/10.1108/S2046-6072202004

Pullen, A., & Rhodes, C. (2018). Anxiety and organization. *Culture and Organization, 24*(2), 95–99. https://doi.org/10.1080/14759551.2017.1412576

Richardson, L. (1994). Writing: A method of inquiry. In N. K. Denzin & Y. S. Lincoln (Eds.), *Handbook of qualitative research* (pp. 516–529). Thousand Oaks, CA: Sage.

Richardson, L. (2000). New writing practices in qualitative research. *Sociology of Sport Journal, 17*(1), 5– 20.

Rodriguez, D. (2011). Silent rage and the politics of resistance: Countering seductions of whiteness and the road to politicization and empowerment. *Qualitative Inquiry, 17*(7), 589–598.

Ropers-Huilman, B. (2000). Aren't you satisfied yet? Women faculty members' interpretations of their academic work. In L. Hagedorn (Ed.), *What contributes to job satisfaction among faculty and staff: New directions for institutional research* (pp. 21–32). New York: Jossey-Bass.

Schein, V. E. (2007). Women in management: Reflections and projections. *Women in Management Review, 22*(1). 6–18 https://doi.org/10.1108/09649420710726193

Suzuki, D., & Mayorga, E. (2014). Scholar-activism: A twice told tale. *Multicultural Perspectives, 16*(1), 16–20.

Tilley, S. A., & Taylor, L. (2014). Complicating notions of "scholar-activist" in a global context: A discussion paper. *Journal of the International Society for Teacher Education, 18*(2), 53–62.

Treviño, L. J., Gomez-Mejia, L. R., Balkin, D. B., & Mixon Jr, F. G. (2018). Meritocracies or masculinities? The differential allocation of named professorships by gender in the academy. *Journal of Management, 44*(3), 972–1000. https://doi.org/10.1177/0149206315599216

Turner, C. S. V. (2002). Women of color in academe: Living with multiple marginality. *The Journal of Higher Education, 73*(1), 74–93. https://doi.org/10.1080/00221546.2002.11777131

Tzanakou, C., & Pearce, R. (2019). Moderate feminism within or against the neoliberal university? The example of Athena SWAN. *Gender, Work & Organization, 26*(8), 1191–1211. https://doi.org/10.1111/gwao.12336

Van den Brink, M., & Benschop, Y. (2012). Gender practices in the construction of academic excellence: Sheep with five legs. *Organization, 19*(4), 507–524. https://doi.org/10.1177/1350508411414293

Van den Brink, M., Benschop, Y., & Jansen, W. (2010). Transparency in academic recruitment: A problematic tool for gender equality? *Organization Studies, 31*(11), 1459–1483. https://doi.org/10.1177/0170840610380812

Van Miegroet, H., Glass, C., Callister, R. R., & Sullivan, K. (2019). Unclogging the pipeline: Advancement to full professor in academic STEM. *Equality, Diversity and Inclusion: An International Journal, 38*(2), 246–264. https://doi.org/10.1108/EDI-09-2017-0180

15 Of wellbeing and self-care in academia

Moreoagae Bertha Randa

As women academics, we have responsibilities as mothers, and also as women due to our social gender role (Castaneda & Isgro, 2013). One has so many duties as an academician, the first of which is to give as many lectures as our colleagues, then fulfill a mother's and a wife's role. For domestic workers, 80 per cent of whom are women, the situation has been dire; around the world; a staggering 72 per cent of domestic workers have lost their jobs (UN Women, 2020). With the lockdown making unemployment rates high, working women are struggling to balance their families and jobs at the same time. The full-time work shifts for women have become a major issue that has led to a disrupted lifestyle for many families. One could be working either on a full-time or contractual basis along with taking care of the family, cooking, and doing household chores without maids, therefore dealing with challenges daily.

Working women are encouraged to recognise that the perfect balance between work and home life is an unattainable myth (American Psychological Association [APA], 2020) However, women academics continue to try hard to keep the balance between their academic life and family roles. These dual responsibilities can increase stress, compromise physical and emotional health, and lead to burnout and lower work productivity (APA, 2020; Michailidis, 2008). In the past, one succeeded in keeping the balance between academic life and motherhood by not bringing work home. Academics had, for the most part, the freedom to decide where, how, and even when to work. Most come close to being their own supervisors even if they are employees. Autonomy is closely related to flexibility, and it has been argued that flexibility at work improves work-family balance (Rafnsdóttir & Heijstra, 2013), which is no longer the case. Time disposal was partly determined by the individual, partly by social or legal coercion, and partly through negotiations with others (Davies, 1989, cited by Rafnsdóttir & Heijstra, 2013). The outbreak of the Novel Coronavirus disease has drastically affected the lives of everyone around us (Brazeau et al., 2020). The pandemic has affected all sectors, most importantly the academic sectors, which mainly comprise women workers. Balancing the demands of an academic career while simultaneously raising a family is a source of potential conflict for academic parents, as they often find themselves unable to meet all these demands (Harris et al., 2019; van Engen et al., 2021). With the rapid spread of the virus and the universities and schools closing down, inadequacy in catering to the needs of students and of the family arose. Nonetheless,

DOI: 10.4324/9781003341482-18

teaching in Higher Education Institutions had to continue, and teaching innovation, including technology with online teaching, had to be phased in (Rapanta et al., 2020). With the continued global pandemic, the education environment was forced to change from traditional classroom or blended teaching modes to an online learning teaching model (Jin et al., 2021).

The flexibility allowed by technology has disintegrated the traditional work-life boundary for most professionals (Aczel et al., 2021). I am geographically located within the sub-Saharan Africa (SSA) continent in the region of South Africa, and am employed in a historically disadvantaged Higher Education Institution (HEI) as a woman academic. My job responsibilities include those of being a lecturer, a facilitator, a researcher, a coordinator, and a supervisor, amongst other roles. I also serve in different committees, for example, as Head of Research Portfolio, member of the teaching and learning committee and management committee, where I have to develop learning guides, documents for practice, and standard operating procedures. Additionally, I also have to read and publish articles, as that is a performance area.

Gender inequality

Gender inequality is also very high, and note should be taken that every country will progress towards gender equality at a different pace. There is no systematic government policy to support and promote gender equality in academia, and systematic institutional policies are very rare (Shore & Wright, 2015; Windsor & Crawford, 2020).

The prevailing view is that supporting women in their academic careers just means not actively holding them back. Any active support for women is viewed as giving them an unacceptable advantage (Van den Brink, Benschop & Jansen 2010; Van den Brink & Benschop, 2012). Not surprisingly, during the Covid-19 pandemic, female scientists suffered a greater disruption than men in their academic productivity and time spent on research, most likely due to the demands of childcare (King & Frederickson, 2021; Myers et al., 2020). The conditions for combining work and care make it even more difficult for women to fit into the standard model of a research career (Sallee, 2008). Whilst studying for my doctoral degree, my academic responsibilities still had to be met for me to achieve the key performance area goals. My employer does not offer full-time study leave for academics to pursue post-graduate studies. I had to juggle between work and studying.

Subject to a successful application process, a sabbatical leave or a 50/50 study leave of six months to a year can be granted towards completion, where one focuses on writing a dissertation/thesis. Despite having met the stipulated criteria and all the required documents submitted, my request was unsuccessful with unjust reasons. It was my journey, and driven by determination, I devised some means to enable me to complete my studies and meet the extended submission deadline. That meant having to work extended hours during the week, with no weekends off, and free time was used to write. This negatively impacted on my family time and resulted in conflicts. In contrast, a male colleague pursuing the same doctoral degree was granted a full six-month sabbatical leave. His application was approved without a hassle, and that gave him an opportunity to complete and submit his thesis on time. The evidence that occupational class disparities among women continue to widen is worrying (González Ramos et al., 2015), and it is, therefore, essential that policy focusing on the creation of "good jobs" be informed by an understanding of the intersections of gender and occupational class (Warren & Lyonette, 2018; Howe-Walsh & Turnbull, 2016). In his book, George Orwell (1945) said, "All animals are equal, but some animals are more equal than others."

Women are disadvantaged by organisations which lack formality and transparency with regards to the criteria for recruitment, promotions, or pay negotiation (Ceci et al., 2014). In the absence of such criteria, decisions on pay and promotion are more likely to be made via a process of social cloning, whereby those in a position of power champion those like them (Jones, 2019). There is a need to improve women's progression in the workplace, an aspect which I need to explore further as a researcher.

Despite continuous efforts by governments to promote gender equality in research and innovation (R&I) and to increase the number of women in science, statistics indicate resistance to these trends in many countries (Linková, 2017).

A large body of literature has shown that neoliberal governmentality has strongly gendered consequences for academic careers. Murgia and Poggio (2019) found that many committee members depict women as non-competitive, modest, non-committed, and non-mobile, which hampers women's career development and impedes their escape from precariousness. It influences the organisational, individual, and epistemic aspects of research and reproduces and increases inequalities within research domains and institutions and among individuals. Women's career paths do not usually fit this model as well because their careers are usually interrupted and less spatially and temporally flexible.

Extensive research has shown that what is declared as excellent is highly political, gender-biased, and not at all value-free. Amongst the facets of gender bias in research is the lack of incorporation of gender data into evidence-based medicine (Raine et al., 2002), as well as the UK National Health Service (NHS) guidelines for management, which are not gender-specific (Doyle et al., 2003). Women usually occupy lower ranks in the academic hierarchy, work in less prestigious and resourced institutions, and are less integrated into scientific networks (Moss-Racusin et al., 2012). They have fewer chances of attaining a tenure-track position. Women who try to juggle both a family and an academic job are usually at greater risk of work-family conflicts than men because they often have more household and care responsibilities (Wolfinger et al., 2009; Fox et al., 2011). Data suggests that early-career researchers and women especially are being increasingly relegated to precarious academic positions, while the system reinforces the privileged work status of the older generation (Vohlídalová, 2018).

Resilience in academia

Since the last decade, the study of resilience has grown rapidly, particularly in developmental psychology, family psychology, counseling, rehabilitation, and clinical psychology (Kumpfer, 2002). Resilience has been conceptualised as an individual characteristic, and the term "resiliency" has been used to refer to good, stable, and consistent adaption under challenging conditions. Recently, some researchers have considered resilience as a domain-specific concept. This approach suggested different aspects of resilience, such as academic, emotional, and behavioral, among others. Of these, academic resilience required more attention compared to other aspects (Wang & Gordon, 2012).

Positive affect and mindfulness are the psychological resources that positively relate to the levels of resilience of women leaders in higher education institutions. As with positive affect, there is a growing body of research which suggests that mindful individuals tend to display an increased propensity to be resilient in the face of challenges (Pillay, 2020).

Historical events in South African society have given rise to a cycle of under-representation of women in leadership roles in tertiary institutions. However, higher education institutions are making steady advances towards a positive transformation, which is evidenced by the increase of women in leadership (Moodly & Toni, 2015). The volatile environment that characterises the South African higher education system presents a barrier to leadership growth. It is stated that these barriers are persistent and require women leaders to continuously use resilience as a key resource to resume optimal functioning following the experience of a setback (Pillay, 2020). To this end, the concept of resilience serves as a crucial resource for women leaders, and, as a result, higher education institutions need to prioritise resilience development for these women to adapt to uncertainty (Sanaghan, 2016).

For women leaders to remain persistent and overcome these barriers, they need to access the resources necessary to resist disruptions that threaten their career journey (Weatherspoon-Robinson, 2013), especially in an environment that is less than optimal (Pillay, 2020). Institutions can assist in increasing positive affect through the creation of positive experiences for women leaders such as opportunities for coaching and mentoring. Additionally, institutions can encourage the practice of mindfulness through creating opportunities for meditation and exercises to increase attention and awareness (Halliday, 2018; Keye & Pidgeon, 2013).

Career development

Academic life is based on continuous development. Understanding career advancement as something purely promotional is a narrow concept of professional life. Professional life must be understood as an integrated concept that includes both career advancement and professional development (Jones & O'Brien, 2011). Multiple factors influence the social context in which professional development takes place. Yet the evidence is that social and situational concepts of learning development, particularly those of the professional development of teachers, provide a sound basis for the design of professional development opportunities for academic staff.

Women in academic careers face notable challenges that may go unrecognised by university management and/or policy makers (Lantsoght et al., 2021). The current Covid-19 pandemic has shed light on some of these challenges, as academics shifted to WFH while some simultaneously had to care for children. On the other hand, many women academics found that the shift to WFH offered new opportunities such as working more flexible hours, development of digital skillsets, and increased involvement in the education of their children (Lantsoght et al., 2021).

The work-life balance

The Covid-19 pandemic required academics to work from home and switch to blended teaching, requiring a quick shift in teaching materials and style. Simultaneously, school and university closures and the loss of other forms of child-care required a greater contribution by parents towards both the education and care of their children.

The situation created increased challenges for academic parents. In particular, academic parents experienced intensified workloads associated with shifting work from in-person to virtual platforms in conjunction with expanded childcare and/ or homeschooling (Lantsoght et al., 2021). Short-term solutions transitioned to long-term obstacles as parents began planning for extended periods with reduced or no childcare.

Balancing the demands of an academic career while simultaneously raising a family is a source of potential conflict for academic parents, as they often find themselves unable to meet all these demands (Palumbo, 2020).

The transition to WFH afforded parents new opportunities, such as working flexible hours, self-development (research-, teaching-, or admin-oriented careers) with the advantage of new digital tools, and increased involvement in the education of one's children. On the flip side, increased flexibility also came with the potential for heavy workloads (Poronsky et al., 2012), undefined and extended working hours, intense work pressure, and meetings scheduled beyond the traditional working hours, including on the weekends (Wilton & Ross, 2017).

This personally felt like a double-edged sword, as I could not distinguish between free time, work time and family time (see Figure 15.1).

As an individual, I cannot say that I have a balance between the jobs in my life. I believe it is not an easy thing to do so, by the way. By any means necessary, I try to manage motherhood, academic life, and being a researcher by changing my focus constantly. For example, if there is something urgent regarding my academic work or if I try to complete a manuscript, I neglect my family and focus on my work. However, if the situation is reversed, then my focus is on my family, and I neglect my academic life.

I attest that I can better achieve certain aspects of research in one place than the other. However, I miss the traditional office, sharing thoughts with colleagues and keeping in touch with the team. In contrast, at home, it can be very lonely.

When analysing the visual narrative, one can conclude that time management is a challenge. There is no proper self-care in terms of detaching from the workspace. Longer working hours don't mean more productivity (Kazekami, 2020), but they may eventually lead to job burnout and decreased productivity.

However, WFH is one initiative that has been promoted as a way of improving the work-life balance. WFH can increase the permeability of the boundary

Figure 15.1 Here is to spending my large portion of my days sitting behind the laptop. As a self-care routine, I have multiple cups of coffee whilst reading and typing. To take a proper break is a luxury I cannot afford when chasing deadlines.

between work and family domains, causing attempts to juggle work and family schedules to become more difficult (Moore & Crosbie, 2012).

The pursuit of a balance between work and the rest of our daily lives is a fairly recent concern. Williams (2001) suggests that we can map people's work-life needs within three different but connected areas of their lives. Firstly, there is personal time and space: what do we need for the care of self and maintenance of body, mind, and soul? Secondly, social time and space: what do we need to care properly for others? And thirdly, there is work time and space: what do we need to enable us to gain economic self-sufficiency? According to Williams (2001), a balance between work and daily life could be said to be achieved when each of these areas is in equilibrium.

Work-life balance: Women academics

Academic life mainly consists of teaching, preparing lectures, mentoring students, grading students' papers, publishing scientific research and papers, wiring textbooks, preparing for and participating in scientific conferences, administrative (various reports, analyses) and managerial work (chiefs of departments, vice deans, etc.), and participating in academic and scientific bodies and organisations, scientific projects, professional and consulting projects. Academics are evaluated, and their advancement is, first and foremost, based on research in terms of the number of publications in high impact academic journals (Hammarfelt, 2017).

Personal life consists of various roles: family life, raising children, home chores, maintaining friendships, emotional relationships, travel, leisure, hobbies, and so forth (McCutcheon & Morrison, 2018). Academic and professional responsibilities are mounting and are overflowing into our private lives. The thin line between the academic and the private life of academics is thus disappearing, and we are already having a hard time balancing work and other aspects of our lives.

As it is currently, I work much longer than the traditional 40-hour working week. I do have the motivation to WFH and stay productive; however, I am having a hard time preserving healthy boundaries between my professional and personal life. In fact, many of us continue to work after official workhours, sometimes sending emails as late as 10:00 p.m. This has an unintentional snowballing effect on other colleagues, who feel compelled to respond right away, even when the emails are not urgent. One of the extremely important consequences of increasing responsibilities is elevated levels of stress in academics, as we want to meet deadlines and promote output. While WFH can be great, there are challenges to navigate too.

Creating boundaries between work and personal life to create a work-life balance is a far-fetched theory (Misra et al., 2012), as I still don't have fixed working hours, with the potential for increased stress and inevitable burnout. Amongst other things, I must make an effort to get a change of scenery and deal with home distractions. The truth is that I am getting used to a sedentary lifestyle with improper eating habits and sleep deprivation. As such, I tend to employ negative coping strategies to alleviate the stress.

Home and work balance

Work-life balance today, especially in these times of Covid, where home and the workplace have overlapping boundaries, is an imperative precursor for the wellbeing of an individual (Bhat, 2021). Relevant to my context, there is a need for an improved institution's infrastructure and its facilities, which have to be adequate. Furthermore, a good working environment will promote elimination of stress and motivate me as an academic to improve my work-life balance. Personnel organisations and institutions need to be better equipped for the digital workspace.

Due to the Covid-19 pandemic, teaching innovation technology was phased in to enable continuous teaching activities. The challenge I encountered was due to lack of adaptation to digitalisation. There was an urgent need for me as an academic to familiarise myself with the learning management system that was put in place. For that I managed to do self-recording for presentations of lectures and created wizzes, group discussion sessions to facilitate problem-based learning for students online. This enabled me to balance activities, as I could juggle around work and be able to prepare an assessment tool or questions whilst the class was on.

A satisfying job well integrated into their life balances the overall mental and emotional quotient of working women, particularly in the current pandemic, where the workplace is posing a new and unfamiliar set of challenges and problems for women (Rawal, 2021). Carrying on with online classes remotely has become the order of the day, and it is becoming stressful when both work and personal life operate in the same space.

WFH is effective in improving quality of life, employee happiness, and work satisfaction (Azarbouyeh & Naini, 2014); however, WFH also has challenges. These are discussed next in relation to Williams' areas of life necessary for work-life balance.

Personal time and space

The creation of personal space and time has both psychological and personal benefits. One finds it easy to set a personal target to complete work, however the question to be answered is "*do you stick to the plan?*" When one works from home, personal time becomes fragmented, as one does not get time to relax.

To manage time effectively, the three key factors be considered are:

-*priorities were set*: I had tasks scheduled on a daily and weekly basis
-*getting on with it*: wrote my plans down and planned when, where, and how I was going to do it
-*working practices to avoid*: I stopped doing things that were impractical, for example, carrying on with work over the weekends (Bomert & Leinfellner, 2017).

In my experience, I have noticed that one must either let go of or challenge impossible expectations – be it my own, those of my field, my workplace, or society as a whole. Being a morning person has helped immensely in preserving my sanity, as I have some time alone in the workplace, before everyone else is up, to get the work done.

Social time and space

Some of the cited advantages of WFH include familiarity, comfort, flexibility, self-management, a quiet and undisturbed workspace, no travel, being with the children and family (Royal College of Art, 1999). It is a fact that WFH affords some level of flexibility in how to use one's time. However, there are tensions inherent in these advantages, as being with the children does not support working undisturbed (Windsor & Crawford, 2020).

Prior to the pandemic, a system was in place whereby I would wake up and prepare myself for work, whilst my helper prepared my granddaughter for school. With the lockdown imposed, all systems came to a standstill. Even with the easing of the lockdown rules, as schools re-opened, transport was still a problem, and this necessitated dropping off and picking up my granddaughter from school. Fearing Covid-19, the house helper also asked that she be recused from her duties, and this added to my already full plate of tasks. I had to make sure that my granddaughter was prepared and ready for school, have breakfast ready, and lastly drop her off at school before starting with my online classes. Seeing that I couldn't cope, I added her name to the special pick-up transport service arranged by her school to lessen my responsibilities. This afforded me ample time to prepare a proper breakfast before the day began, let alone for the rest of the day.

Work time and space

Sharing resources and a workspace can either help or hinder productivity. Having a dedicated workspace is essential, as it brings a sense of legitimacy to your work environment, encourages discipline, and improves productivity (Sullivan, 2000). This tendency to work long hours has caused problems in my familial relationships. A key impact of long work hours on my family was the reduction in time available to spend with my children, and this put my relationship with my spouse under a lot of stress with resultant fights. There was also limited or no time to socialise or visit friends and extended family members, which contributed to the poor health of family members.

This is similar to the findings of Parasuraman and Simmers (2021) and Yavas et al. (2008), who shared that in order to meet tedious problems, such as the negative social, emotional, and cognitive demands of the workplace to secure their jobs, employees have to work for longer hours, leaving them with very little time to relax, refresh, and unwind, which ultimately results in negative impacts on their family's wellbeing and leading to work-family conflict. This is a big obstacle preventing parents from spending quality time with their children (Baral & Bhargava, 2010).

Discussion

Work engagement lessens the perceptions of work-life unbalance. The increased work-related fatigue triggered by remote working may produce physical and emotional exhaustion in home-based tele-workers (Palumbo, 2020). Women academics are encouraged to recognise that the perfect balance between work and home life is an unattainable myth. Balance isn't obvious with remote work. I have noted the importance of a dedicated workspace, going for walks to break up the day, and communicating unique family needs to one's boss and team. Yet, we may still feel like work-life balance eludes us. The expected results include having to consider work among the multiple life roles that women academics manage.

Work-life balance has been negatively associated with family wellbeing (Akhtar, Kashif, Arif & Khan, 2012). Balancing the demands of academic work with the needs of the family has been a great challenge among academicians, especially among mothers. Previous studies have shown that most employees think that family is a great hindrance to career advancement (Wilkinson, 2008).

Firstly, prioritising one's role can assist in deciding how one can best manage the time across various roles and responsibilities (Forbes Coaches Council, 2018). Committing to a schedule and setting boundaries are the best ways to balance my life. Choosing what best serves my priorities and avoiding what doesn't is a must. Whether it be working on a Saturday or spending time with family, I become totally engaged and fully present. Engaging in self-care does not mean going out or yoga and a face mask. I often ask myself "What do I need to do to completely unwind?" I engaged in cooking, watching reality television, napping, or reading a romance novel. The activities turned out to be healthy as I could get my work done and still meet other obligations. A good self-care activity entails recharging and turning your brain off work mode. However, it can mean whatever it means to me, and may be different for everyone. More importantly, one must acknowledge one's feelings and practice self-compassion.

Conclusion

A satisfying job that has been well integrated into life balances the overall mental and emotional quotients of working women, particularly in the current pandemic, in which the workplace is posing a new and unfamiliar set of challenges and problems for women. The attainment of work-life balance is a very circumstantial phenomenon and isn't permanent. Work-life balance is all about individual achievement and enjoyment and feeling satisfied with whatever one does. It is crucial to have a proper work-life balance as it will help you feel more in control. When everything is in order, most of us tend to feel calmer. On the other hand, productivity is likely to be boosted, not only at work, but also in one's personal pursuits.

References

Aczel, B., Kovacs, M., van der Lippe, T., & Szaszi, B. (2021). Researchers working from home: Benefits and challenges. *PLoS ONE, 163*, e0249127. https://doi.org/10.1371/journal.pone.0249127

Akhtar, C. S., Kashif, A., Arif, A., & Khan, A. (2012). Impact of long working hours on family wellbeing of corporate family. *World Applied Sciences Journal, 16*(9), 1302–1307.

APA Committee on Women in Psychology. (2020). *How working women can manage work-life balance during COVID-19.* https://www.apa.org/topics/covid-19/working-women-balance

Azarbouyeh, A., & Naini, S. (2014). A study on the effect of teleworking on quality of work life. *Management Science Letters, 4*(6), 1063–1068.

Baral, R., & Bhargava, S. (2010). Work-family enrichment as a mediator between organizational interventions for work-life balance and job outcomes. *Journal of Managerial Psychology, 25*(3), 274–300.

Bhat, M. V. (2021). Work life balance (WLB) of primary school teachers in new normal: Learn, unlearn & relearn – a theoretical study. *Asia Pacific Journal of Research*, Special Issue XV, (2), 46–51.

Bomert, C., & Leinfellner, S. (2017). Images, ideals and constraints in times of neoliberal transformations: Reproduction and profession as conflicting or complementary spheres in academia. *European Educational Research Journal, 16*(2–3), 106–122.

Brazeau, G. A., Frenzel, J. E., & Prescott, W. A. (2020). Facilitating wellbeing in a turbulent time. *American Journal of Pharmaceutical Education, 84*(6). https://doi.org/10.5688/ajpe8154

Castaneda, M., & Isgro, K. (Eds.) (2013). *Mothers in academia.* New York, NY: Columbia University Press.

Ceci, S. J., Ginther, D. K., Kahn, S., & Williams, W. M. (2014). Women in academic science: A changing landscape. *Psychological Science in the Public Interest, 15*(3), 75–141.

Davies, K. (1989). *Women and time. Weaving the strands of everyday life.* Lund: Grahns Boktryckeri.

Doyle, L., Payne, S., & Cameron, A. (2003). Promoting gender equality in health. University of Bristol. https://www.researchgate.net/publication/237484761_Promoting_Gender_Equality_in_Health

European Commission (EC). (2019). *She figures 2018.* Brussels: EC.

European Commission Research (EC). (2010). Study on mobility patterns and career paths of EU researchers (Technical Report). https://cdn5.euraxess.org/sites/default/files/policy_library/more_extra_eu_mobility_report_final_version.pdf

Forbes Coaches Council. (2018, November 21). Nine ways you can improve your work-life balance during the holidays. https://www.forbes.com/sites/forbescoachescouncil/2018/11/21/nine-ways-you-can-improve-your-work-life-balance-during-the-holidays/

Fox, M. F., Fonseca, C., & Bao, J. (2011). Work and family conflict in academic science: Patterns and predictors among women and men in research universities. *Social Studies of Science, 41*(5), 715–735.

George Orwell. (1945). *Animal farm: A fairy story.* London, England: Secker & Warburg.

González Ramos, A. M., Navarrete Cortes, J., & Cabrera Moreno, E. (2015). Dancers in the dark: Scientific careers according to a gender-blind model of promotion. *Interdisciplinary Science Reviews, 40*(2), 182–203.

Halliday, A. J. (2018). Mindful resilience: Investigating mindfulness and resilience in relation to a broad range of adversity. Unpublished doctoral thesis. University of Western Ontario, Canada.

Hammarfelt, B. (2017). Recognition and reward in the academy: Valuing publication oeuvres in biomedicine, economics and history. *Aslib Journal of Information Management, 69*(5), 607–623. https://doi.org/10.1108/AJIM-01-2017-0006

Harris, C., Myers, B., & Ravenswood, K. (2019). Academic careers and parenting: Identity, performance and surveillance. *Studies in Higher Education, 44*(4), 708–718. https://doi.org/10.1080/03075079.2017.1396584

Howe-Walsh, L., & Turnbull, S. (2016). Barriers to women leaders in academia: Tales from science and technology. *Studies in Higher Education, 41*(3), 415–428.

Jin, Y. Q., Lin, C. L., Zhao, Q., Yu, S. W., & Su, Y. S. (2021). A study on traditional teaching method transferring to E-learning under the COVID-19 pandemic: From Chinese students' perspectives. *Frontiers in Psychology, 12*, 632787. https://doi.org/10.3389/fpsyg.2021.632787

Jones, K., & O'Brien, J. (2011). Professional development in teacher education: European perspectives. *Professional Development in Education, 37*(5), 645–650.

Jones, L. (2019). Women's progression in the workplace. In *Global Institute for Women's Leadership.* London: Government Equalities Office: King's College London. Crown copyright

Kazekami, S. (2020). Mechanisms to improve labor productivity by performing telework. *Telecommunications Policy, 44*(2), 101868.

Keye, M. D., & Pidgeon, A. M. (2013). Investigation of the relationship between resilience, mindfulness, and academic self-efficacy. *Open Journal of Social Sciences, 1*(6), 1–4. https://doi.org/10.4236/jss.2013.16001

King, M. M., & Frederickson, M. E. (2021). The pandemic penalty: The gendered effects of COVID-19 on scientific productivity. *Socius, 7.* https://doi.org/10.1177/23780231211006977

Kumpfer, K. L. (2002). *Factors and processes contributing to resilience.* New York: Plenum Publishers.

Lantsoght, E. O., Tse Crepaldi, Y., Tavares, S. G., Leemans, K., & Paig-Tran, E. W. (2021). Challenges and opportunities for academic parents during COVID-19. *Frontiers in Psychology* https://doi.org/10.3389/fpsyg.2021.645734

Linková, M. (2017). Excellence and its others: Gendered notions of what it takes to succeed in science. In M. Vohlídalová & M. Linková (Eds.), *Gender and neoliberalism in czech academia* (pp. 159–197). Praha: Slon.

Masten A. S. (1994). Resilience in Individual Development: Successful Adaptation Despite Risk and Adversity. In M. C. Wang & E. W. Gordon, (Eds.), *Educational Resilience in Inner-City America: Challenges and Prospects* (pp. 3–25). Hillsdale, NY: Lawrence Erlbaum.

McCutcheon, J. M., & Morrison, M. A. (2018). It's "like walking on broken glass": Pan-Canadian reflections on work-family conflict from psychology women faculty and graduate students. *Feminism & Psychology*, *28*(2), 231–252. https://doi.org/10.1177/0959353517739641

Michailidis, M. P. (2008). Gender-related work stressors in tertiary education. *Journal of Human Behavior in the Social Environment*, *17*(1–2), 195–211. https://doi.org/10.1080/10911350802171203

Misra, J., Lundquist, J. H., & Templer, A. 2012. Gender, work time, and care responsibilities among faculty. *Sociological Forum*, *27*(2), 300–323. https://doi.org/10.1111/j.1573-7861.2012.01319.x

Moodly, A. L., & Toni, N. (2015). Women's access to higher education leadership: Where are the role models? *Journal of Social Sciences*, *45*(1), 45–52.

Moore, J. & Crosbie, T. (2002). 'The homeworking experience: the effects on home and family life'. *University of Teesside*.

Moss-Racusin, C. A., Dovidio, J. F., Brescoll, V. L., Graham, M. J., & Handelsman, J. (2012). Science faculty's subtle gender biases favor male students. *Proceedings of the National Academy of Sciences*, *109*(41), 16474–16479.

Murgia, A. & Poggio, B. (2019). *Gender and precarious research careers: A comparative analysis*. London and New York: Routledge.

Myers, K. R., Tham, W. Y., Yin, Y., Cohodes, N., Thursby, J. G., Thursby, M. C., & Wang, D. (2020). Unequal effects of the COVID-19 pandemic on scientists. *Nature Human Behaviour*, *4*(9), 880–883.

Palumbo, R. (2020). Let me go to the office! An investigation into the side effects of working from home on work-life balance. *International Journal of Public Sector Management*. *33*(6/7), 771–790. https://doi.org/10.1108/IJPSM-06-2020-0150

Parasuraman, S., & Simmers, C. A. (2001). Type of employment, work-family conflict and well-being: A comparative study. *Journal of Organizational Behavior: The International Journal of Industrial, Occupational and Organizational Psychology*.

Pillay, D. (2020). Positive affect and mindfulness as predictors of resilience amongst women leaders in higher education institutions. *SA Journal of Human Resource Management*, *18*(1), 1–10.

Poronsky, C. B., Doering, J. J., Mkandawire-Valhmu, L., & Rice, E. I. (2012). Transition to the tenure track for nurse faculty with young children: A case study. *Nursing Education Perspectives*, *33*(4), 255–259.

Rafnsdóttir, G. L., & Heijstra, T. M. (2013). Balancing work–family life in academia: The power of time. *Gender, Work & Organization*, *20*(3), 283–296.

Raine, R., Goldfrad, C., Rowan, K., & Black, N. (2002). Influence of patient gender on admission to intensive care. *Journal of Epidemiology & Community Health*, *56*(6), 418–423.

Rapanta, C., Botturi, L., Goodyear, P., Guàrdia, L., & Koole, M. (2020). Online university teaching during and after the Covid-19 crisis: Refocusing teacher presence and learning activity. *Postdigital Science and Education*, *2*(3), 923–945. https://doi.org/10.1007/s42438-020-00155-y

Rawal, D. M. (2021). Work life balance among female school teachers [k–12] delivering online curriculum in Noida [India] during COVID: Empirical study. *Management in Education*. https://doi.org/10.1177/0892020621994303

Royal College of Art. (1999). *Work at home*. London: Helen Hamlyn Research Centre.

Sallee, M. W. (2008). Work and family balance: How community college faculty cope. *New Directions for Community Colleges, 142*, 81–91.

Sanaghan, P. (2016). *Building leadership resilience in higher education*. Denver: CR Mrig. https://www.academicimpressions.com/sites/default/files/0116-leadership-resilience-md.pdf

Shore, C., & Wright, S. (2015). Audit culture revisited: Rankings, ratings, and the reassembling of society. *Current Anthropology, 56*(3), 421–444.

Sullivan, C. (2000). Space and the intersection of work and family in homeworking households. *Community, Work & Family, 3*(2), 185–204.

UN Women. (2020). COVID-19 and its economic toll on women: The story behind the numbers. https://www.unwomen.org/en/news/stories/2020/9/feature-covid-19-economic-impacts-on-women

Van den Brink, M., & Benschop, Y. (2012). Slaying the seven-headed dragon: The quest for gender change in academia. *Gender, Work & Organization, 19*(1), 71–92. https://doi.org/10.1111/j.1468-0432.2011.00566.x

Van den Brink, M., Benschop, Y., & Jansen, W. (2010). Transparency in academic recruitment: A problematic tool for gender equality? *Organization Studies, 31*(11), 1459–1483. https://doi.org/10.1177/0170840610380812

Van Engen, M. L., Bleijenbergh, I. L., & Beijer, S. E. (2021). Conforming, accommodating, or resisting? How parents in academia negotiate their professional identity. *Studies in Higher Education, 46*(8), 1493–1505. https://doi.org/10.1080/03075079.2019.1691161

Vohlídalová, M. (2018). *Akademici a akademičky: zpráva z dotazníkového šetření akademických a vědeckých pracovnic a pracovníků ve veřejném sektoru*. Praha: Institute of Sociology, Czech Academy of Sciences.

Wang, M. C., & Gordon, E. W. (2012). *Educational resilience in inner-city America: Challenges and prospects*. New York: Lawrence Erlbaum Associates, Inc.

Warren, T., & Lyonette, C. (2018). Good, bad and very bad part-time jobs for women? Re-examining the importance of occupational class for job quality since the "Great Recession" in Britain. *Work, Employment and Society, 32*(4), 747–767.

Weatherspoon-Robinson, S. (2013). *African American female leaders: Resilience and success. Unpublished doctoral dissertation*. Malibu, CA: Pepperdine University.

Wilkinson, S. J. (2008). Work-life balance in the Australian and New Zealand surveying profession. *Structural Survey, 26*(2), 120–130.

Williams, F. (2001). In and beyond New Labour: Towards a new political ethics of care. *Critical Social Policy, 21*(4), 467–493. https://doi.org/10.1177/026101830102100405

Wilton, S., & Ross, L. (2017). Flexibility, sacrifice and insecurity: A Canadian study assessing the challenges of balancing work and family in academia. *Journal of Feminist Family Therapy, 29*(1–2), 66–87. doi: 10.1080/08952833.2016.1272663

Windsor, L. C., & Crawford, K. F. (2020). Best practices for normalizing parents in the academy: Higher-and lower-order processes and women and parents' success. *Political Science & Politics, 53*(2), 275–280. doi: 10.1017/S1049096519001938

Wolfinger, N. H., Mason, M. A., & Goulden, M. (2009). Stay in the game: Gender, family formation and alternative trajectories in the academic life course. *Social Forces, 87*(3), 1591–1621.

Yavas, U., Babakus, E., & Karatepe, O. M. (2008). Attitudinal and behavioral consequences of work-family conflict and family-work conflict: Does gender matter? *International Journal of Service Industry Management, 19*(1), 7–31.

Index

Note: *Italic* page number refers to figure; **Bold** page number refers to table and Page number followed by n refers to notes respectively.

Taylor & Francis Group
an **informa** business

Taylor & Francis eBooks

www.taylorfrancis.com

A single destination for eBooks from Taylor & Francis
with increased functionality and an improved user
experience to meet the needs of our customers.

90,000+ eBooks of award-winning academic content in
Humanities, Social Science, Science, Technology, Engineering,
and Medical written by a global network of editors and authors.

TAYLOR & FRANCIS EBOOKS OFFERS:

A streamlined
experience for
our library
customers

A single point
of discovery
for all of our
eBook content

Improved
search and
discovery of
content at both
book and
chapter level

REQUEST A FREE TRIAL
support@taylorfrancis.com

 Routledge
Taylor & Francis Group

 CRC Press
Taylor & Francis Group

Ingram Content Group UK Ltd.
Milton Keynes UK
UKHW021105170323
418657UK00018B/215